Coraline

ANIMATION: KEY FILMS/FILMMAKERS

Series Editor: Chris Pallant

Coraline

A Closer Look at Studio LAIKA's Stop-Motion Witchcraft

Edited by
Mihaela Mihailova

BLOOMSBURY ACADEMIC
LONDON • NEW YORK • OXFORD • NEW DELHI • SYDNEY

BLOOMSBURY ACADEMIC
Bloomsbury Publishing Inc
1385 Broadway, New York, NY 10018, USA
50 Bedford Square, London, WC1B 3DP, UK
29 Earlsfort Terrace, Dublin 2, Ireland

BLOOMSBURY, BLOOMSBURY ACADEMIC and the Diana logo are
trademarks of Bloomsbury Publishing Plc

First published in the United States of America 2021
This paperback edition published 2023

For legal purposes the Acknowledgements on pp. x–xi, 36 and 184 constitute an
extension of this copyright page.

Series design: Louise Dugdale
Cover image: Film, *Coraline* © Laika Inc. Courtesy of Ronald Grant
Film Archive/Mary Evans Picture Library

Library of Congress Cataloging-in-Publication Data
Names: Mihailova, Mihaela, editor.
Title: Coraline : a closer look at Studio LAIKA's stop-motion witchcraft /
edited by Mihaela Mihailova.
Description: New York : Bloomsbury Academic, 2021. | Series: Animation :
key films/filmmakers | Includes bibliographical references and index.
Identifiers: LCCN 2021007999 (print) | LCCN 2021008000 (ebook) |
ISBN 9781501347863 (hardback) | ISBN 9781501347870 (ebook) |
ISBN 9781501347887 (pdf)
Subjects: LCSH: Selick, Henry–Criticism and interpretation. |
Gaiman, Neil. Coraline–Film adaptations. | LAIKA (Firm) | Coraline (Motion picture) |
Stop-motion animation films–United States–History and criticism. |
Stop-motion animation films–Production and direction. |
Animation (Cinematography)–United States.
Classification: LCC PN1997.2.C669 C67 2021 (print) | LCC PN1997.2.C669
(ebook) | DDC 791.43/72–dc23
LC record available at https://lccn.loc.gov/2021007999
LC ebook record available at https://lccn.loc.gov/2021008000

ISBN: HB: 978-1-5013-4786-3
PB: 978-1-5013-8143-0
ePDF: 978-1-5013-4788-7
eBook: 978-1-5013-4787-0

Series: Animation: Key Films/Filmmakers

Typeset by Newgen KnowledgeWorks Pvt. Ltd., Chennai, India

Dedicated to the memory of my grandfather Dimitar Angelov,
who watched cartoons with me before anyone else,
and to my grandmother Dobra Angelova, who still watches
them whenever I visit

Contents

Part 3 Puppet politics: Ideology, identity, representation

Figures

Acknowledgements

This book began, as many books do, over a pint. Then it ended, as all of them do, over lukewarm coffee.

There was never a doubt in my mind regarding which animated film I would like to spend years of my life thinking about, once given the option. To quote Neil Gaiman's own manuscript, when I first saw *Coraline*, 'the sky had never seemed so sky; the world had never seemed so world'.

The power of animation to transport us has never felt more relevant – indeed, more *urgently needed* – than it does now, many months into a devastating, soul-crushing global pandemic. Even as I miss my animation community, I remain keenly aware of how our shared love for this magical, stunning, liberating medium continues to bring us together. To the Society for Animation Studies, thank you for keeping my spirit in motion.

I am grateful to Chris Pallant for inviting me to put this volume together, and most of all for responding to all kinds of panicked Facebook messages with endless calm and adorable photos of his lovely family. Many thanks to Erin Duffy, Katie Gallof and Kalyani Kanekal at Bloomsbury for all their patience and professionalism. At the University of Michigan, I'd like to thank my UROP research student Miranda Kranz.

My all-star team of contributors deserves all the credit for their brilliant, thought-provoking and beautifully written chapters *and* for valiantly putting up with dangerously elevated levels of nitpickery. For meeting my twitchy ways with witchy insight, each of them should get at least one garden in the shape of their face. Alas, in this economy, I hope a complementary copy of this book will suffice.

The editing of this volume coincided with my extended sojourn to the frozen lands of Michigan, Coraline's home turf. I would like to thank all the wonderful friends I met here, for all the company, support and various shenanigans: Kaveh Askari, Nilo Couret, Lyn Goeringer, Blake Gutt, Ungsan Kim, Mikki Kressbach, Kristin Mahoney, Yuki Nakayama, Melissa Phruksachart, Veerandra Prasad, Mingzhe Wang and Joshua Yumibe.

Many, many thanks to the best boys, Evan Granito and Bagel, for getting me through the last, frantic stretch of this journey. You are my pandemic demon slayers.

Friends who listened to me complain about the academic editorial process for years deserve recognition for their emotional labor: Milena Arsova, Annie Berke, Jason Cody Douglass, Daria Ezerova, Cristina Formenti, Alla Gadassik, Leon Gurevitch, Eric Herhuth, Chris'pher 'Double L' Holliday, Timothy Jones, Iliana Nissimova, Ila Tyagi. Your support and occasional gentle mockery will not be forgotten.

Much love to my four-legged siblings: Chocolate, Felix, Kaspar, Maxie, Sir E and Tiger.

As always, the greatest debt of gratitude goes to my indomitable mother, Veselina Angelova, who is infinitely cooler, stronger and more fascinating than any fictional mothers in this or any other universe.

Coraline: A twitchy, witchy girl in stop-motion land

Mihaela Mihailova

In 2009, a small puppet named Coraline crawled through a tunnel and emerged on the pages of animation history. A decade later, this image of a young, blue-haired girl advancing through a mysterious passage, eyes alight with wonder, has become emblematic of a transformative moment for contemporary stop-motion production. This volume delves into the mystery of that moment, seeking to explain how a newly (re)formed Oregon-based studio managed to unlock a new dimension to one of the oldest forms of filmmaking.

An adaptation of British fantasy writer Neil Gaiman's children's book of the same name, *Coraline* (Henry Selick) was the first feature-length movie produced by LAIKA, a stop-motion company established in 2005 following Nike co-founder Phil Knight's takeover (and renaming) of Will Vinton Studios.[1] Selick and LAIKA had already collaborated before, on an eight-minute animated short titled *Moongirl*, 'the first computer generated experience for both parties'.[2] However, it was the veteran stop-motion director's past credits, notably the spooky 1993 classic *The Nightmare Before Christmas*, that made him a perfect fit for Gaiman's eerie tale of haunted domesticity.

In his chapter for this volume, Malcolm Cook calls attention to the fact that *Coraline*'s premiere was widely seen as coinciding with a contemporary renaissance of stop motion, inaugurated by the success of Selick's earlier features, as well as Tim Burton's *Corpse Bride* (2005) and Aardman Animations' early 2000s claymation films. In fact, 2009 marked the release of an unprecedented number of stop-motion features from around the world, including Australian animator Adam Elliot's *Mary and Max*, American live-action auteur Wes Anderson's first foray into the medium with *Fantastic Mr. Fox*, and Stéphane Aubier and Vincent Patar's European co-production *A Town Called Panic*.

However, as Cook points out, while both the global nature of this phenomenon and the sheer volume of releases were certainly noteworthy, 'many sources went no further than noting it'.

While attempting to fully account for and unpack this stop-motion renaissance is beyond the scope of this volume, the following pages situate *Coraline* within an interconnected network of historical, industrial, discursive, theoretical and cultural contexts. They place the film in conversation with the medium's aesthetic and technological history, broader global intellectual and political traditions, and questions of animation reception and spectatorship. In doing so, they invite recognition – and appreciation – of the fact that *Coraline* occupies many liminal spaces at once. It straddles the boundary between children's entertainment and traditional 'adult' genres, such as horror and thriller. It complicates a seemingly straight(forward) depiction of normative family life with gestures of queer resistance. Finally, it marks a pivotal point in stop-motion animation's digital turn. Following the film's recent tenth anniversary, the time is right to revisit its production history, evaluate its cultural and industry impact and celebrate its legacy as contemporary stop-motion cinema's gifted child.

Coraline and stop motion's digital turn

As Jane Shadbolt notes in her chapter for this collection, *Coraline* 'marked a particular point in a near two-decade-long watershed in technical developments in US mainstream stop-motion production', using digital tools in a way that allowed it to expand the storytelling vocabulary of its traditional animation technique. Indeed, *Coraline*'s production was made possible by two technological 'firsts' in stop-motion filmmaking: rapid prototyping and stereoscopic photography.[3] Both would prove historically significant to the medium, as they not only unlocked new creative avenues for animation directors but also, by garnering widespread positive critical attention, solidified stop motion's position in the popular imagination as a technique with unique and ever-expanding expressive potential.

LAIKA's rapid prototyping process, first developed for *Coraline*, was recognized by the Academy of Motion Picture Arts and Sciences with a Scientific and Engineering Award in 2016, accepted by director of rapid prototyping Brian McLean and former LAIKA facial animation designer Martin Meunier.[4] As Ken A. Priebe explains, 'rapid prototyping was a method for printing out 3D computer models of replacement animation and props into physical resin materials in order to combine the technical smoothness of CG into a stylized stop-motion set'.[5] In other words, rapid prototyping allowed LAIKA to use contemporary 3D printing technology to modernize and optimize its use of replacement animation, a traditional stop-motion method 'whereby puppet parts (such as the head) are replaced (one frame at a time) with slightly dissimilar ones'.[6] Specifically, according to Brian McLean, the process was developed to 'harness the power of the computer' in order to provide the production with 'more facial options' for the puppets, rendering them capable of an unprecedented range and sophistication of expressions. As a result, while earlier stop-motion features, such as Selick's own *The Nightmare before Christmas*, 'used a few hundred hand-sculpted faces, *Coraline* used 6,333 printed faces, which could be combined to make 207,000 possible facial expressions'.[7] To achieve this, LAIKA relied on Stratasys's Objet Eden260 3D printer, which used white resin subsequently cured by UV lights. McLean has praised this method for its 'precision and accuracy, especially [with] fine feature details', while also pointing out its limitations, notably the fact that each puppet face had to be hand-painted, with the printer's single material system limiting 'the level of sophistication that could be used when painting the characters'.[8]

LAIKA has continued to rely on increasingly sophisticated 3D printing for its subsequent productions. Most recently, on *Missing Link* (Chris Butler, 2019), the Stratasys J750 printer, which offers over five hundred thousand different colour combinations, was used to create over 106,000 3D-printed faces.[9] In that sense, *Coraline* heralded the studio's ongoing search for technical and visual complexity. However, while rapid prototyping remains notable as a technological breakthrough, its significance to stop-motion filmmaking lies in its impact on stop-motion aesthetics. *Coraline*'s 3D-printed face, with its individually hand-painted freckles, is certainly a testament to digitally enhanced craftsmanship, but it is the puppet's performance – marked by an exceptional level of nuance and subtlety in every slight eyebrow raise or sly smirk – that distinguished LAIKA's film and raised the bar for what is considered attainable in stop-motion animation.

In addition to pioneering the use of rapid prototyping, *Coraline* has also claimed the title of 'first stop-motion feature film to be shot entirely in stereoscopic 3-D'.[10] As Scott Higgins explains in his study of the film's approach to stereoscopic photography, 'Selick's crew shot each scene of *Coraline* frame by frame with a digital still camera that was moved laterally between each exposure, generating two slightly different shots for every frame. IoD [interocular distance] could be adjusted between frames for a meticulous control of stereo space … unheard of in live-action'.[11] Higgins credits *Coraline* with offering 'a historically significant aesthetic solution to the 3D conundrum', namely how to draw on the creative potential of 3D without 'assaulting the viewer'.[12] According to him, LAIKA's feature helped 'define a depth-oriented aesthetic that binds stereoscopic effects to character-oriented narrative tasks [and] controls protrusion while seeking expressive methods for handling the space behind the screen'.[13]

Indeed, accounts of *Coraline's* production suggest that the film's use of 3D was primarily driven by narrative considerations. Pete Kozachik, the director of photography, has elaborated on the ways in which *Coraline* manipulates depth cues in order to distinguish its two parallel universes and also convey the protagonist's impressions of them:

> We all agreed 3-D had to be used to enhance story and mood, like any other photo technique. Along with the story arc, lighting arc and colour script, we decided to impose a complementary 'stereo arc' on the show. Henry [Selick] wanted 3-D depth to differentiate the Real World from the Other World, specifically in sync with what Coraline is feeling. To do that, we kept the Real World at a reduced stereo depth, suggesting Coraline's flat outlook, and used full 3-D in the Other World. At first, full 3-D opens up a better world for Coraline, but when things go bad, we carefully exaggerate stereo depth to match her distress.[14]

This 'stereo arc' has been analysed in great detail in scholarly writing on the film. For example, Stephen Prince unpacks the ways in which the camera's movements through stereo space in the Other World 'visually convey the irony of Coraline's situation'. As he notes, 'her desire to be in the Other Mother's world is stereoscopically portrayed using this emphatic Z-axis information'. Then, as soon as the Other Mother's true nature and intentions are revealed, 'the design of stereoscopic space becomes more aggressive yet, with greater use of theatre space as sinister objects come at Coraline and at the viewer'.[15]

Coraline's stereoscopic vision was praised by film critics, who tended to describe the film's use of 3D as a welcome respite from live-action Hollywood's conventional approach to the technology. For example, Kenneth Turan of the *Los Angeles Times* wrote that 'the third dimension comes of age with *Coraline*. The first contemporary film in which the 3-D experience feels intrinsic to the story instead of a Godforsaken gimmick, *Coraline* is a remarkable feat of the imagination, a magical tale with a genuinely sinister edge'.[16] A. O. Scott praised the 3D aspects of LAIKA's feature as 'unusually subtle', writing that Selick 'uses the technology to make his world deeper and more intriguing'.[17] In his book on the history of modern stereoscopic cinema, Ray Zone attributes to the film the invention of a 'new visual grammar for stereoscopic narrative, ... with new thinking about the narrative use of the z-axis' that 'dispenses with the gimmicks of 3-D, which often thrust the viewer out of the story by foregrounding the technology, and simply emphasizes the immersive and real nature of the imagery on-screen'.[18]

Finally, many commentators have framed *Coraline* as a prestige production whose favourable reception contributed to a popular and critical legitimization of 3D. For instance, Caetlin Benson-Allott argues that the film 'bestowed RealD stereoscopic filmmaking with artistic and cultural prestige, affirming theatre owners' and cinemagoers' growing interest in digital cinema'.[19] Similarly, Scott Higgins observes that '*Coraline* participates in a more general stylistic trend in prestigious 3D production that limits out of frame effects in favour of exploring depth and volume', helping 3D 'shed its reputation for artless gimmickry'.[20]

Coraline's approach to stereoscopic 3D, as well as its use of rapid prototyping, affirms the film's core creative goal – to bring to life a world (or, more accurately, *worlds*) that is immersive, full of subtle, enchanting detail and, above all, inviting. That it would so persistently, purposefully push the boundaries of its own medium in order to build that world is only fitting. After all, from its very inception as a story about – and *for* – brave children, *Coraline* has been a narrative about the limits, dangers and, ultimately, rewards of curiosity – and the exhilarating terror of plunging into the unknown.

Coraline's production history: Embracing children's horror

'There are many scenes and images in "Coraline" that are likely to scare children. This is not a warning but rather a recommendation.'[21] Thus begins A. O. Scott's glowing *New York Times* review of *Coraline*. Alas, his enthusiasm for the story's horror elements and his glib attitude towards the question of age-appropriate content proved to be the exception, rather than the norm, when it comes to *Coraline*'s initial critical reception. Concerns about the narrative's straddling of the boundary between adult and children's media have accompanied the project from its earliest days, as Neil Gaiman was repeatedly told that his book draft was 'not publishable'. In 1991, an editor at British book publisher Victor

Gollancz advised that 'nobody can publish something that is for *both* kids and adults', especially a horror novel for children.[22] Ten years later, already on the other side of the Atlantic, Gaiman's New York City literary agent said 'you can't let children read this'.[23] The author has since concluded that, when the book eventually got the green light, it was thanks to a changed publishing landscape, due largely to the massive popularity of the *Harry Potter* series.[24] His novel ended up becoming wildly successful, receiving several reprints and selling more than a million copies worldwide, having been translated into more than thirty languages.[25]

LAIKA's film is not *Coraline*'s only adaptation. In fact, Gaiman's heroine has traversed multiple media worlds: a stage play by Irish theatrical puppet troupe Púca Puppets in 2006, a Swedish children's and youth theatre production by Mittiprickteatern in 2007, and a graphic novel adaptation by P. Craig Russell in 2008, among others.[26] More recently, a family-friendly opera adaptation composed by Mark-Anthony Turnage premiered at the Barbican Centre in London.[27] However, it is Henry Selick's vision that brought the story into the mainstream – and reignited debates surrounding its genre status and age rating.

Coraline appears to have been waiting for Selick all along. The stop-motion auteur, who had been on Neil Gaiman's radar, thanks to *The Nightmare before Christmas* and *James and the Giant Peach* (1996), was sent an advance manuscript of *Coraline* by Gaiman's agent.[28] The British author considered Selick an obvious choice because the latter 'understands something that people often forget – that children love to be scared'.[29] As Rayna Denison's chapter for this volume reveals, film critics in the book's and film's respective homelands did indeed frequently fail to remember this. Denison points out that American and British journalists 'questioned the extent to which children's horror is desirable', even as they united in praising the film's harnessing of stop motion's uncanny qualities. As she concludes, *Coraline*'s noteworthy status as a genuinely unsettling PG-rated feature ended up offering 'a window onto a set of debates about the place of animation within culture'.

In particular, *Coraline* contributed to – and indeed brought new urgency to – a critical re-evaluation of animated and children's horror. Using LAIKA's feature as one of her case studies, Megan Troutman has argued that 'children's animated horror serves as a tool to question childhood mythologies'.[30] Specifically, she contends that films like *Coraline* 'rewrite mainstream depictions of children as passive and vulnerable' and 'allow child characters to play the types of agentic, heroic roles that are typically reserved for adult and, until recently, almost exclusively male protagonists'.[31] *Coraline* also resonates strongly with Catherine Lester's analysis of the children's horror film as an 'impossible subgenre' that relies on typical genre conventions while being 'simultaneously able to deviate and become "child-friendly" by excluding—or finding strategic ways to alleviate—horrific elements that might be thought to distress child viewers'.[32] While not addressing the horror aspects of *Coraline* directly, this volume engages with their implications across several of its chapters, notably Ann Owen's discussion of the relationship between the film's animation technique and the sensations of threat it generates, as well as Jane Batkin and Nicholas Andrew Miller's studies of the film's approach towards depicting a child's capacity to face, overcome and learn from danger.

Coraline's legacy: (Hand-)Crafting the LAIKA brand

As discussed above, *Coraline's* production relied heavily on advanced digital technologies and coincided with a defining moment in the development of several techniques that have altered the face(s) of contemporary stop-motion filmmaking. Thus, in much the same way it found itself at the centre of debates regarding the status and meaning of children's animated horror as a cinematic genre, the film also emerged at the forefront of discussions regarding the changing technological and aesthetic profile of the traditionally analogue art of stop-motion animation and related anxieties about its future in a mainstream filmmaking landscape dominated by the digital. Specifically, *Coraline's* promotional discourse repeatedly emphasized the film's hand-made aspects in order to affirm LAIKA's commitment to traditional animation craftsmanship and, in doing so, set the tone for the studio's ongoing effort to build a brand around notions of traditional craftsmanship.[33]

In her analysis of the ways in which contemporary American stop-motion filmmakers (including LAIKA) 'have grappled with the logics of the digital', Andrea Comiskey has shown that 'they value, and strive to make visible, certain traces of the earlier medium – particularly the "handmade" and sculptural qualities that are connected to materiality and indexicality', but at the same time 'they also seek to efface or limit the incursion of the digital in order to uphold the computerised/handmade binary that is central to both their professional identities and the medium's cultural cachet'.[34] As she explains, while significantly benefitting from digital technologies, *Coraline* nevertheless strove to emphasize the analogue imperfections of stop-motion filmmaking, such as the irregular texture and sheen of the gravy in the 'gravy train' scene.[35] The film's press coverage was similarly keen on highlighting traditional production processes; as Malcolm Cook points out in his chapter for this collection, discussions of *Coraline* 'frequently turned to the hand-crafted qualities of stop motion as a way of contrasting these films with digital animation', suggesting that the feature was 'indicative of a new historical moment in which the visible materiality of stop motion was understood to relieve the clinical flawlessness of CGI'.

Indeed, this particular rhetoric continues to dominate accounts of the film's production. For instance, Ken A. Priebe writes that 'even with this new technology and state-of-the-art compositing effects, every effort was made to keep *Coraline* as handcrafted as possible. Amazing miniature work was done in the puppet fabrication department, in the realms of posable hair, tiny knit sweaters, and innovative animated plants for a fantastic garden sequence'.[36] In an interview about the feature, Brian Gardner, who worked as LAIKA's stereoscopic adviser, notes that he 'found that the spirit of *Coraline* was really about handcrafting and a love for classic art forms'.[37] *Coraline*'s own behind-the-scenes materials actively contributed to this line of discourse. For example, the film's companion book emphasizes Travis Knight's description of LAIKA as a 'place where we value stuff that's handmade and hand-crafted'.[38]

Caroline Ruddell and Paul Ward argue that 'recently, craft has become an increasingly valued phenomenon in contemporary culture', wherein the 'notion of the "handmade", the "authentic", is used as part of the marketing of products sold by major corporations'.[39] Starting with *Coraline*, LAIKA's marketing has leaned on this strategy very consistently. The obsession with being seen as the successor to a global legacy of traditional stop-motion craft (which I unpack in my chapter for this volume) has remained the cornerstone of the studio's publicity efforts across its entire oeuvre. Notably, mid- and post-credits sequences depicting behind-the-scenes work, featured in every LAIKA film to date, have become a recognizable company trademark.

In *The Boxtrolls* (Graham Annable and Anthony Stacchi, 2014) bonus scene, two puppets engage in tongue-in-cheek banter about the extreme laboriousness of stop-motion production as a time-lapse video shows animator (and LAIKA CEO) Travis Knight working on them day after day. This may play like an inside joke, but it is also an example of one of LAIKA's leading promotional tactics, namely the dual focus on the meticulousness of stop-motion animation labour and the time-intensive nature of every step of this filmmaking process. This resonates with Carla MacKinnon's observation that 'the romanticisation of handmade animation is particularly evident in commentary surrounding stop-motion production', especially when it comes to 'the fascination ... for the *experience* of making stop-motion animation, with its long and physically challenging process'.[40]

Thus, *Coraline* can be read as contributing to the broader overvaluation of the handmade during a historical moment marked by omnipresent digital technology, and it should also (in retrospect) be recognized as a foundational text for LAIKA's brand not only in terms of technology and aesthetics but also in relation to the studio's (self-)image, specifically defined in relation to its signature animation technique. However, this is not to say that the studio's creative and promotional strategies have not evolved since 2009; in fact, Travis Knight credits the retention of *Coraline*'s 'core team' as a major factor in the continual refinement of the studio's production process and the gradual embrace of advanced technologies, as it allowed studio members to draw and build upon their shared production experience. As he has explained,

> by going from film to film together like we have, all the innovations that happen over the course of making a film, from 3-D printing our characters' faces in colour to advances in rigging or lighting, stay with us. All of the things we learned on *Coraline* we applied to *ParaNorman*, and all of the things we learned on *ParaNorman* and *Coraline* we applied to *The Boxtrolls*.[41]

Indeed, in recent years, there has been a shift towards a more complete embrace of digital filmmaking at LAIKA. This culminated in a widely publicized Academy Award nomination for visual effects for the studio's 2016 feature *Kubo and the Two Strings* (Travis Knight, 2016).[42] Marking a tonal shift away from the (over)emphasis on the handmade discussed above, the *Hollywood Reporter* identified the film as a 'hybrid' production which combined stop motion and computer animation.[43] Travis Knight, meanwhile, acknowledged the centrality of visual effects to his feature but – very much in line with LAIKA's established brand – attempted to reframe his studio's reliance on twenty-first-century effects as true to the roots of the stop-motion medium: '[The nomination is] shocking, not because I don't think it's deserving, but because it required the visual effects branch to look at what we do in a different way. Really, the whole thing is a visual effect. If you go back to the dawn of cinema, stop motion was one of the first visual effects.'[44]

Rhetorical exercises aside, Birgitta Hosea has rightly pointed out that LAIKA's most recent films 'could just as well have been CGI animation as the result is so perfect that it no longer looks handmade'.[45] Perhaps in response to this very visible blurring of the boundaries between stop motion and a conventional digital aesthetic, LAIKA marked the release of its latest feature, *Missing Link*, with a promotional video ('Inside the Magic of LAIKA') in which Knight is more forthcoming about the fact that, while LAIKA's filmmaking is 'craft-based', it does rely on blending traditional animation with the latest computer technologies.[46] This (belated) recognition of the impact of digital production methods on LAIKA's ability to remain at the vanguard of contemporary commercial stop-motion animation echoes Jane Shadbolt's observation, in her chapter for this book, that, 'ironically, … the same digital processes that threatened to make stop motion redundant as a special effect have propelled this very analogue style into the feature film mainstream'. Digital processes have certainly propelled LAIKA into the mainstream, too, and will likely continue to shape both the studio's filmmaking approach and its creative identity for years to come.

Writing about stop-motion pioneer Willis O'Brien's work, Dan North observes the following:

> Out-takes from *The Lost World* show that O'Brien, animating at speed, would sometimes appear in the frame for a split-second, mistakenly caught on camera between model movements. Even if we are always aware that the dinosaurs are miniature models, it is only through examination of the vestigial traces of the artist that we can discern their exact scale and gain a glimpse at the interstitial spaces in which the art of special effects is performed. It is a compelling act of concealment, making the puppeteer invisible.[47]

As I write this introduction, nearly a century after *The Lost World*'s release, the days of concealed stop-motion labour are long gone. *Coraline* helped usher in a new era of stop-motion visibility – for mainstream audiences, critics and the commercial animation industry. What is more, LAIKA's foregrounding of the craft within the film (examined in various chapters across this collection) and in numerous paratexts invited a new appreciation for the form as both a traditional art and a medium capable of rising to – and conquering – the challenges of the digital age.

Exploring (with) *Coraline*

Coraline is a narrative about discovery; it celebrates the impulse to venture into the dark, unearth the hidden and make sense of the unknown, however daunting it may be. This essay collection honours its namesake's explorer spirit by delving into her story from a variety of analytical angles in order to knit together a web of interconnected readings by animation scholars and practitioners from around the globe. Divided into three sections, the volume examines *Coraline*'s place in history, evaluates its cultural impact, dissects its politics and unpacks its role in the technological and aesthetic development of its medium. More broadly, it celebrates stop motion as a unique and enduring artform while embracing its capacity to evolve in response to cultural, political and technological changes, as well as shifting critical and audience demands.

Part 1 places the film in a range of historical contexts, tracing its roots back to earlier forms of art and entertainment (Chapters 1 and 4) and situating it within the history of stop-motion and LAIKA's larger body of work (Chapters 2 and 3). In Chapter 1, Malcolm Cook explores the function of drawing in *Coraline*, advocating for a re-evaluation of the role of graphic arts in contemporary mainstream animation filmmaking. He analyses the film's evocation of the Victorian period, focusing on the resonance between cultural shifts in the understanding of vision that occurred during that time and *Coraline*'s commentary on the similarly transformative moment that contemporary animation is currently undergoing due to the rise of digital technologies. Chapter 2 places *Coraline* within LAIKA's larger oeuvre, discussing the studio's signature approach vis-à-vis its fusion of disparate stylistic sources that offers an alternative to other leading American animation producers such as Disney/Pixar. Miriam Harris identifies hybridization as one of LAIKA's leading creative strategies, arguing that, starting with *Coraline*, the studio's features have consistently combined aesthetic influences and narrative tropes while also blending analogue and digital technology. Using queer theory, she also considers the degree to which hybridization allows LAIKA to challenge normative structures in its approach to animation production and its representation of human experience. My own study, Chapter 3, focuses on LAIKA's self-reflexivity, interpreting it as fundamental to the studio's subtextual historicization effort, wherein *Coraline* functions as a network of intertextual references to pivotal moments in stop motion's past. This chapter unpacks the ways in which the film's exploration of the stop-motion process unfolds through allusions to seminal works and directors, as well as key technological and aesthetic developments that have shaped the medium. In doing so, my discussion illuminates LAIKA's efforts to frame *Coraline* as the heir apparent and torch bearer of a global creative legacy. In all three chapters, intertextual analysis is employed in order to root *Coraline* within a network of intellectual and creative traditions, tracing and historicizing the aesthetic and technological connections and reference points that have shaped its style and LAIKA's production philosophy. Chapter 4 goes even further, situating the film at the centre of a 'multiverse' of artistic and epistemological endeavours spanning several centuries and numerous literary, political and creative traditions and schools of thought. In his poetic study of what he has termed *Coraline*'s 2½ D – contrasting parallel dimensions, flatness crashing into 3D, dead space left to ambiguity – Norman M. Klein takes the reader on a whirlwind historical tour, touching upon Baroque Artifice, modernist aesthetics, early industrialism and Russian literary theory (to name a few trajectories), finding provocative ways to put them in conversation with LAIKA's film.

Part 2 looks at *Coraline* through the lens of industry, focusing on its production process and the underlying technologies that render it both aesthetically distinct and historically significant. This section of the volume also pursues questions of spectatorship, unpacking both the broader critical reception of the film and individual perceptual responses to its signature technique. Chapter 5 offers an in-depth discussion of the use of replacement animation in *Coraline*, analysing the theoretical, narrative and aesthetic implications of LAIKA's engagement with this traditional stop-motion method. Dan Torre reads the studio's employment of replacement animation as a key metanarrative that permeates *Coraline*, demonstrating how 'the very concept and process' of the technique is thematically mirrored throughout the film. In Chapter 6, Jane Shadbolt contends that *Coraline* marked a pivotal moment in the recent history of stop-motion technological development, offering a production-oriented analysis of the impact of computer-controlled camera rigs and digital still cameras on LAIKA's storytelling vocabulary. As she demonstrates, *Coraline*'s use of digital and computer-controlled production tools enabled it to borrow from the cinematic language of live-action filmmaking, resulting in a visual style distinct from earlier generations of stop-motion features. The following two chapters of the collection engage with two different aspects of spectatorship. In Chapter 7, Ann Owen takes an innovative approach to the subject by drawing on neuroscientific and neuroaesthetic research on human visual processes in order to study the relationship between the visual signifiers in *Coraline*, stop-motion's unique embodied spectatorship qualities and the narrative needs of the story. Building on interdisciplinary knowledge, she asks if – and how – LAIKA may have activated 'some neural process that links artifact, medium and content, and that benefits from some elements of the stop-motion technique remaining visible'. Zooming out from the individual to the global, Rayna Denison's chapter rounds off this section's analysis of spectatorship by comparing the initial critical response to *Coraline* in the United States to its reception upon the film's later release in the UK. Chapter 8 examines news, magazine and trade reviews in both countries, revealing *Coraline*'s position as a challenging text that pushed against established ratings categories and conventional children's film review tropes. Through a close analysis of critical debates surrounding the film, Denison highlights the emergence of a contradictory discourse of 'darkness and delight', which shaped the film's paradoxical reception, marked by positive evaluations of the animation, offered alongside alarmist rhetoric regarding its potential negative impact on young audiences.

Part 3 of this collection examines the sociopolitical and ideological dimensions of *Coraline*, asking how the film addresses questions of identity, reflects on familial relationships and evolving notions of the contemporary family and models queer representation in animated cinema. Chapter 9 picks up on and, crucially, brings to the forefront of the discussion key intellectual and theoretical threads woven throughout the volume's earlier pages, such as Miriam Harris's discussion of *Coraline*'s opposition to normativity and Rayna Denison's study of the film's resistance to conventional categorization. Kodi Maier draws on witchcraft as a metaphor for queer power, arguing that Coraline, the Other Mother and the Misses Forcible and Spink manifest aspects of the Triple Goddess deity. Maier's analysis challenges heteronormative interpretations of LAIKA's film, demonstrating how *Coraline* can be read as a text deeply engaged with queer identity, political resistance and the ongoing, ever-relevant fight against social oppression. Chapter 10 examines the threat of losing one's identity as comparable to becoming a puppet, arguing that, in *Coraline*, this central narrative and aesthetic motif functions as commentary on recent technological developments (particularly the growth of digital media production) and a platform for exploring philosophical questions 'about what is alive, intelligent, and autonomous'. Putting *Coraline* in conversation with various theoretical conceptualizations of the puppet, Eric Herhuth proposes that the film ultimately reinforces liberal subjectivity and 'copes with the state of having already become a puppet'. In Chapter 11, Jane Batkin explores questions of child identity, child displacement and the reimagined contemporary American family unit by focusing on the image of the wandering child in *Coraline*. Tracing the ways in which Selick's young protagonist navigates and overcomes fears of abduction and abandonment, Batkin demonstrates how the heroine 'eventually finds herself in her quest to establish firmer ideas of home and family'. The final chapter of the volume challenges conventional readings of *Coraline* as a mother-daughter narrative by exploring the ways in which *Coraline*'s 'paternal dyad', consisting of a fictional father and an Author Father (Neil Gaiman), fundamentally shapes and structures the story. Nicholas Andrew Miller reflects on *Coraline*'s origin as a tale composed by a father for his daughters, explores the narrative's relationship with the legacy of father figures in literary representations of maternal evil and argues that Selick's adaptation offers a constructive critique of this tradition by resisting and challenging a normative view of fatherhood defined in terms of power and discipline.

The title of this volume – *A Closer Look at Studio LAIKA's Stop-Motion Witchcraft* – is a tip of the hat to Maier's chapter and the transformative power it locates at the heart of *Coraline*. However, on a broader level, it is also a recognition of stop motion's unique flavour of cinematic magic. Like witchcraft, puppet craft remains poorly understood and frequently branded as a relic of a bygone era – and yet, it has endured, an art form equal parts mystifying and awe-inspiring. The goal of the following pages is to dispel some of that mystery, while preserving all of the wonder.

Finally, this volume, too, is a form of witchcraft. Its chapters peek through Coraline's hag stone in search of the film's hidden soul. What they find is a kaleidoscopic hall of mirrors, simultaneously miniature and vast, enchanting and cursed. More than a decade after *Coraline*'s release, her world still shimmers at the edges, as elusive as it is tantalizing.

Notes

1   Ken A. Priebe, *The Advanced Art of Stop-Motion Animation* (Boston, MA: Cengage Learning, 2010), p. 56.

2   Joe Fordham, '*Coraline*: A Handmade World', *Cinefex*, no. 117 (2009), p. 42.

3   Priebe, *The Advanced Art of Stop-Motion Animation*, p. 57.

4 Carolyn Giardina, ' "Coraline" Makers Reveal How They Sculpted 6,333 Faces Fast', *The Hollywood Reporter*, 12 February 2016. https://www.hollywoodreporter.com/behind-screen/coraline-makers-reveal-how-they-863155 (accessed 3 November 2020).

5 Priebe, *The Advanced Art of Stop-Motion Animation*, p. 57.

6 For a detailed analysis of replacement animation in *Coraline*, see Dan Torre's chapter in this volume.

7 Giardina, ' "Coraline" Makers Reveal How They Sculpted 6,333 Faces Fast'.

8 Sarah Saunders, 'LAIKA's Brian McLean Talks about 3D Printed Faces for Studio's New Stop Motion Animation Film', *3D Print*, 20 March 2019. https://3dprint.com/238607/brian-mclean-talks-3d-printed-faces-for-laika-stop-motion-animation/ (accessed 4 November 2020).

9 Saunders, 'LAIKA's Brian McLean Talks about 3D Printed Faces'.

10 Stephen Jones, *Coraline: A Visual Companion* (New York: HarperCollins, 2009), p. 114.

11 Scott Higgins, '3D in Depth: *Coraline, Hugo*, and a Sustainable Aesthetic', *Film History: An International Journal*, vol. 24, no. 2 (2012), p. 200.

12 Ibid., p. 196.

13 Ibid., p. 207.

14 Pete Kozachik, '2 Worlds in 3 Dimensions', *American Cinematographer*, vol. 90, no. 2 (2009), p. 28.

15 Stephen Prince, *Digital Visual Effects in Cinema: The Seduction of Reality* (New Brunswick, NJ: Rutgers University Press, 2012), p. 215.

16 Kenneth Turan, 'Review: "Coraline" ', *Los Angeles Times*, 6 February 2009. https://www.latimes.com/entertainment/la-et-coraline6-2009feb06-story.html (accessed 18 November 2020).

17 A. O. Scott, 'Cornered in a Parallel World: Coraline', *New York Times*, 6 February 2009, p. C1.

18 Ray Zone, *3-D Revolution: The History of Modern Stereoscopic Cinema* (Lexington: University Press of Kentucky, 2012), p. 319.

19 Caetlin Benson-Allott, 'The *Chora* Line: RealD Incorporated', *South Atlantic Quarterly*, vol. 110, no. 3 (2011), p. 621.

20 Higgins, '3D in Depth', p. 205.

21 Scott, 'Cornered in a Parallel World'.

22 Jones, *Coraline: A Visual Companion*, p. 4.

23 Ibid., p. 13.

24 Ibid., p. 14.

25 Ibid., p. 23.

26 Ibid., pp. 199–206.

27 Tim Ashley, '*Coraline* Review – Creepy Adaptation of Neil Gaiman's Tale Will
    Turn Kids on to Opera', *The Guardian*, 30 March 2018. https://www.theguardian.
    com/music/2018/mar/30/coraline-review-neil-gaiman-barbican (accessed 5
    November 2020).

28 Jones, *Coraline: A Visual Companion*, p. 33.

29 Ibid., p. 55.

30 Megan Troutman, 'It's Alive … AGAIN: Redefining Children's Film through
    Animated Horror', in Casie Hermansson and Janet Zepernick (eds), *The Palgrave
    Handbook of Children's Film and Television* (Cham, Switzerland: Palgrave
    Macmillan, 2019), p. 165.

31 Ibid., p. 149.

32 Catherine Lester, 'The Children's Horror Film: Characterizing an "Impossible"
    Subgenre', *The Velvet Light Trap*, no. 78 (2016), p. 34.

33 For an extended discussion of LAIKA's approach to building a brand rooted in
    notions of historical continuity, see Chapter 3 of this volume.

34 Andrea Comiskey, 'Special Effects in Contemporary Puppet Animation', in Dan
    North, Bob Rehak and Michael S. Duffy (eds), *Special Effects: New Histories/
    Theories/Contexts* (London: BFI Palgrave, 2015), p. 59.

35 Ibid., p. 57.

36 Priebe, *The Advanced Art of Stop-Motion Animation*, p. 57.

37 Zone, *3-D Revolution*, p. 323.

38 Jones, *Coraline: A Visual Companion*, p. 73.

39 Caroline Ruddell and Paul Ward, 'Introduction', in Caroline Ruddell and Paul Ward
    (eds), *The Crafty Animator: Handmade, Craft-Based Animation and Cultural Value*
    (Cham, Switzerland: Palgrave Macmillan, 2019), p. 2.

40 Carla MacKinnon, 'Autobiography and Authenticity in Stop-Motion Animation',
    in Caroline Ruddell and Paul Ward (eds), *The Crafty Animator: Handmade, Craft-
    Based Animation and Cultural Value* (Cham, Switzerland: Palgrave Macmillan,
    2019), pp. 105–6.

41 Caitlin Roper, 'The Man Who Brought Stop-Motion Animation to the 21st
    Century', *Wired*, 18 September 2014. https://www.wired.com/2014/09/travis-
    knight-stop-motion-boxtrolls/ (accessed 23 September 2020).

42 Notably, the last time an animated feature appeared in this category was in 1993,
    with *The Nightmare Before Christmas*.

43 Carolyn Giardina, 'Oscars: "Kubo and the Two Strings" is Rare Animated Feature
    to be Nominated in VFX', *The Hollywood Reporter*, 24 January 2017. https://www.
    hollywoodreporter.com/behind-screen/oscars-2017-kubo-two-strings-is-rare-
    animated-feature-be-nominated-vfx-967979 (accessed 16 November 2020).

44 Ibid.

45 Birgitta Hosea, 'Made by Hand', in Caroline Ruddell and Paul Ward (eds), *The Crafty Animator: Handmade, Craft-Based Animation and Cultural Value* (Cham, Switzerland: Palgrave Macmillan, 2019), p. 33.

46 Carlos Aguilar, 'Take a Look at the Painstaking Craft behind Laika's "Missing Link", *Cartoon Brew*, 10 April 2019. https://www.cartoonbrew.com/stop-motion/take-a-look-at-the-painstaking-craft-behind-laikas-missing-link-172509.html (accessed 10 May 2020).

47 Dan North, *Performing Illusions: Cinema, Special Effects and the Virtual Actor* (New York: Wallflower Press, 2008), p. 77.

Part One

Historical contexts and perspectives

1

Drawing *Coraline*: Illustration, adaptation and visuality

Malcolm Cook

Towards the end of the 2009 film adaptation of *Coraline*, directed by Henry Selick, we are confronted with an unsettling moment that plays on the film's relationship with drawing, juxtaposing the graphic with digital and sculptural ways of representing the world, and engaging with questions about the limits of vision. In this sequence, Coraline, aiming to escape the increasingly disturbing 'Other Mother', leaves the 'other house' that mirrors her own original home, and goes outside. As she walks away from the house through the gardens and orchard, the world seems to melt away (see Figure 1.1).

The landscape becomes overexposed blank white space and the trees become two-dimensional lines, before disappearing. As Coraline and the cat continue walking, they unintentionally find themselves returning to the house, which rematerializes as if from mist, first resembling a black and white line drawing, then a pixelized shimmer and finally the three-dimensional model seen earlier in the film. *Coraline* is a stop-motion animation production, but this sequence evokes the moving line drawings that have dominated animation history and the wire-frame spaces used to pre-render computer-generated images before the time-consuming calculations of a final render. The viewer's perplexed response, arising from uncertainty about how the scene was shot, echoes Coraline's realization that the visible Other World she sees is not all it seems.

This sequence is emblematic of the ideas raised in this chapter through an exploration of the function of drawing in this film, which is concealed but significant in many ways: in the film's production, in the process of adapting the book for the screen and in the story's thematic and conceptual concerns. At a practical level, *Coraline*'s production relied heavily on development and

Figure 1.1 The Other World collapses.

concept drawings by artists including Mike Cachuela, Dan Krall, Stef Choi and Tadahiro Uesugi, and traces of this remain in the film, for instance, in set designs and character models. Adapting Neil Gaiman's novel (2002) also meant engaging with Dave McKean's graphic contributions to that source, as well as with the longer history of illustrated books.[1] The story of *Coraline* introduces ideas about drawing and media specificities, which are reformulated in each adaptation of the source novel. This in turn involves epistemological questions about vision generally and the representation of the world in art in particular. *Coraline* was marketed as a hand-crafted film and heralded as spearheading a renaissance of stop-motion animation at a time when digital techniques and computer animation were transforming cinema and our way of seeing the world.[2] Looking at the film's evocation of the Victorian period, when vision and its relationship to knowledge were undergoing a comparable change, offers a way to understand *Coraline*'s contribution to, and commentary on, twenty-first-century developments in animation.

Drawing and the influence of Victorian illustration

The 2002 novel written by Neil Gaiman and illustrated by Dave McKean explicitly acknowledged an inheritance from late-nineteenth- and early-twentieth-century children's literature and fairy tales in its epigraph from G. K. Chesterton: 'Fairy tales are more than true: not because they tell us that dragons exist, but because they tell us that dragons can be beaten.'[3] Later critics of both novel and film adaptation have recognized in the story allusions to Victorian texts, especially Lewis Carroll's *Alice's Adventures in Wonderland* (1865) and *Through the Looking-Glass, and What Alice Found There* (1871). Other stories that are commonly cited as having a direct influence include J. M. Barrie's *Peter Pan* (1904/1911), Lucy Clifford's *The New Mother* (1882), Frances Hodgson Burnett's *Behind the White Brick* (1881), Christina Rossetti's *Speaking Likenesses* (1874), Juliana Horatia Ewing's *Amelia and the Dwarfs* (1870), Jean Ingelow's *Mopsa the Fairy* (1869) and Anna M. Richards's *A New Alice in the Old Wonderland* (1895).[4] These readings of the *Coraline* novel identify in it intertextual references to Victorian and early-twentieth-century literature that are used to comment upon themes of childhood, gender and psychoanalytical theories of the uncanny.[5] These influences have also been used to read subsequent versions, such as P. Craig Russell's graphic novel and the film, even if they have been necessarily altered in the process of adaptation.[6]

Largely absent from previous discussion of these Victorian influences on *Coraline* is the role of drawing. All of the aforementioned Victorian stories were accompanied by drawings that served many functions, but a critical one for this analysis is the ability of drawing to visualize new fantastical worlds and occurrences.[7] Just as the text of *Coraline* makes extensive references to Victorian children's literature, the incorporation of Dave McKean's drawings into the finished book echoes the functions and practices of Victorian illustration. Gaiman and McKean had already collaborated on a number of prior works, including the *Violent Cases* graphic novel (1987), McKean's covers for *The Sandman* comic book series (1989–96) and the serial *Signal to Noise* in *The Face* magazine (1989) later published as a standalone book (1992). McKean's drawings for *Coraline* help visualize the fantastical moments of the book, such as the Other Mother's button eyes, or the collapsing world sequence that also appears in the film adaptation.[8] The illustrations are typically presented at the start of each chapter, or within one or two pages of it. Rather than being situated in direct alignment with the narrative moment they relate to, the drawings precede the corresponding text description, often by many pages. The effect, at least for first-time readers, is a disconcerting foreshadowing of narrative events. This is reinforced by McKean's drawings, which are in keeping with his prior collaborations with Gaiman but are highly unusual for a children's imprint. Their expressionist style, rejection of conventional linear perspective and ambiguous and uncanny subjects all contribute to the unsettling tone of the novel.

The key point here is that *Coraline* was a visual work from the outset. While McKean's drawings precede the narrative events in the pagination of the finished typeset novel, Gaiman's words anticipate the process of their own visualization, reflecting the writer's sensitivity to the relationship between text and images honed in the comics medium. This includes a moment where Coraline herself becomes illustrator of a story she has written on her father's computer.[9] Selick received Gaiman's manuscript before it was published, another indication that the author always had its visualization in mind.[10] The film's production likewise incorporated drawing and visualization as a crucial preliminary process that preceded full animation and greatly shaped the finished stop-motion film. Storyboard artists including Mike Cachuela, and conceptual and character design artists including Dave Krall, Tadahiro Uesugi and Stef Choi contributed drawings and other graphic art that adapted and visualized the story.[11] The use of these graphic pre-production processes is, of course, common in animation of all kinds, as seen in the 'Art of ...' genre of behind-the-scenes publicity material. The extent to which drawing remains integral to the finished *Coraline* film is notable and suggests a broader need to reconsider the way graphic arts continue to play a formative role in animated films, even those using stop-motion and computer animation.

The work of well-known Japanese illustrator Tadahiro Uesugi became central to the development of the look of the film through his pre-production concept art, which combined characters with set and background designs. His work reveals a strong influence of 1950s 'cartoon modern' American commercial illustration and animation design, which was itself indebted to pre-war European artists such as Raoul Dufy.[12] This is evident in Uesugi's use of colour, reminiscent of Fauvist painters, but his work also retains the original roughly sketched outlines that anchor it in the practice of drawing, rather than the lines being 'cleaned up' as they might be in other commercial illustration. In an interview Uesugi points to the way these qualities were incorporated into the design of *Coraline*: 'What amazed me was the professional sense of the set designers, who were trying their best to re-create jagged lines on the edge of the sets, which is a typical style when I'm drawing the outlines on my illustrations'.[13] Cinematographer Pete Kozachik corroborates this direct effect on the film, stating that 'Uesugi supplied a valuable influence for the show; his work has a graphic simplicity'.[14]

Mike Cachuela provided further insight into this in an interview conducted for this chapter. Cachuela worked as co-director on *Coraline* throughout its pre-production and early animation and is credited as co-storyboard supervisor on the finished film.[15] He told me a key aim of the visual development of the film was to 'try to create a look that was hand drawn' and that the question of 'how do you turn a drawing into 3D' was an active and difficult challenge for the production team.[16] To replicate the concept art as stop-motion sets, a series of mock-up cardboard models were created to understand 'how to realise these drawings and illustrations in 3D'.[17] These required extensive experimentation and revision because 'if you're trying to do something that really represents a drawing it's not going to be your standard set construction or model making'.[18] Professional industrial practices were insufficient here, suggesting a transformation of the very idea of how stop-motion films should be made. One technique attempted to achieve the desired effect was to dip wire into glue and lay it in sand to give a textured line that could be applied to edges of models to give them the loose improvised feel of Uesugi's illustrations.[19] In contrast to that craft-based idea, which was impractical for full-scale production, digital technology could provide assistance. The pixelated house described in this essay's introduction was inspired by 'a really crude scan of one of the sets of the house – it wasn't a very good scanner – so you had this really fragmented scan'.[20] Drawing thus went beyond a simple design tool to inspire innovative techniques that changed the production process of stop-motion animation.

Adaptation and medium

As described above, the Victorian influence on *Coraline* resulted in an extensive and nuanced incorporation of drawing as practice into the novel and later adaptations. Beyond this practical relationship, the dialogue between the Victorian period and the early twenty-first century raises two further resonances that may explain the film's contemporary reworking of these seemingly antiquated literary works. First is the way Victorian publishing underwent a redefinition of the place of illustration within literary works, and second are broader cultural shifts in the understanding of vision occurring in both historical and contemporary moments.

The place and valuation of illustration within the transatlantic anglophone literary tradition changed considerably over the Victorian period and as a result greatly affected subsequent designations of medium specificities.[21] Early Victorian novels were routinely illustrated, but over time commentators increasingly denigrated illustrations of any kind.[22] By the early twentieth century, the literary novel eschewed illustration, which had become associated with specific types and genres of book, notably children's literature.[23] Later critics looking back on the period ignored the illustrations that accompanied classic novels by authors such as Dickens and Thackeray, while Tenniel's illustrations for Carroll's work continued to be celebrated, adopting and reinforcing the association between the art of illustration and juvenile content.[24]

The details here are less significant than the influence they had and the principles they demonstrate. This contextual history of illustration challenges fixed, ahistoric accounts of individual media and perceived medium specificities. Where once the literary novel incorporated illustration, the very definition of the novel changed over time to exclude drawings.[25] This reshaping and altered judgement of the illustrated novel supports Noël Carroll's theoretical critique of the idea of medium specificity.[26] Media, including novels and stop-motion animation, do not have inherent and eternal qualities but rather are the product of historically and culturally specific developments, even if that process is often denied or hidden.

The specificity of words and images, and value judgements about a hierarchy between them, is directly addressed within the story of *Coraline*. Gaiman's text invites a direct comparison of the capacity of words and images to communicate an idea. Mist and fog provide a repeated circumstance for this.[27] In chapter 2, early in the story, Coraline's boredom leads her to start drawing:

> Coraline tried drawing the mist. After ten minutes of drawing she still had a white sheet of paper with
>
> M   ST
>
>   I
>
> written on it in one corner[28]

Other commentators have noted the potential semiotic or psychoanalytical readings of shifting the personal pronoun out of this word.[29] However, this can also be read as a reflection on writing and drawing as distinct media. Neither drawing nor writing seem able to fully represent the elusive appearance and quality of this meteorological phenomenon. Instead Gaiman/Coraline adopt an amalgam of the two, as the word is treated in a graphic manner, acquiring both linguistic and pictorial meaning. The combination of word and image here becomes a microcosm of the book as a whole, as the juxtaposition of Gaiman's words and McKean's illustrations merge to make a meaning not inherent in the individual elements, returning the novel to its Victorian conditions. Similar concerns arise in consideration of the *Coraline* 'graphic novel' adaptation by P. Craig Russell.

The decision to adapt *Coraline* as a stop-motion film extended this negotiation to animation media boundaries and definitions.[30] Publicity and trade press discussion of the film consistently raised different animation techniques and offered historical arguments about them, albeit in simple terms. The idea of a 'golden age' or 'renaissance' of stop motion was noted in a range of sources.[31] *Coraline* had been preceded by a number of financially and critically successful stop-motion features, including Selick's *The Nightmare before Christmas* (1993) and *James and the Giant Peach* (1996), along with Tim Burton's *Corpse Bride* (2005), Aardman's *Chicken Run* (2000) and *Wallace & Gromit: The Curse of the Were-Rabbit* (2005). Alongside *Coraline*, 2009 also saw the release of Wes Anderson's *Fantastic Mr. Fox*, Stéphane Aubier and Vincent Patar's *A Town Called Panic* and Adam Elliot's *Mary and Max*, as well as the announcement of Tim Burton's *Frankenweenie* (2012). This was a global phenomenon going beyond the dominant American industry, involving Australian, British, French and other European countries, as well as several international co-productions. This unprecedented volume of feature films produced using stop-motion animation techniques was noteworthy, but many sources went no further than noting it.

If a closer analysis of this growth was applied by commentators, it was to contrast stop motion with the rise of computer-animated films. The *Calgary Herald* stated this boldly in its headline 'Stop-motion putting end to CGI domination', while *Animation World Network* had the film 'bucking the CG toon trend'.[32] Following the exceptional success of *Toy Story* (John Lasseter, 1995), computer animated films from Pixar, DreamWorks and others had become a dominant part of mainstream cinema and the principal form of animation feature production.[33] Discussion of *Coraline*, and the other films mentioned above, frequently turned to the hand-crafted qualities of stop motion as a way of contrasting these films with digital animation. In doing so, they argued that *Coraline* was indicative of a new historical moment in which the visible materiality of stop motion was understood to relieve the clinical flawlessness of computer-generated imagery (CGI).[34] The contrast with CGI was part of the initial marketing message from LAIKA and the filmmakers, with Selick quoted as saying 'it's the imperfections (in stop-motion animation) that I think make it attractive, that bring the audience in ... there would be no point [in perfection]. We would be doing CG.'[35] This viewpoint was echoed in publicity and reviews. The *Daily Telegraph* contrasted 'quick-fire computer-generated (CG) animation' with 'painstaking stop-motion process', in the process misrepresenting the relative labour involved in the two media.[36] *Slate* similarly distinguished the two, saying, 'Unlike CGI, stop-motion animation is a tactile medium, its textures and volumes vividly palpable ... [unlike] the shimmering gradients of computer-generated animation.'[37] Exceptionally, the Chicago *Daily Herald* compared the film to both computer and cel animation, praising the filmmakers' choice of stop motion because 'digital animation would look too sterile; hand-drawn 2-D animation would look too flat'.[38]

These accounts of the film are helpful in indicating that *Coraline*, in common with its source novel and the Victorian inspirations for it, was an active participant in debates about medium specificities. Yet the focus on stop-motion animation in competition with computer animation underplayed both the extensive use of digital tools within the film's production and the role of drawing as a third medium. Discussions of adaptations are commonly centred on questions of fidelity.[39] This is apparent in many reviews of the film, such as the *Daily Telegraph*'s write-up, which praised the film because 'it has all the eerie, surreal tang of Gaiman's novel'.[40] Given the original source novel had a number of close links with drawing, as discussed above, it might be expected that the choice of three-dimensional stop-motion techniques over drawn cel animation would receive criticism for lacking fidelity, but this was not the case and drawing was largely absent from popular discussions of the film. Similarly, while popular press lingered on the hand-crafted production of the film, specialized industry sources reveal the more extensive and hybrid analogue and digital workflow in use.

In a *Studio Daily* interview, Selick suggested up to 90 percent of *Coraline* was practical, with digital techniques used purely for 'compositing, some manipulation, [and] some repair work'.[41] However, it is also clear that while the finished film image may be of a physical object, the workflow that produced it was intensively hybrid and incorporated considerable use of digital technology. This includes use of CGI for the 'starry night' sequence when Coraline sees three ghost children and most extensively the 'replacement face animation' that was used for key characters, including Coraline and both mothers.[42] *Post* magazine explains that 'the flow of movement in facial expression was also gauged in the computer – using Autodesk Maya software – and the expressions we see in Coraline have been precisely directed by the keen eye of Selick in previs and during the shoot'.[43] Only after this process were these computer animated facial expressions made into physical models with the aid of a 3D printer. Vera Brosgol, at that time a storyboard artist at LAIKA, likewise indicates that during the production of *Coraline* the studio was rapidly transitioning to a technologically enhanced storyboard process, shifting from paper-based drawings to digital drawing tablets and animatics.[44]

The result of these digital technologies, combined with the heavy influence of drawing described earlier, is that the finished film is not a revival of archaic manual techniques but rather a meditation on the different materials and methods of animation. Like the marketing and publicity for the film, the opening credit sequence does initially seem to foreground the hand-crafted, showing a household space in which a puppet is being manually constructed. We see the metallic needle-like hands and fingers of an otherwise unseen person unpick a toy doll, turn it inside out and fill it with sawdust, and then remake the doll in the likeness of Coraline. Most shots are extreme close-ups that afford a detailed visual examination of the materials being handled, evoking their textures and tactility. The frames of individual shots are filled by, respectively, a well-worn toolbox containing implements with aged patina, the ridged cloth of the doll held together with woollen stitching and a shiny and leathery doll's coat. The sequence thus serves as an unambiguous self-reflexive account of the stop-motion animation process and its use of puppets made from everyday materials, evoking their tangible qualities. Yet even here there are subtle reminders of the two-dimensional drawings that preceded the film. The first view we have of the doll's coat is of the drawn lines of a tailor's pattern, showing the process of the translation from two-dimensional planes to a three-dimensional object. A close-up of the doll's face reveals its lips and cheeks to be painted on.

A similar tension between stop motion and other animation techniques emerges throughout *Coraline*. As raised earlier, mist and fog play a significant role in the source novel, and they subsequently provide a test case for adapting it to animated representation. In the novel, mist obscures and is described in optical terms: 'mist hung like blindness around the house'.[45] Similarly, midway through the book, when Coraline awakes in the 'other house' she is disorientated, but after putting the stone with a hole in her pocket 'it was as if her head had cleared a little. As if she had come out of some sort of a fog'.[46] Gaiman's interest in this weather phenomenon is multifaceted. In dramatic terms, mist provides an atmospheric setting for the unsettling story, but it is also used as an analogy for the capacities and limits of vision, and this underpins the discussion of medium specificity and language. What does mist look like? How should it be represented?

In the production of the film, the mist posed a problem for its representation using stop-motion techniques, just as it did for writing and drawing in the novel. According to stop-motion animator Barry Purves, nebulous phenomena like mist, fog and smoke 'notoriously look unconvincing when used with miniature models' and furthermore are difficult to manipulate frame by frame over many days, as would be required for the normal stop-motion workflow.[47] Mike Cachuela suggests early attempts to animate the fog using stop-motion footage of cotton wool were abandoned as unsuccessful.[48] A purely digital approach was also considered, but ultimately a hybrid method was used, combining physical effects with digital compositing. Theatrical dry ice and smoke were poured and blown over different object shapes, and then individual elements and movements were composited to create a 'collage of fog' that could be combined with the stop-motion model footage.[49] The adaptation of images and ideas between different media challenges their perceived capacities and stimulates new representational strategies. In this case, words, drawings and object animation each offer us a different perspective on the elusive nature of mist, but these media also acquire new capabilities in the process.

The hybrid techniques for creating the fog remain clearly evident and contribute to its unsettling appearance in the finished film. However, possibly the most extensive and complex hybridization of different animation media in *Coraline* is also one of the less obvious: the creation and animation of many of the characters themselves, especially Mr Bobinsky. Mr Bobinksy is the first character we see in the story world after the title sequence, performing his callisthenics on the roof of the Pink Palace apartments. His extreme body shape and gravity defying movements signal the non-naturalistic stylization of this world and anticipate his mixed-media origins discussed further below. Coraline's own first encounter with the character recapitulates the production process of the film, from novel to drawings to dimensional characters. Her initial introduction to him is through text: his name and address on the postal packages she finds on the porch and takes up to his apartment. She is then directed to him by a piece of graphic art: a sign pointing to his apartment. The sign is reminiscent of Russian Constructivist art in its primary colour palette, geometric shapes and sans serif typeface, hinting at his personality and ethnicity through drawing before it is alluded to in other details, such as his accent, clothes and accompanying music.

When Coraline finally meets Mr Bobinsky, he is evidently one of the most stylized and caricatured inhabitants of this world. The visual style of *Coraline* – especially Mr Bobinsky's design – was heavily influenced by British cartoonist Ronald Searle, as can be seen in pre-production artworks from artists including Shane Prigmore, Stef Choi and Dan Krall.[50] Mr Bobinsky's elongated limbs and bulbous torso resemble the cartoonist's characters, such as the famous St Trinian's schoolgirls. The final puppet of Mr Bobinsky retains a very strong trace of the film's pre-production line drawings, especially in the distinct individual strands in his moustache and body hair, as well as the gravity-defying caricatured physique.

Yet his model is also very clearly a stop-motion puppet in three dimensions. His items of clothing, including wristbands and woollen vest, have a tactile quality to them. Likewise, his facial movement has the characteristic irregularity of object animation, although his expressions rely upon the combination of digital animation and 3D printing described above. Unlike with other characters in the film, the seams produced by replacement face animation were not erased in digital post-production, so the lines by his eyes are a further reminder that we are looking at a physical model. However, his stylized body does rely on digital manipulation in other ways. His spindly legs are insufficient to support a heavy stop-motion puppet that could be reliably manipulated, so support rigs were necessary to carry the weight and avoid unintended movement.[51] These rigs were then erased in digital post-production, with a similar method used for many other scenes and characters in the film.[52] Mr Bobinsky therefore represents a truly hybrid animated character: an extreme caricature derived from drawing, the physicality and materiality of a stop-motion puppet, and the reality-defying posture and movement enabled by digital manipulation.

Visuality

As suggested above, the renegotiation of stop-motion aesthetics seen in *Coraline* can be considered a response to new developments in digital technology in a practical and industrial manner. The film's marketing distanced its stop-motion techniques from computer animation, even while the production workflow heavily incorporated digital manipulation. Yet the film can also be understood to engage with a more pervasive epistemological challenge that digital technology poses for animation. In broad terms, film theory has become preoccupied with the way the 'digital turn' has undermined the truth-value of the cinematic image by breaking its photochemical indexical trace of the world, in turn opening questions about the ontology of cinema.[53] Yet there are implications of this technological shift that are especially relevant to animation and have received less attention.

Throughout the twentieth century, viewers could make distinctions between different animation modes simply through close inspection of the final images. Stop motion and drawn or cel animation had characteristic production methods and materials, but these could also be readily discerned from the finished films. Hybrid or experimental techniques might require more attention but would reveal their construction with close scrutiny. Even when early computer animation appeared in the latter half of the century, it had distinguishing features that were plainly evident to the observer without recourse to production history. However, in the twenty-first century and the time of *Coraline*'s production, digitally manipulated animation images have been increasingly challenging the capacity of human vision to discriminate between them and identify their origins and methods. Akin to Coraline's initial inability to see the Other World for what it is, viewers face a potentially unsettling uncertainty about their ability to recognize and categorize animated images. As well as breaking down the boundaries between animated media and perceived specificities in them, recognizing these limits to vision raises pervasive existential questions. This contemporary shift in our ways of seeing and knowing the world can be seen as another way in which the film echoes the Victorian period and can explain the attachment to this otherwise distant historical moment.

In his book *Techniques of the Observer*, Jonathan Crary has persuasively demonstrated that the nineteenth century saw a radical shift in the cultural understanding of vision and the role of the observer in constructing what is seen.[54] Prior to this period an enlightenment model was dominant, in which 'observation leads to truthful inferences about the world'.[55] Scientific investigation of vision in the nineteenth century changed this, as the role of the observer in constructing what they saw was recognized. The stereoscope is, for Crary, emblematic of this shift because it provided practical demonstration that the observer and observed are inextricably linked.[56] In viewing images through a stereoscope, a viewer becomes aware of the disjunction between the sensory data that is provided (two slightly different two-dimensional images) and the single unitary image with depth they perceive. The term 'visuality' is helpful here to distinguish a cultural history of vision from its basic physiology. Hal Foster differentiates the two, stating that 'vision suggests sight as physical operation, and visuality sight as social fact' while recognizing that the two are not entirely discrete.[57] Crary does not argue that the basic mechanics of human vision changed in the nineteenth century but that visuality, our understanding of vision, was transformed.[58]

The attention to visuality Crary describes is closely connected to the earlier discussion of drawing and medium specificity. The Victorian stories that preceded *Coraline* can be seen as a reflection of a new way of looking at the world.[59] Of particular relevance here, the changes described in the use of drawing and illustration can also be seen in this light. New ways of seeing the world resulted in new ways of representing the world. Crary explicitly highlights canonical modernist painting as an example of this, but other forms of commercial graphic art can equally be considered in this way.[60] The concern here is not directly with unpacking these historical precedents, but rather understanding them as they are incorporated and refigured in the various versions of *Coraline*. *Coraline*'s self-conscious evocation of Victorian literature can be seen as a way of making connections between the historical changes in visuality those novels were part of and the comparable, but distinct, challenge digital technologies brought to present-day understanding of vision and their implications for distinguishing different types of animation.

Thematically and aesthetically, vision and visuality are central to *Coraline*, an inheritance from the source novel and its Victorian influences. The opening title sequence, showing the construction of a doll, lingers on the moments relating to eyes and the foreshadowing of the use of buttons to replace them in the main story. We see a large drawer full of pairs of button eyes and an extreme close-up of a sharp needle protruding through cloth out through the button eye (and for those watching in stereoscopic 3D, it disturbingly extends beyond the screen and threatens to pierce our own eyes). Many of the characters in the film are distinguished by ophthalmic quirks. Wybie is introduced wearing a strange facemask with multiple lenses that offer different perspectives on the world. Miss Spink's trademark is an exaggerated wink, while Miss Forcible is 'blind as a bat', and we are given a point of view shot through her *lorgnette* long-handled glasses that are another regression to the nineteenth century. The theatrical posters in the two spinsters' flat use puns on sight ('Julius Sees-Her', 'King Leer') to humorously draw attention to their earlier careers as objects of the 'male gaze'.[61] Coraline's father is given an absent-minded scholarly tone with his half-frame glasses.

The main plot involves the Other Mother attempting to persuade, trick or compel Coraline to give up her eyes, to be replaced with buttons. She constructs an illusory world that appears more colourful and dimensional, more alive, more desirable, than Coraline's original home. A range of production techniques were used to differentiate the two worlds, such as including different lighting and colour schemes, and variations in forced perspective set design.[62] The use of stereoscopic 3D plays a significant role in enhancing this effect when the film is experienced using this technology, creating an even stronger contrast between the claustrophobia and flatness of Coraline's original home and the space and depth of the Other World. The most telling example is the tunnel through the door that links the two worlds, which seems to extend into the screen, drawing Coraline, and viewers, into it. Cinematographer Pete Kozachik describes the 'stereo arc' across the film where 'at first, full 3-D opens up a better world for Coraline, but when things go bad, we carefully exaggerate stereo depth to match her distress'.[63] This was in part achieved by 'animating IO' in some shots, that is dynamically adjusting the interocular distance (the distance between the left and right images, copying the distance between our eyes) giving a greater or lesser sense of the depth to the stereoscopic image, evident in the trapeze act towards the end of the film.[64] Crucially, this adheres to Crary's characterization of stereoscopic technologies reinforcing an awareness of the role of the observer in constructing what is seen. Stereoscopic 3D here does not contribute to a Bazinian progression to 'total cinema'.[65] Rather it is used to further unsettle and disturb the viewer, aligning with Coraline's growing sense that all is not what it seems.

The climax of the film further dramatizes visuality and the idea that vision is a construction rather than providing access to an unfettered truth. Coraline is given a stone with a hole in it by Miss Spink and Miss Forcible, which she discovers allows her to see the Other World in a quite different way. Not only does the single hole mean Coraline must rely on flattened monocular vision, but it also drains the world of its vivid colours. The stone does not provide a 'true' picture of the Other World but rather discloses its illusion and construction, allowing Coraline to locate and retrieve what she is looking for. Importantly, the world the stone reveals resembles a drawing (see Figure 1.2). Highlights provide distinct linear edges to objects, while depth and texture are lost in the monochromatic colour. Despite the film's many departures from the source novel, in this respect the lineage is clear. In the novel, the stone also makes everything 'grey and colourless, like a pencil drawing'.[66] Through the stone, the world is returned to a form in which the construction of visual representation is foregrounded rather than hidden.

Figure 1.2 Coraline looks through the stone.

Conclusion

The centrality of drawing to *Coraline* revealed in this chapter indicates the continuing place this longstanding art practice has in contemporary mainstream animation in both practical and conceptual terms.[67] Traditional cel animation no longer holds the dominant position it had at the height of the studio system, but drawing remains a primary step in animation production through storyboards, character designs and development drawings, which are in turn integrated into digital workflows. This foundational role of drawing has profound effects upon the finished films like *Coraline*, whose origins in drawing abound once you look for them. Drawing also raises conceptual questions about representation and the truth-value of images. As *Coraline* both demonstrates and dramatizes, our relationship with drawn worlds is different from the physical objects of stop motion, the digital worlds created using computers, or indeed language.

More than this, we see a development of the place and definition of illustration and drawing and especially an increasing hybridity in which distinctions between animation media are dissolving. The late nineteenth century that provides so much of the inspiration for *Coraline* saw far-reaching changes in visuality and ways of representing the world. The rise of digital technology constitutes a similar transformative moment, and this can explain why the various adaptations of *Coraline* revive that earlier moment. The case study of *Coraline* presented here allows us to move beyond broad epochal claims to see how these changes are enacted in specific ways. Like Coraline herself, we may never look at the world in the same way again.

Acknowledgements

The author wishes to express his gratitude to Mike Cachuela for generously sharing his time and thoughts during the writing of this chapter.

Notes

1   A new edition of the book with alternative illustrations by Chris Riddell was released after the film in 2013.

2   Vanessa Farquharson, 'Stop-Motion Putting End to CGI Domination; Technique Enjoys Resurgence in Animated Market', *Calgary Herald*, 27 November 2009, p. E15.

3   Neil Gaiman and Dave McKean, *Coraline* (London: Bloomsbury, 2002), p. 9.

4   Chloé Germaine Buckley, 'Psychoanalysis, "Gothic" Children's Literature, and the Canonization of Coraline', *Children's Literature Association Quarterly*, vol. 1, no. 1 (2015), p. 58; Elizabeth Parsons, Naarah Sawers and Kate McInally, 'The Other Mother: Neil Gaiman's Postfeminist Fairytales', *Children's Literature Association Quarterly*, vol. 33, no. 4 (2009), p. 388; Maryna Matlock, '"What's in the Empty Flat?": Specular Identity and Authorship in Neil Gaiman's Coraline', in Sara K. Day

and Sonya Sawyer Fritz (eds), *The Victorian Era in Twenty-First Century Children's and Adolescent Literature and Culture* (London: Routledge, 2018), p. 45.

5   Richard Gooding, ' "Something Very Old and Very Slow": Coraline, Uncanniness, and Narrative Form', *Children's Literature Association Quarterly*, vol. 33, no. 4 (2008); Parsons, Sawers and McInally, 'The Other Mother: Neil Gaiman's Postfeminist Fairytales'; David Rudd, 'An Eye for an I: Neil Gaiman's Coraline and Questions of Identity', *Children's Literature in Education*, vol. 39, no. 3 (2008).

6   Meghann Meeusen, 'Framing Agency: Comics Adaptations of *Coraline* and *City of Ember*', in Michelle Ann Abate and Gwen Athene Tarbox (eds), *Graphic Novels for Children and Young Adults: A Collection of Critical Essays* (Jackson: University Press of Mississippi, 2017); Lindsay Myers, 'Whose Fear Is It Anyway? Moral Panics and "Stranger Danger" in Henry Selick's Coraline', *The Lion and the Unicorn*, vol. 36, no. 3 (2012), pp. 245–57.

7   Perry Nodelman, *Words About Pictures: The Narrative Art of Children's Picture Books* (Athens: University of Georgia Press, 1988), pp. 4–5, 69–71.

8   Gaiman and McKean, *Coraline*, pp. 32, 123.

9   Ibid., pp. 63–4.

10 John Clark, 'Adding Dimension to the Storytelling' *New York Times*, 1 February 2009, p. 16.

11 Amid Amidi, 'A Peek into the Art of "Coraline" Book That Never Was', *Cartoon Brew*, 2 July 2015. https://www.cartoonbrew.com/auctions/a-peek-into-the-art-of-coraline-book-that-never-was-gallery-108716.html (accessed 11 October 2019).

12 Bill Desowitz, 'Tadahiro Uesugi Talks "Coraline" Design', *Animation World Network*, 23 January 2009. https://www.awn.com/animationworld/tadahiro-uesugi-talks-coraline-design (accessed 11 October 2019); Amid Amidi, *Cartoon Modern: Style and Design in Fifties Animation* (San Francisco: Chronicle Books, 2006).

13 Desowitz, 'Tadahiro Uesugi Talks "Coraline" Design'.

14 Pete Kozachik, '2 Worlds in 3 Dimensions', *American Cinematographer*, vol. 90, no. 2 (2009), p. 27.

15 Dann Gire, 'Creepy Stop-Motion Animation Highlights Fantasy Turned Nightmare', *Daily Herald*, 5 February 2009, p. 19.

16 Mike Cachuela interview by Malcolm Cook, London, 25 September 2018.

17 Ibid.

18 Ibid.

19 Ibid.

20 Ibid.

21 For more on the bidirectional literary relationship between Britain and the United States see Robert Weisbuch, *Atlantic Double-Cross: American Literature and British*

Influence in the Age of Emerson (Chicago: University of Chicago Press, 1986); Paul Giles, *Virtual Americas: Transnational Fictions and the Transatlantic Imaginary* (Durham: Duke University Press, 2002).

22 Kamilla Elliott, *Rethinking the Novel/Film Debate* (Cambridge, MA: Cambridge University Press, 2003), pp. 37–8, 46.

23 Nodelman, *Words About Pictures: The Narrative Art of Children's Picture Books*, pp. 2–3; Patricia J. Cianciolo, *Picture Books for Children*, 4th edn (Chicago: American Library Association, 1997), pp. 1–41.

24 Elliott, *Rethinking the Novel/Film Debate*, p. 46.

25 Ibid.

26 Noël Carroll, 'The Specificity of Media in the Arts', *Journal of Aesthetic Education*, vol. 19, no. 4 (1985), pp. 5–20; Noël Carroll, 'Medium Specificity Arguments and Self-Consciously Invented Arts: Film, Video and Photography', *Millennium Film Journal*, no. 14/15 (1984–5), pp. 127–53.

27 Gaiman and McKean, *Coraline*, pp. 31, 84, 87, 89, 102, 133, 148.

28 Ibid., p. 26.

29 Rudd, 'An Eye for an I: Neil Gaiman's Coraline and Questions of Identity', p. 160; Parsons, Sawers and McInally, 'The Other Mother: Neil Gaiman's Postfeminist Fairytales', p. 377; Buckley, 'Psychoanalysis, "Gothic" Children's Literature, and the Canonization of Coraline', p. 75.

30 Similarly, Catherine Lester has shown how *Coraline*, along with other stop-motion films, including those from LAIKA and Tim Burton's contributions to the field, have played a significant role in the genre classification of 'children's horror films': Catherine Lester, 'The Children's Horror Film: Beneficial Fear and Subversive Pleasure in an (Im)Possible Hollywood Subgenre' (PhD thesis, University of Warwick, 2016); Catherine Lester, 'The Children's Horror Film: Characterizing an "Impossible" Subgenre', *Velvet Light Trap*, no. 78 (2016).

31 Sheila Johnston, 'A Delicious Way to Scare Your Little Darlings to Death; The New Animation from the Director of *The Nightmare before Christmas* is a Creepy Treat', *Daily Telegraph*, 9 May 2009, p. 14; Vanessa Farquharson, 'Stop-Motion Putting End to CGI Domination; Technique Enjoys Resurgence in Animated Market', *Calgary Herald*, 27 November 2009, p. E15; Susan Wloszczyna, '3-D and Stop-Motion Find "Coraline"; Visuals Pop with Old, New Images', *USA Today*, 18 November 2008, p. 1D; Ellen Wolff, 'Systems Go for Stop Motion', *Daily Variety*, 13 November 2009.

32 Farquharson, 'Stop-Motion Putting End to CGI Domination', p. E15; Thomas J. McLean, 'On the Set with "Coraline": Where the Motion Doesn't Stop', *Animation World Network*, 16 September 2008. https://www.awn.com/animationworld/set-coraline-where-motion-doesnt-stop (accessed 5 July 2019).

33   Christopher Holliday, *The Computer-Animated Film: Industry, Style and Genre* (Edinburgh: Edinburgh University Press, 2018).

34   For more on the tension between craft and the digital, see Caroline Ruddell and Paul Ward, 'Introduction', in Caroline Ruddell and Paul Ward (eds), *The Crafty Animator: Handmade, Craft-Based Animation and Cultural Value* (Cham, Switzerland: Palgrave Macmillan, 2019), p. 9.

35   McLean, 'On the Set with "Coraline"'.

36   Johnston 'A Delicious Way to Scare Your Little Darlings to Death', p. 14.

37   Dana Stevens, 'Button Eyes', *Slate*, 5 February 2009. http://www.slate.com/articles/arts/movies/2009/02/button_eyes.html (accessed 7 May 2019).

38   Gire, 'Creepy Stop-Motion Animation', p. 19.

39   Thomas M. Leitch, *Film Adaptation and Its Discontents: From Gone with the Wind to the Passion of the Christ* (Baltimore: Johns Hopkins University Press, 2007), pp. 127–50; Colin MacCabe, Kathleen Murray and Rick Warner, *True to the Spirit: Film Adaptation and the Question of Fidelity* (Oxford: Oxford University Press, 2011).

40   Johnston 'A Delicious Way to Scare Your Little Darlings to Death', p. 14.

41   Debra Kaufman, 'Director Henry Selick on Coraline', *Studio Daily*, 6 February 2009. http://www.studiodaily.com/2009/02/director-henry-selick-on-coraline/ (accessed 5 July 2019).

42   Ibid.

43   Ken McGorry, 'Cover Story: "Coraline" Animated via Stop-Motion', *Post*, 1 February 2009. http://www.postmagazine.com/Publications/Post-Magazine/2009/February-1-2009/cover-story-coraline-animated-via-stop-motion.aspx (accessed 11 October 2019).

44   Chris Pallant and Steven Price, *Storyboarding: A Critical History* (Basingstoke: Palgrave Macmillan, 2015), p. 162.

45   Gaiman and McKean, *Coraline*, p. 31.

46   Ibid., p. 84.

47   Barry J. C. Purves, *Stop-Motion Animation: Frame by Frame Film-Making with Puppets and Models* (London: Bloomsbury, 2014), p. 38.

48   Mike Cachuela interview by Malcolm Cook, London, 25 September 2018.

49   *The Making of Coraline* (UK Blu Ray Release, 2013).

50   Amidi, 'A Peek into the Art of "Coraline"'; Dan Krall, 'Coraline', http://www.dankrall.com/coraline/ (accessed 5 July 2019).

51   Joe Fordham, '*Coraline*: A Handmade World', *Cinefex*, no. 117 (2009), p. 51; Andrea Comiskey, '(Stop)Motion Control: Special Effects in Contemporary Puppet Animation', in Dan North, Bob Rehak and Michael S. Duffy (eds), *Special Effects: New Histories, Theories, Contexts* (London: British Film Institute, 2015), p. 49.

52 McGorry, 'Cover Story: "Coraline" Animated via Stop-Motion'.

53 Stephen Prince, 'True Lies: Perceptual Realism, Digital Images, and Film Theory', *Film Quarterly*, vol. 49, no. 3 (1996); Mary Ann Doane, 'The Indexical and the Concept of Medium Specificity', *differences: A Journal of Feminist Cultural Studies*, vol. 18, no. 1 (2007).

54 Jonathan Crary, *Techniques of the Observer: On Vision and Modernity in the Nineteenth Century* (Cambridge, MA: MIT Press, 1990).

55 Ibid., p. 29.

56 Ibid., pp. 116–36.

57 Hal Foster, 'Preface', in Hal Foster (ed.), *Vision and Visuality* (Seattle, WA: Bay Press, 1988), p. ix.

58 Crary, *Techniques of the Observer: On Vision and Modernity in the Nineteenth Century*, p. 2.

59 Hilary Fraser, 'Through the Looking Glass: Looking Like a Woman in the Nineteenth Century', in Francesca Orestano and Francesca Frigerio (eds), *Strange Sisters: Literature and Aesthetics in the Nineteenth Century* (Bern: Peter Lang, 2009), pp. 190–1.

60 Crary, *Techniques of the Observer: On Vision and Modernity in the Nineteenth Century*, p. 5.

61 Laura Mulvey, 'Visual Pleasure and Narrative Cinema', *Screen*, vol. 16, no. 3 (1975).

62 Kozachik, '2 Worlds in 3 Dimensions', pp. 29–30.

63 Ibid., p. 29.

64 Ibid., pp. 30, 34.

65 André Bazin, 'The Myth of Total Cinema', trans. Hugh Gray, in *What Is Cinema? Vol. 1* (Berkeley: University of California Press, 2005), pp. 17–23.

66 Gaiman and McKean, *Coraline*, p. 114.

67 Drawing also remains an important practice in experimental animation: Vicky Smith and Nicky Hamlyn (eds), *Experimental & Expanded Animation: New Perspectives and Practices* (London: Palgrave Macmillan, 2018); Maryclare Foá et al. (eds), *Performance Drawing: New Practices since the 1960s* (London: I.B. Tauris, 2019).

2

Mixing it up: *Coraline* and LAIKA's hybrid world

Miriam Harris

Alternative outlooks, new ways of seeing and the pushing of creative boundaries are terms frequently associated with LAIKA's objectives as an animation studio. For instance, *Coraline* (2009) illustrator and concept artist, Tadahiro Uesugi, recalls director Henry Selick's encouragement – in the previsualization stages of *Coraline* (2009) – to 'design with your own ideas, but [create] something we've never seen before!'[1] This impulse towards innovation has extended to methods of storytelling and the depiction of characters and content, with LAIKA CEO, director and animator Travis Knight reflecting that he wanted 'to tell these weird, thought-provoking, thematically challenging, emotionally resonant stories, but [he] wanted [the studio] to do it in a new way'.[2] In this chapter, I will focus upon hybridization as one of the chief strategies employed by LAIKA in the creation of fresh and emotionally charged perspectives, enabled through techniques such as the fusion of disparate stylistic sources, the intermingling of narrative tropes and a blending of analogue and digital technology. The communicative implications of such amalgamations will be explored by looking at examples found not only in *Coraline* but also in other LAIKA films. In turn I will consider the extent to which innovation arises in LAIKA animated features, or whether in the zealous drive to break new ground, instances occur where the viewer is ironically returned to the point of origin and 'old' viewpoints are maintained.

The LAIKA oeuvre builds upon a range of traditional constructs, references and craftmanship while forging connections with modern narratives and new technologies. For instance, *Coraline* offers a twenty-first-century take on a variety of global fairy tale and fantasy tropes; the eponymous character's discovery of the door that accesses the shiny menace of the Other Mother and Father's world summons memories of other narratives requiring portals to reach alternate worlds. There is the rabbit hole in *Alice in Wonderland*, the wardrobe in *The Chronicles of Narnia* series, the path to the bathhouse in *Spirited Away* (Hayao Miyazaki, 2001). Coraline's adventures occur in a contemporary Oregon setting, in which an updated miniature version of the classic Volkswagen Beetle car is parked adjacent to a Victorian Gothic house, and the characters are modelled upon traditional ball-and-socket metal armature puppets. This combination of old and new sources is further echoed by the puppets being clad in intricately handmade Lilliputian-sized clothes, while also drawing upon new processes aided by digital technology such as 3D-printed facial replacement parts.

In a similar fashion, LAIKA's subsequent animations take recognizable plot and genre structures and form new composites by marrying these structures with unexpected bedfellows from other narratives, while extending the capacities of both analogue and digital production processes with each new film. *ParaNorman* (Chris Butler and Sam Fell, 2012), for instance, combines signatures of the horror movie genre (obsessively collected by Norman), with a set of characters reminiscent of the iconic 1980s film *The Breakfast Club* (John Hughes, 1985) and reminders of Arthur Miller's play *The Crucible* (1953). *The Boxtrolls* (Graham Annable and Anthony Stacchi, 2014), in the fashion of *Coraline* being based upon Neil Gaiman's novella for children, stems from the fantasy novel *Here Be Monsters!* (2005) by Alan Snow – and blends evocations of Dickens and a steampunk aesthetic with a visual style reminiscent at times of the work of French director Sylvain Chomet. *Kubo and the Two Strings* (Travis Knight, 2016) intermingles epic dimensions in the work of both Japanese director Akira Kurosawa and English director David Lean, and *Missing Link* (Chris Butler, 2019) fuses together elements from the *Indiana Jones* trilogy, buddy movies and narratives about English imperialism. A range of cultural and stylistic influences therefore informs these films and echoes the questing of the central protagonists for an identity that is multidimensional and often happily peripheral to normative frameworks.

In this chapter, a variety of sources – both theoretical and production-related – will inform my exploration of the communicative implications of such hybridization. Julia Kristeva and Jonathan Culler's writings on intertextuality consider the meanings generated through a plurality of aesthetic and narrative voices and are therefore highly pertinent. I will refer to Lev Manovich's observations regarding digital hybridization and Andrea Comiskey's investigation into the digital presence in stop-motion animation. Hybridization offers much more than the strict binaries that can populate mainstream productions and which are embodied in areas that range from materiality to the depiction of sexuality and gender. Given that queer theory examines identities outside of so-called normative structures, and Eve Kosofsky Sedgwick cautions against the ring-fencing and exclusion that can occur through strict binary dualities, such a theoretical perspective has the potential to yield fruitful insights; Jack Halberstam has in fact analysed Pixar animations such as *Finding Nemo* (Andrew Stanton and Lee Unkrich, 2003) and Aardman's *Chicken Run* (Peter Lord and Nick Park, 2000) through the lens of queer theory. And information gleaned through interviews with LAIKA directors and crew – both online and in journals and magazines – offers a valuable understanding of the studio's production process. I will also refer to the comments of three members of LAIKA's production crew – two of whom are still working with the studio, and one who has left – who kindly responded to my emailed questions.

In my exploration of both the new ground and well-worn territory that LAIKA encompasses in its approach to hybridization, I will examine two key areas. Firstly, I will investigate several of the intertextual elements within *Coraline* and a selection of LAIKA films, from the perspective of aesthetics and narrative structure. I will then scrutinize the particular hybrids that have emerged from the LAIKA stable, through a cross-breeding of analogue and digital techniques, and the extent to which such a blend might be viewed as creatively trailblazing. Employing the lens of queer theory, I will explore LAIKA's approach to hybridization, considering the degree to which this creative strategy challenges normative structures and offers a new perspective in relation to both the production of animated films and the human experience.

Intertextuality

The plurality of aesthetic and narrative voices encountered in LAIKA animations seems to embody the 'mosaic of quotations' that Julia Kristeva refers to in her 1967 essay 'Word, Dialogue, and Novel', in which she initially coined the term 'intertextuality'. Extending Mikhail Bakhtin's notion of the novel as dialogic and referencing a multitude of voices, Kristeva writes that 'any text is the absorption and transformation of another'.[3] This statement need apply not just to direct quotations but also to literary and socio-historical codes that the reader deciphers, based upon their familiarity with previous texts and experiences.

As *Coraline* unfolds, it is clear to a spectator that the narrative not only invokes literary sources – the evil stepmother in Grimm's fairy tales, the tunnel to an alternate world in Lewis Carroll's *Alice in Wonderland* – but also alludes to animated films from diverse temporal and geographical zones. The highly tactile title sequence, for example, with its close-ups focusing on the materiality of leather, thread, fabric and buttons, and its recourse to the disintegrating effects of time in faded wallpaper, cobwebs and a scratched old sewing machine, summons associations with the work of Czech animator Jan Švankmajer and the eerie life he awakens in used objects. Such an influence might spring to mind for a viewer familiar with independent and fine arts-related animation, and this equation is further enhanced with the surreality of a doll, created with aged fabric, being cut open with animated scissors and woollen stuffing spilling from its head. Parallels can also be drawn with animations by the Quay Brothers, who cite Švankmajer as a primary influence: in their film *The Cabinet of Jan Svankmajer* (1984), stuffing tumbles from the cranium of a curious doll-hybrid. If one is purely familiar with more commercial productions, memories of the artful tactility and stylized horror lurking in Tim Burton's films and animations, together with the Henry Selick-directed stop-motion film *The Nightmare before Christmas* (1993), might instead be activated.

Jonathan Culler, in his chapter 'Presupposition and Intertextuality', asserts that for a discussion to be significant, it needs to take place in relation to a pre-existing discourse 'which it implicitly or explicitly takes up, prolongs, cites, refutes, transforms – the presuppositions of a piece of writing'.[4] Henry Selick's animated films implicitly reflect the influence of certain Czech animators, and there are passages, such as the title sequence in *Coraline*, in which the conversation with their work is quite explicit. In a 2009 interview with Michael Leader, Selick cites works within the Czech animation tradition that have had a significant impact upon his own creative direction, noting that Švankmajer's short films made a strong impression upon him during his studies at California Institute of the Arts, together with Jiří Trnka's *The Hand* (1965). He also refers to 'the disciples of Švankmajer', the Brothers Quay, as being influential, and their film *Street of Crocodiles* (1986).[5]

With its ball-and-socket metal armatures, attention to tactile detail and eerie undertone, *Coraline* draws upon the legacy of Eastern European – particularly Czech – puppet animation – but transforms it by situating it firmly within an American context. The resultant hybrid ushers in a new take upon stop-motion animation; the character of Coraline combines a fierce individuality with contemporary Americana, with her knitted sweater, jeans, glittery dragonfly clip and ultramarine coiffure. She represents the first example of an early-twenty-first-century American 11-year-old brought to life through commercial stop-motion animation, and her rebellious spirit is further signalled by the fact that the film integrates Czech animation aesthetic reminders and its own seditious streak. Several iconic Czech stop-motion animations evince subversion and irreverence in relation to the political and social sphere; in Švankmajer films such as *Dimensions of Dialogue* (1982) and *The Death of Stalinism in Bohemia* (1990), the oppressive power of Soviet rule is challenged and parodied through the use of symbols and metaphor. Likewise, Trnka's free-spirited harlequin in *The Hand* defies an autocrat's tyrannical demand for obedience and conformity through symbolic actions such as artistic activity, cultivating a flower and escaping from a cage.

This particular approach to creativity, which connects within *Coraline* the disparate ingredients of contemporary Americana and Czech animation, also echoes Jonathan Culler's observation that intertextual elements can take up, cite and transform a pre-existing discourse. While maintaining traditional tropes associated with fairy tales – a genre frequently explored by studios such as Disney – *Coraline* also assimilates influences from outside of American studios and challenges messages of heteronormativity, conformity and stereotypical gender roles that Disney and in turn other American institutions have touted for decades. A scene that particularly illustrates this rebellious impulse occurs on a shopping expedition for school uniforms. Coraline's mother rummages through racks of identical grey shirts, whereas her colourfully clad daughter disdains the lack of choices and instead proffers the liberating symbol of a pair of multihued gloves. She is intent on expressing her own individuality rather than being like everyone else – an anti-conformist desire shared by Eastern European animation, and in turn LAIKA.

In 2013, I visited the LAIKA studios and gave a presentation on Czech and Polish animation to a group of LAIKA employees. The invitation had been extended due to my curation of an exhibition on the topic installed at the Pacific Northwest College of Art in Portland. That this subject area might potentially appeal to employees makes sense in light of LAIKA's incorporation of Eastern European animation influences. A drive of about forty minutes from Portland's city centre, along highways lined with forest, took us to the LAIKA studio, and in the foyer stood display cases with models and scenes from *Coraline* and *ParaNorman*. Coraline's blue hair gleamed as she struck a feisty pose, and a tour of the studio revealed a Willy Wonka-like magical hive of activity. Approximately four hundred people, within different departments, were labouring over the exquisite detail of puppets, clothing, intricate moving mechanics and sets from *The Boxtrolls*. In the sketches on the walls, I was reminded of animated films directed by Sylvain Chomet, due to the wonky linework and vivid evocation of streetscapes reminiscent of *The Triplets of Belleville* (2003). In fact, the French graphic novelist Nicolas de Crécy, who has collaborated with Chomet, was chosen by LAIKA to create early concept art for *The Boxtrolls*. Michel Breton, who was a background artist on *The Triplets of Belleville*, took de Crécy's concept art and developed it still further.[6]

Just as *Coraline* integrates aesthetic influences such as Jan Švankmajer and Eastern European puppet animation, that heighten the sense of absurdity as well as the creepy quotient, *The Boxtrolls* absorbs de Crécy's distinctive blend of illustrative beauty, incongruity and the grotesque. This gives rise to a world that is very different in tone to works from the Pixar, DreamWorks and Disney fold. After all, de Crécy is an artist who narrated his graphic novel *Celestial Bibendum* (1990) from the perspective of a severed, grinning head and lampooned neo-liberalism, with collaborator Chomet, in the satire *Léon la Came* (1993–8). Such a predilection for the grotesque, coupled with humorous social commentary, can be seen in *The Boxtrolls* in Archibald Snatcher's mutating form that sprouts bulbous protuberances as an allergic reaction to his consumption of cheese. Despite the injurious ramifications, Snatcher insists on continuing his cheese-eating practice in a bid to join the upper echelons of Cheesebridge, for whom cheese is a sign of status. An intertextual evocation of elements from Charles Dickens's novel *Oliver Twist* (1838) further deepens the message linking extreme wealth with class inequality and an abuse of power and also intensifies passages of terror. With his Cockney accent, yellowing teeth, Victorian garb and predatory menace, Snatcher is an embodiment of Dickens's murderous character William Sikes.

Through similar strategies of multi-textual referencing that integrate dark literary and cinematic tropes within the body of the film, *Coraline*, *ParaNorman* and *Kubo and the Two Strings* also challenge the threshold for what is considered too terrifying for animated children's fare. In doing so, the films foreground young protagonists with an emotional dimensionality and resilience, inhabiting environments that are alternately supportive and threatening. *ParaNorman* in fact overtly references terror through an intertextual allusion to the horror movie genre, with familiar tropes such as jagged typography, zombies, witches, ghosts, suspenseful music and an encounter in a dark wood. From the very beginning of the film, in which Norman and his grandmother's ghost are watching a zombie film together, we learn that Norman is obsessed with horror movies, and this is entertainingly detailed by the fact that virtually every surface in his bedroom is adorned with phantoms and monsters, ranging from the wallpaper through to his toys, slippers and even his electric toothbrush. As the film progresses, it acquires a more sombre tone, due to the fusion of horror tropes with references to films such as *The Breakfast Club* that reflect the 1980s American high school experience. Signifiers from these films such as lockers, the jock and the cheerleader are amalgamated with actual horror in *ParaNorman*. Norman witnesses spectres, has the word 'freak' smeared across his locker and is publicly humiliated during the school play in a fashion that is suffused with dread and menace. The analogy communicates the fact that for some kids, school is indeed a horrific experience.

Thus far I've offered some examples of the unorthodox angles explored by LAIKA through the hybridization of aesthetic influences, and over the next paragraphs in this section I will consider examples in which innovation is developed through the merger of identifiable narrative tropes. *Coraline*, for instance, is an intriguing potpourri of horror, comedy, sensitively depicted inter-personal relationships and absurdity. One of the reasons that its horrific extremes – such as the Other Mother's metamorphosis from an American homemaker with an insincere smile into a nightmarish monster – can be tolerated is due to the presence of humour and nuanced characterization. An example of this occurs when the Other Mother, in her most terrifying incarnation, expresses her love for Coraline. However, rather than capitulate to such a declaration, Coraline retains her pluckiness and asserts that 'you have a very funny way of showing it'.

These twists and turns in narrative expectations, the blending of tropes and the presence of ambiguity rather than rigid binary divisions constitute a nuanced dimensionality that does not occur with the regularity one might wish for in American animated feature films for children. Such an approach relates to Eve Kosofsky Sedgwick's cautioning against binary thinking and the degree to which such dualistic thought supports a heteronormative status quo. Seeking the integration of psychoanalytical theories that are less dualistic than Freud's notion of 'sexual difference' and 'sexual sameness', in a bid to enlarge the frame of reference to include queer identities, Sedgwick notes the damaging sense of shame that has been routinely assigned to 'non-normative' positions, such as queerness. 'Normative' narratives can be revised, and reparative alternatives sought, so that 'selves and communities succeed in extracting sustenance from the objects of a culture – even of a culture whose avowed desire has often been not to sustain them'.[7] Jack Halberstam, in writing about queer gaming, observes that 'the world as we know it was not designed for queer subjects'[8] and echoes Sedgwick's exhortation to nurture alternatives; in order to establish their own agency, 'queer subjects have to hack straight narratives and insert their own algorithms for time, space, life, and desire'.[9]

LAIKA films can be viewed through a queer lens, due to the fact that the traditional, mythic structure that Joseph Campbell has termed 'the hero's journey' is fused with more unorthodox narratives. A space is thereby created in which normative views are destabilized and questions raised about their legitimacy. As an illustration of a queer script, Jack Halberstam analyses the animation *Wreck-It Ralph* (Rich Moore, 2012), describing it as 'both highly conventional and highly innovative',[10] with the motif of the glitch disrupting the conventional storyline in a way that allows for 'unpredictable and improvised modes of transformative opportunity'.[11] In contrast, recent animations from American commercial studios, while introducing a more progressive sociological and cultural slant, have tended to adopt the predictable and normative narrative arc of the hero's journey. For instance, in the Pixar features *Toy Story* (John Lasseter, 1995) and *The Incredibles* (Brad Bird, 2004) and the Disney animation *Moana* (Ron Clements et al., 2016), the hero or heroine encounters difficulties, makes progress despite several obstacles and ultimately vanquishes oppositional forces and resolves adversity. The hero journey's inexorable drive to solve problems in an adventurous fashion – a trajectory that is regularly foregrounded in commercial US animation – allows little time for ruminating on the grey areas that are part of the human condition.

Halberstam regards games such as *Braid* (2008) and *Monument Valley* (2014) as displaying queer codes, because they diverge from action-packed, goal-oriented killing rampages and instead offer qualities such as wonder, a melancholic reflectiveness, experimental temporal and spatial experiences, and 'an immersion in alternative dimensions that exceed and confound one's experience about virtual realities, affect, and potential'.[12] One can ascribe similar features to *Coraline*; it draws upon the horror, drama and binary portrayals within fairy tales but also injects stretches of wonder and absurdity, unexpected forks in the road and interpersonal dramas containing depth. The temporal and spatial mind-bending evinced by the world of the Other Mother and Father does not solely connote the trappings of a terrifying realm but also an astonishing, boundless creativity. Coraline gazes in awe and delight at the glowing plant mutations, the Van Gogh-inspired sky, the mouse circus and Misses Spink and Forcible's physics-defying stunts. These scenes exhibit an attention to exquisite handmade detail, together with ingenious animatronics and digital additions. In the parallel 'real' world, there is also a subtly delineated narrative strand that explores contemporary mother and daughter relationships, in which Coraline's mother moves from irritation to a touching acceptance of her daughter: her gifting of the colourful gloves is a queer celebration of difference. It is the mash-up of all these elements that leads to Coraline growing in confidence and maturity during the course of the film and not just the linear saga of her vanquishing a monstrous foe.

Hybrid narrative perspectives are embedded within several LAIKA animations and possess a queer slant in a fashion that is both explicit and implicit. From an angle that is inclusive of a range of identities, there are queer characters: in *ParaNorman*, football jock Mitch confounds expectations of heteronormativity with the casual revelation that he has a boyfriend who loves watching 'chick flicks'. In *Missing Link*, the central protagonist is a Sasquatch who presents as male but prefers to be addressed as Susan. That a portion of the heterosexual population possesses narrow conceptions, defined by stereotypes, regarding homosexual identities is highlighted by the fact that Norman's sensitivity is conflated with possible queerness in his father's eyes. He hollers at his wife – upon hearing the boy conversing with his dead grandmother – that 'that limp-wristed hippy garbage needs to be nipped in the bud'. In *The Boxtrolls*, Archibald Snatcher dresses up as Madame Frou Frou, and theatrically enacts a female identity on stage; theorist Judith Butler has noted drag performativity's potential to challenge traditional conceptions of gender. Coraline's own attire and actions do not register as stereotypically 'girly' – she dons a naval cap above her glittery dragonfly clip and, although she benefits at times from the assistance of Wybie, remains pluckily independent.

In addition, (hetero)normative expectations are challenged through not only the inclusion of queer identities but also – as in *Coraline* – swimming against the tide of cinematographic convention. *Kubo and the Two Strings*, for instance, offers a remarkable hybridization of Western and East Asian influences by referencing both David Lean and Akira Kurosawa epics; characters negotiate vast landscapes, as in *Lawrence of Arabia* (1962) and *Ran* (1985), and the fighting scenes contain parallels with those in *Seven*

Samurai (1954). Considerable research and labour have gone into costumes and environments that are not generically Japanese but rather reflect specific Japanese cultural outputs; the architecture is from the Heian Era, and the main visual influence is artist Kyoshi Saito.[13] This striving for cultural authenticity is unfortunately kneecapped by the voice talent being predominantly White, an issue that has sparked controversy and protest.[14] Ancient Japan being depicted through a lens that privileges contemporary commercial American marketing objectives casts a pall over the film's hybrid potential. Overall, the animation's trajectory resists the happy ending convention that occurs at the conclusion of numerous animations for children. Instead, Kubo's parents remain dead and their lives are not miraculously restored; over the course of the film, members of his biological family have in fact been hellbent on his destruction, with a vicious grandfather and a pair of aunts mercilessly tracking him down. Kubo must learn to live with his loss, and in a queer outcome that embraces ties that go beyond the biological family unit, his village becomes a surrogate family.

By resisting rigid binaries, and embracing a range of perspectives and references, these LAIKA animations achieve an ambiguity and dimensionality that go beyond dualistic paradigms such as 'good' and 'bad'. This can be seen in the fact that, despite the terror Coraline encounters in the Other World, she also delights in the creative imagination that is unleashed. In *ParaNorman*, the bullies and townsfolk baying for blood come to recognize that their behaviour is similar to the zombie characters they are trying to eradicate; in their intolerance of difference, they resemble the Puritans from the past who were 'stupid and scared'. In *ParaNorman*, it is not only the characters who are initially repudiated for deviating from norms – Norman for his weirdness, Neil because of his weight – that eventually come to be valued by their family and peers. Seemingly stereotypical figures such as Mitch the jock, Courtney the cheerleader and Alvin the bully are also invested with an increased emotional dimensionality. The inhabitants of Cheesebridge in *The Boxtrolls* likewise realize that the Boxtrolls – contrary to popular legend – are benign tinkerers who are not intent on slaughtering them in their beds. This broadened perspective enables the Boxtrolls to come out – or rather come up – from their underground lair and freely mingle with the townsfolk. All these examples, demonstrating an open inclusiveness, accord with Sedgwick's valuing of difference.

Analogue and digital

LAIKA's commingling of the tactility and imperfections of the analogue with the capacity for malleability aided by the digital – an alternative to the 3D computer-generated imagery (CGI) outputs of Disney and Pixar – is another strategy that manifests the studio's desire to go beyond narratives that are formulaic, heteronormative and lacking in innovation. Both analogue ingenuity and digital enhancement contribute to the films' emotional dimensionality and pushing of conventional boundaries. But a danger exists that LAIKA might skirt perilously close to the thrills of digital spectacle and wind up creating animated passages that too closely resemble the very films from which they wish to differentiate themselves. In this section, I will explore some examples of analogue and digital innovation and expressivity in both *Coraline* and subsequent LAIKA animations and will examine the implications of the studio's increased integration of analogue/digital hybridity.

What kind of fresh vision is hatched through an intermingling of the century-old medium of stop motion and contemporary digital techniques? LAIKA's particular blend of analogue and digital processes creates a complex set of responses from an affective perspective. The animations draw upon the capacity of analogue elements to immerse the viewer in a sense of warmth and tactility, while digital strategies further extend the potentialities of facial expression, animated movement, camera angles and set design, and thereby bring the cinematography closer to that of the live-action film. Yet this is only part of the equation; while such techniques conjure a cinematic familiarity associated with live action, and endow the animated characters with keenly observed nuances that move us and with which we can identify, both analogue and digital processes also take us into a world of the imaginary.

This world is lined with physics-defying stunts, outlandish creatures and vivid transformations that induce both fear and a sense of rapturous delight. However, at the same time as being transported by reminders of our humanity and these surges of fantasy, a viewer is also aware that they are seeing a miniature, constructed world. This is intimated through the tactility of surfaces, an illustrative stylization and the slight shimmer commensurate with physical frame-by-frame filmmaking. From a phenomenological perspective, such a composite fosters an assortment of perceptions and emotions, that I will explore in the next paragraphs through specific examples from *Coraline* and other LAIKA animations. I will make some connections between what is communicated during the viewing experience and Sedgwick's advocacy of multiple viewpoints, as compared to a dualistic outlook. Her notion of a reparative reading can also be applied in these instances, as a message associating creativity with boundless possibilities crops up in several LAIKA films and communicates a subversion of societal rules and the status quo.

'Warmth' and 'magic' are qualities that viewers typically ascribe to the handmade, observes Andrea Comiskey, while also pointing out the extent to which digital processes are relegated to the backseat in promotional material, in order to foreground the meticulously handcrafted puppets and sets of these stop-motion films.[15] When viewing *Coraline*, we are immersed on the analogue level in the haptic tactility of surfaces and materials that actually exist in the physical world; wood, metal and fabric are integrated through recognizable, exquisitely miniature versions such as a parquet floor, kettle and Coraline's bed linen. Analogue elements dominate LAIKA's first feature, in comparison with subsequent films where the ratio with the digital is more equal. On the analogue/digital spectrum, Henry Selick has been viewed as more of a stop-motion 'purist', whereas Travis Knight has enthusiastically embraced the 'hybrid' label since the release of *ParaNorman* and regards the computer as a tool 'like an exacto blade'.[16] In a 2009 interview, Selick estimated that at least 90 percent of *Coraline* draws on analogue techniques, due to 'a decision to keep as much of it as hand-made and real as possible'. Yet 10 percent digital is still a significant presence, and Selick viewed the CGI as being 'there to extend what we do and to help glue the world together and make things a little more seamless'.[17]

Do both analogue and digital processes contribute to a pushing of the creative envelope in *Coraline*? And do we respond to each approach differently, or does a merger of the two cultivate ambiguity? Some answers to these dilemmas can be found through a phenomenological interpretation, as in theorists Suzanne Buchan and Laura Marks's investigation of haptic tactility in the animated films of the Brothers Quay. Buchan notes that *Street of Crocodiles* 'strongly triggers intellectual, emotional and sensual engagement with its visual surfaces and poetic structures',[18] and that even objects like screws acquire a sentient agency. LAIKA hair and fur specialist, Jessica Lynn, recalls Henry Selick being seized with a similar drive to confer lifelike properties upon inanimate elements, such as hair. A powerful example is the scene where Coraline is looking under the bed, and 'Henry expressed really wanting to see all those individual strands of hair falling down, so a special "stunt" wig was created that was fully wired to help the animator give it that gravity-induced cascading effect'.[19] This vivid treatment immerses us fully in the nuanced portrayal of a plucky girl, who, instead of gingerly peering into the darkness, encounters the unknown with such daring that her hair acquires its own life force (see Figure 2.1).

Further analogue elements in *Coraline* affect a viewer on an equally visceral level. One example is the revulsion we share with Coraline when her father offers her some gelatinous-looking vegetable bake. Although the model's composition probably includes glue and paper, its viscosity reminds us of bodily secretions, which Julia Kristeva links with the abject.[20] The substance's abject nature is further echoed by the stains on the surrounding kitchen cupboards, the bleak pyrex dish and a lonely cup sitting in the dish rack. This response can be contrasted with the titillation of our taste buds prompted by the distinctive textures defining the Other Mother's dinner: a gleaming golden chicken, fluffy mashed potatoes and buttery corn on the cob. These scenes also take the stop-motion film into firmly contemporary territory from a social perspective, because we witness Coraline's parents dividing domestic labour in a modern fashion – 'your Dad cooks, I clean' – while the Other Mother attempts to lure Coraline with all the trappings and gender divisions of a 1950s world.

These vignettes illustrate the power of the analogue to emotionally engage a viewer and portray a fresh vision informed by societal progress (if not the progress of the father's culinary skills). Rather than presenting as analogue's polar opposite, one of the few overtly digital passages in *Coraline* also contains a

Figure 2.1 Coraline's ultramarine strands are as untameable as her spirit.

powerful sense of warmth and magic, while being different from the rest of the movie in style. The sequence occurs later in the film, when the ghost children appear to warn Coraline of impending danger, and her bedroom ceiling is transformed into the swirling colours and glowing constellations of Vincent van Gogh's iconic painting *The Starry Night* (1889). Tactility enters this digital rendition through animated brushstrokes, and the viewer shares Coraline's sense of awe before van Gogh's vision, now pulsing with animated life. From a semiotic perspective, the various attributes associated with the Dutch painter – his unique outlook, creative brilliance and break with convention – find certain parallels within the LAIKA film. The analogue puppet and digital sky forge a new illustrative style that mixes Post-Impressionist painting, electronic media and the influence of Czech stop motion. Such a mixed-media approach is made possible by digital compositing, and the fusion of these disparate elements would have been hard to achieve in the past with optical printers.

Lev Manovich has argued, in his pivotal essay 'Understanding Hybrid Animation', that the fusion of different media – 3D, 2D, physical and virtual, joined together through compositing software such as After Effects – has since the mid-1990s generated 'a new kind of visual aesthetics that did not exist previously'.[21] Such fluid amalgamations are enabled by converting different media into algorithmic data, which in turn enables further manipulation. The night scene in *Coraline* exemplifies such innovation, with Coraline being shot against a green screen, the keyed-out green producing a transparency that reveals the animated sky and digital colour adjustment bringing the separate elements together. There is an evocative layering of temporal zones as well, with the recourse to van Gogh's painting from the nineteenth century, Czech stop motion and contemporary aesthetics reflected in the latest technology.

From a less visible standpoint, the digital also joins forces with analogue elements in *Coraline* to celebrate creative expression and a refreshing eccentricity. As Comiskey notes, the digital makes possible Bobinsky's contorted acrobatics, which are unprecedented in stop-motion animation. These are engineered through an arrangement of rigs and clamps that are removed in post-production through digital compositing; his wiry legs and protruding belly means that the puppet topples over without support, and his spry leaps would not have been possible through purely analogue means.[22] Miss Spink's and Miss Forcible's ample bosoms and extraordinary flying trapeze antics meant the puppets required a similar analogue support and digital compositing treatment. The animation of such top-heavy puppets was initially deemed impossible, yet Selick pressed for the investigation of solutions. Jeanne McIvor, who worked on *Coraline* in the armature department, observed in an email that Selick's boundary-pushing 'raised the bar for every crew member no matter what their background'.[23]

Raising the bar definitely figures in LAIKA's much-touted approach to facial replacement parts, which are modelled in the computer and then printed in resin through state-of-the-art 3D digital printers. LAIKA has actively researched and stretched to the hilt the capacity of 3D printing, taking the medium into uncharted territory. While resin faces were hand-painted in the case of *Coraline*, subsequent films have incorporated an inbuilt colourization through technological advances.[24] For LAIKA's most recent animation, *Missing Link*, a commercial 3D Stratasys printer produced over 103,000 faces in colour.[25] But is innovation necessarily a signifier of quality? Although the sheer number of facial variations boggles the mind, it prompts the question of whether boundary-pushing is always the best solution in creative terms. The animation in fact begins to look too smooth and cannot be differentiated from CGI sequences. As Emily Myers, who worked in the armature department from *ParaNorman* to *Kubo and the Two Strings*, writes, 'LAIKA is married to the idea of innovation, and sometimes the overall goal of a well-functioning puppet is lost on innovation for the sake of innovation'.[26] Myers notes that in both the analogue and digital departments, precious time can be lost in pursuit of the holy grail of innovation: a quest that proceeds despite 'strong recommendations from the fabricators themselves'.[27]

In the creation of a hybrid composed of both analogue and digital processes, LAIKA faces some soul-searching as to future directions, if it is to maintain its distinctive identity as a trailblazing studio, telling nuanced narratives through a patchwork of influences that depart from convention. In recent LAIKA animations, the digital threatens at times to overwhelm the unique properties of analogue elements; the studio's striving for an expressive realism veers in some cases dangerously close to the very Hollywood animations from which it seeks to differentiate itself. For instance, in *Kubo and the Two Strings*, an entire puppet of the Moon Beast was constructed with 130 individual printed pieces, animated by hand and infused with additional digital visual effects.[28] The fact that the result is indistinguishable from CG animation evidences the difficulty in achieving just the right calibration of analogue and digital proportions. Subsuming the physicality of the Moon Beast through VFX generated by the computer deprives the scene of the wonder bestowed by the slight jitter of haptic ingredients being animated by hand.

In contrast, there are notable examples in LAIKA's later films where the unique properties of different media are preserved, and a blend of approaches extends visual possibilities. For instance, a subtle use of CGI in *The Boxtrolls* extends sets and augments crowds; extra Boxtrolls and ballroom dancers have been modelled and textured and are indistinguishable from their analogue brethren.[29] Digital camera work is also effectively integrated. Earlier in this chapter, I referred to the hybridization of David Lean and Akira Kurosawa influences in *Kubo and the Two Strings*, evidenced in sweeping camera moves and crane shots, which bring a uniquely epic dimension to the stop-motion film and are based on live action codes. In *Coraline*, one witnesses a similar use of digitally controlled motion rigs that enable aerial shots and enhance the sense of wonder; a notable example occurs when Coraline and the Other Father survey the magically lit garden from a great height. From *ParaNorman* onwards, each LAIKA animation has featured a climactic scene with supernatural elements that draws heavily on digital visual effects. However, this does not have to always produce a result akin to CG blockbusters, as illustrated by Norman's nail-biting encounter in the dark wood with a fiery Aggie bent on revenge. This scene is an extraordinary composite of analogue puppets, 2D hand-drawing, 3D models and glowing VFX and communicates an excitingly fresh vision in which no singular medium has the power to cancel out another.

Conclusion

In this chapter, I have argued that LAIKA's hybrid approach to aesthetics, narrative tropes and the merger of analogue and digital processes fosters an innovative creativity with ambiguity and emotional range. A host of influences and their accompanying associations are integrated through strategies such as intertextuality and the merger of disparate media, and an alternative is thereby offered to films in which more cut-and-dried, dualistic messages are reinforced. This expansive inclusivity can be aligned, I believe, with Eve Kosofsky Sedgwick's challenging of the traditional binaries associated with heteronormative conventions and therefore imbue the narrative trajectory with a queer subversive power.

A more extensive creative repertoire acknowledges the currency of twenty-first-century life, rather than investing the stop-motion medium with an overriding nostalgia by purely drawing upon traditional tropes and techniques.

Consequently, a message is communicated that the exacting, time-consuming, beautiful craftsmanship of the past can coexist in the twenty-first century with the accelerated pace engendered by digital technology and that the digital itself also involves significant labour and skill. However, in LAIKA's pursuit of innovation as a trademark signature, one perceives a number of potential speed bumps. A certain caution needs to be exercised that such strategies are indeed providing alternatives to mainstream fare, rather than ironically replicating an outlook that restores a more conventional status quo.

Notes

1 Bill Desowitz, 'Tadahiro Uesugi Talks *Coraline* Design', *Animation News Network*, 23 January 2009. https://www.awn.com/animationworld/tadahiro-uesugi-talks-coraline-design (accessed 15 July 2019).

2 Mekado Murphy, 'Moving Ahead in Stop Motion', *New York Times*, 10 August 2012. https://www.nytimes.com/2012/08/12/movies/with-paranorman-laika-aims-to-push-animation-boundaries.html (accessed 30 July 2019).

3 Julia Kristeva, 'Word, Dialogue and Novel', in Toril Moi (ed.), *The Kristeva Reader* (New York: Columbia University Press, 1986), p. 37.

4 Jonathan Culler, *The Pursuit of Signs: Semiotics, Literature, Deconstruction* (Ithaca: Cornell University Press, 1981), pp. 100–1.

5 Michael Leader, 'Exclusive: Henry Selick on *Coraline*', *Den of Geek*, 7 May 2009. https://www.denofgeek.com/movies/exclusive-henry-selick-on-coraline/ (accessed 12 August 2019).

6 Philip Brotherton, *The Art of The Boxtrolls* (San Francisco: Chronicle Books, 2014), p. 26.

7 Eve Kosofsky Sedgwick, *Touching Feeling* (Durham, NC: Duke University Press, 2003), pp. 150–1.

8 Jack Halberstam, 'Queer Gaming: Gaming, Hacking, and Going Turbo', in Bonnie Ruberg and Adrienne Shaw (eds), *Queer Game Studies* (Minneapolis: University of Minnesota Press, 2017), p. 187.

9 Ibid., p. 187.

10 Ibid., p. 192.

11 Ibid.

12 Ibid., p. 198.

13 Emily Haynes, *The Art of Kubo and the Two Strings* (San Francisco: Chronicle Books, 2016), p. 10.

14 Erik Pedersen, 'Watchdog Group Chides Laika for "White-Washing" "Kubo and the Two Strings"', *Deadline*, 23 August 2016. https://deadline.com/2016/08/kubo-and-two-strings-protest-white-actors-japanese-characters-manaa-1201807914/ (accessed 12 August 2019).

15 Andrea Comiskey, 'Special Effects in Contemporary Puppet Animation', in Dan North, Bob Rehak and Michael S. Duffy (eds), *Special Effects: New Histories/Theories/Contexts* (London: BFI Palgrave, 2015), p. 46.

16 Haleigh Foutch, '*Kubo and the Two Strings*: Director and CEO Travis Knight on LAIKA's most ambitious film yet', *Collider*, 30 June 2016. https://collider.com/kubo-and-the-two-strings-travis-knight-arianne-sutner-interview/ (accessed 12 August 2019).

17 Debra Kaufman, 'Director Henry Selick on *Coraline*', *Studio Daily*, 6 February 2009. https://www.studiodaily.com/2009/02/director-henry-selick-on-coraline/ (accessed 9 September 2019).

18 Suzanne Buchan, 'The Animated Spectator: Watching the Quay Brothers "Worlds"', in Suzanne Buchan (ed.), *Animated 'Worlds'* (Eastleigh: John Libbey, 2006), p. 28.

19 Jessica Lynn, email communication with the author.

20 Julia Kristeva, *Powers of Horror: An Essay on Abjection*, trans. Leon S. Roudiez (New York: Columbia University Press, 1982).

21 Lev Manovich, 'Understanding Hybrid Media' in Betti-Sue Hertz (ed.), *Animated Painting* (San Diego: San Diego Museum of Art, 2007), p. 37.

22 Comiskey, 'Special Effects in Contemporary Puppet Animation', p. 49.

23 Jeanne McIvor, email communication with the author.

24 Stephen Jones, *Coraline: A Visual Companion* (New York: HarperCollins, 2009), p. 107.

25 Ramin Zahed, *The Art of Missing Link* (San Rafael, CA: Insight Editions, 2019), p. 70.

26 Emily Myers, email communication with the author.

27 Ibid.

28 Martin McEachern, 'Myth in Miniature', *Computer Graphics World*, vol. 39, no. 5 (2016). https://www.cgw.com/Publications/CGW/2016/Volume-39-Issue-5-Sept-Oct-2016-/Myth-in-miniature.aspx (accessed 24 August 2020).

29 Brotherton, *The Art of the Boxtrolls*, p. 138.

3

Armatures in the closet: *Coraline* and the history of stop motion

Mihaela Mihailova

Coraline (Henry Selick, 2009) is, in many ways, a classical witchcraft narrative.[1] But it is also fundamentally the story of a witch's *craft* – the art of (re)animating lifeless objects. Starting with its opening sequence, the film proudly embraces its fascination with its own peculiar brand of magic: puppetry. *Coraline*'s introductory scene depicts a pair of skeletal metal hands (later revealed to belong to the Other Mother) pulling apart a doll in order to refashion it into a lookalike of the young protagonist. The sequence pays meticulous attention to this process. Close-ups zoom in on different steps of constructing the Coraline doll: choosing and attaching the button eyes, filling the body with sawdust, arranging the hair strands and stitching together the fabric. The prominence of the disembodied craftsman hands recalls early animators' tendency to interject themselves into their films, defined by Donald Crafton as self-figuration.[2] The Other Mother's role as animator has been emphasized by Henry Selick, who has shared that, in the original concept for the film, the real world would have been rendered digitally, with stop motion reserved for the environments and creatures crafted by the witch.[3] While this idea was ultimately scrapped, the director has compared the Beldam's labour to that of his crew: 'We, like the Other Mother, hand-made this film for Coraline.'[4] In this way, LAIKA's puppet comes to mirror – and perform – its own creation for the viewer, signalling the studio's proclivity for self-reflexive engagement with the stop-motion process.

Edited in a way that both emulates typical 'behind-the-scenes' videos and anticipates the adoption of such footage as an essential component of LAIKA's end-credit sequences, the crafting of the Coraline doll sets the tone for this film's meta-commentary on stop-motion production. Indeed, *Coraline* regularly foregrounds its animation technique. For example, as Dan Torre notes in his chapter for this volume, the film features sequences 'in which what could be described as external stop-motion rigging devices are also sometimes visible'. He singles out the Other Father's piano, which guides the character's hands via 'Mickey Mouse-styled gloves which are supported and controlled by an elaborate array of external rigs' – an apparatus that is 'somewhat similar to the manner in which such a scene would have been animated in a typical stop-motion shoot'.

The following pages engage with LAIKA's particular brand of self-reflexivity, interpreting it as fundamental to the studio's subtextual historicization effort, wherein *Coraline* doubles as a network of intertextual references to pivotal moments in stop motion's past. This chapter unpacks the ways in which the film's exploration of the stop-motion process unfolds through allusions to seminal works and directors, as well as key technological and aesthetic developments that have shaped the medium. The goal is to illuminate LAIKA's (re)construction of a historical stop-motion lineage wherein *Coraline* can be seamlessly inserted – as both the inheritor of a global creative legacy and a herald of its future.

Early stop motion and the roots of reflexivity

Coraline's self-reflexivity is representative of the particular ways in which stop motion has drawn attention to itself from the earliest moments of its history. In the first decades of the twentieth century, shining a spotlight on the production process by foregrounding authorial presence directly was already common practice in animated media, as mentioned above.[5] However, stop-motion films are notable for consistently incorporating self-reflexivity into the narrative itself in a way that established fascination with the stop-motion process as an organic aspect of stop-motion storytelling.

Take, for example, *King Kong* (Merian C. Cooper and Ernest B. Schoedsack, 1933), a seminal film in the history of stop-motion effects, thanks to the lasting influence of Willis O'Brien's groundbreaking model animation of the titular giant ape. An ambitious filmmaking project about a momentous (fictional) cinematic endeavour, this is a film driven by the 'desire to draw attention to the mechanisms of its own production'. As Dan North explains, 'if, conceptually, *King Kong* is a premise for showcasing the special effects of Willis O'Brien …, the narrative framing devices become more vital as a result'. Indeed, every time Carl Denham, the director of the fictional *Kong* movie at the centre of the film's plot, reminds the audience how astounding it is to be able to show such a formidable beast on the big screen, this self-reflexive rhetorical strategy 'creates a space for unalloyed spectacle and justification for astonished gazing'.[6]

On the other side of the Atlantic Ocean, cotemporaneous stop-motion productions often depicted scenes of puppet construction, typically followed by shots of the model coming to life. In the prelude of the German feature *The Seven Ravens* (*Die Sieben Raben*, 1937), directed by Ferdinand and Hermann Diehl, an actor takes a partially assembled jester puppet out of a box and connects its head to its body. Suddenly animated, the puppet begins narrating. As Ken A. Priebe has pointed out, the Diehl brothers would often reference the stop-motion process in their work, including their short films featuring Mecki the Hedgehog, 'who would come to life after being sculpted right on [a] workshop table'.[7] In Władysław Starewicz's 1933 live-action and stop-motion hybrid film *The Mascot* (*Fétiche Mascotte*), a toymaker sews up a puppy doll for her sick child. A tear rolls from the mother's eye and falls on the toy's chest; the puppy blinks and moves its head and, in the act of coming to life in response to the woman's creative and emotional labour, casts her as an animator.

While critics have pointed out that Henry Selick's earlier films, particularly *The Nightmare before Christmas* (1993), owe a debt to Starewicz more broadly and to *The Mascot* in particular, there is no evidence that Selick referenced this exact scene in his own opening sequence.[8] Nevertheless, there are notable similarities between the two, particularly vis-à-vis their self-reflexive take on the mother as (toy)maker. *The Mascot* features a close-up of the mother's hands moving the needle along the belly of the toy which can be seen as an early precursor to *Coraline*'s introductory sequence. One should note that the scene in question is original to Selick's adaptation, as there is no mention of the Other Mother crafting a Coraline lookalike doll in Gaiman's book. This addition is not a stretch, since the literary Other Mother is certainly a maker; when Coraline attempts to explore beyond the immediate area of her other home, her Other Father explains that 'there isn't anywhere but here. This is all she made: the house, the grounds, and the people in the house'.[9] What is more, while the Beldam is never explicitly described as a puppet maker on the page, a certain episode from the book (which never made the transition to screen) suggests otherwise. In the scene in question, Coraline finds her Other Father, bloated and losing his shape, in a dank cellar. This is what occurs next: 'the creature's twig-like hands moved to its face and pushed the pale clay about, making something like a nose. It said nothing'.[10] This allusion to mouldable clay solidifies the notion of the Other Mother as puppeteer – a self-reflexive idea that the film adaptation integrates much more fully into its narrative and mise-en-scène, following in the footsteps of early stop-motion classics.

The Seven Ravens and *The Mascot* are not isolated examples; the motif of toys coming to life was very prevalent during the first years of stop-motion animation. Brian Sibley attributes the recurrence of this to a 'strong European literary tradition of stories about living toys', while also pointing out that 'toys (particularly ones with jointed limbs) made good actors'. As an example, he refers to *The War and the Dream of Momi* (*La Guerra e il sogno di Momi*, 1917), a collaboration between Segundo de Chomón and Italian director Giovanni Pastrone, which features a young boy falling asleep and dreaming of a battle between puppets.[11] This vision of children's dreams as the space where toys become animated had already appeared in numerous films by that point. For instance, this is the setup for the stop-motion sequences in two British shorts, *Dolly's Toys* (1901) and *A Boy's Dream* (1903).[12] Another British production, Arthur Melbourne-Cooper's *Dreams of Toyland* (1908), features a boy 'tucked up in bed and dreaming of a teeming metropolis of rampant toys'. According to Paul Wells, the function of the child's dream in this film – and, I would add, in all similar narratives from this time period – was to demonstrate 'the very "performance" of animation through quasi-humanoid automata'.[13]

This self-reflexive impulse to play out – and play with – the expressive potential of toys and puppets was equally strong in early US stop motion. Biograph's 1907 short *Dolls in Dreamland* centres on a young boy's dream of toys coming to life.[14] Another American short released in the same year, Edwin S. Porter's *The 'Teddy' Bears* includes a performance by the titular toys, witnessed by a girl looking through a knothole. A century later, Travis Knight would echo this fascination with stop motion as play in an interview about *Missing Link*: 'It feels like a child's plaything being brought to life. It's like we're playing with our dolls, playing with our toys, telling stories that mean something to us.'[15]

In *Coraline*, we already see LAIKA playing with its puppets, who are, in turn, playing with theirs. During her first visit to the Other World, the young protagonist is delighted to find that all the toys inside her bedroom have come to life and are happily moving about. One of them, a jovial felt octopus, even greets her like an old friend. On a less positive note, Coraline's lookalike doll is also animated – by the Other Mother's sinister magic. While the doll is apparently lifeless, it tends to disappear and reappear mysteriously at strategic locations around the house, evoking horror film tropes of cursed objects haunting their owner. For example, when the heroine's father sends her off on a meaningless counting errand, she puts the doll down, only to find it gone a moment later. Shortly after, Coraline discovers the door to the Other World, and the toy materializes anew behind her, seemingly observing with interest as Coraline's real mother uses her key to open the door. In a later sequence, the doll can be seen spying on Coraline and Wybie from a window as they discuss Mrs Lovat's missing sister. Such scenes suggest that, even as it never appears fully alive, the doll is being animated by the Beldam's will.

The mouse circus and the legacy of George Pal

While a number of early shorts self-reflexively celebrate puppets' capacity to come alive through stop motion, one title in particular – *The Humpty Dumpty Circus* (1898) – stands out as a potential key node in LAIKA's network of historical references. As noted in *Coraline: A Visual Companion*, 'the very first example of cinematic stop-motion is usually credited to [this lost film], in which British émigrés Albert E. Smith and James Stuart Blackton used the pioneering technique to bring a toy circus of animals and acrobats to life'.[16] While Neil Gaiman came up with Mr Bobinsky's trained mice in his original text, one crucial difference between the page and screen versions suggests that it was LAIKA that elected to highlight this stop-motion circus performance as one of the centrepieces of its depiction of a magical parallel universe. In the novella, the eccentric neighbour tells Coraline that he is coaching a mouse circus, but there is no follow-up; the extravagant performance depicted in the film is an addition exclusive to this adaptation.[17] In that sense, the mouse circus sequence may or may not be a deliberate nod to a pivotal moment in the evolution of stop-motion filmmaking. Regardless of this, it remains a fitting tribute to the creative roots of the medium that captures the fascination and sense of wonder that characterized its initial years.

Henry Selick has, in fact, singled out the mouse circus number as a scene designed to pay tribute to the history of stop-motion filmmaking, albeit in relation to a different cinematic corpus. In his director's commentary for the home release of *Coraline*, he calls the mice 'maybe the most classic stop-motion feeling creatures in the film, inspired by George Pal's Puppetoons'. Selick goes on to explain that 'Pal wanted this sort of elasticity you get in Disney and Warner Brothers drawn animation in stop motion', which influenced the *Coraline* production team's approach to seeking out a similar squash and stretch effect on the mice.[18] Pal is also referenced in the official *Coraline* companion book, which highlights his use of replacement animation, a technique which, as Dan Torre examines at length in his chapter for this volume, helped shape *Coraline's* aesthetic as well.[19]

The mice's expertly synchronized circus routine is also linked to Pal's work via a shared fascination with visually elaborate, tightly choreographed performance sequences reminiscent of 1930s and 1940s Hollywood musicals. Mette Peters has examined the musical scenes in Pal's *Philips Broadcast of 1938* and *Philips Cavalcade* (1939), concluding that 'the puppets are singers, musicians and dancers and reference contemporary (American) film conventions'. To illustrate this point, she singles out a scene from the former, in which 'the camera films the synchronic pattern of the choreography of the dancers from above, alluding to Busby Berkeley's famous use of the crane shot in his musicals'.[20] *Coraline* appears to have inherited Pal's fascination with this type of cinematic spectacle along with the remarkable plasticity of his puppets. The Other Bobinsky's mice pull off a range of visually striking formations in quick succession; coming together in circles, spirals, stars and, most impressively, a mouse pyramid that spells out the heroine's name, the puppets invoke the spirit of old Hollywood musicals. What is more, the layered spiral structure that rises out of the ground towards the end of the sequence is reminiscent of Berkeley's signature human waterfall, as seen, for instance, in *Footlight Parade* (Lloyd Bacon, 1933). *Coraline* reviews picked up on this, too, often comparing the mice sequence to a Busby Berkeley number.[21]

Following the sawdust trail: Dog taxidermy as a locus of intertextuality

In addition to evoking early stop-motion tropes (such as toys coming to life) and drawing inspiration from historically significant methods (such as Pal's particular brand of replacement animation), *Coraline* often foregrounds the materiality of puppets in ways that evoke traditional puppet crafting techniques while paying tribute to some of the stop-motion classics that have modelled the LAIKA feature's own approach to self-reflexivity. The film does this in two ways: by revealing some of its puppets' stuffing in sequences designed to tap into the resulting sense of visceral discomfort and by alluding to the act of stuffing as an indirect reference to the early years of stop-motion filmmaking. The latter is introduced through Miss Spink and Miss Forcible's penchant for taxidermy, which is exclusive to the film adaptation:[22] as the two explain to an alarmed Coraline, who has just come face to face with their 'sweet departed angels', they 'couldn't bear to part with [the dogs], so [they] had them stuffed'. While the Scottish terriers do not function as puppets within the narrative, their prominent presence in *Coraline*'s menagerie is a visual callback to the puppets of early pioneers such as Władysław Starewicz and Ray Harryhausen. As Richard Neupert has pointed out, Starewicz regularly employed a 'mix of stuffed dead animals and dolls' throughout his career, bestowing upon them a rare fluidity and subtlety of movement, 'thanks in part to his knowledge of anatomy'.[23] While Harryhausen did not make use of stuffed animals for his creature features, he collaborated with taxidermist George Lofgren, who developed a process for 'rubberizing' fur ('an ingenious technique of replacing the skin with rubber') in order to make it more resilient to the touch. It was used in constructing the titular ape in *Mighty Joe Young* (Ernest B. Schoedsack, 1949) in order to ensure that his fur would 'ripple' less than his famous predecessor King Kong's rabbit pelt exterior.[24] Lofgren would go on to work with Harryhausen on several 1950s productions, notably *The 7th Voyage of Sinbad* (Nathan Juran, 1958), for which he fabricated the outward features of the 'Snake Woman' and the two-headed Roc puppets.[25] Later Harryhausen models retain a noticeable taxidermy look: for example, both the big cat in *Sinbad and the Eye of the Tiger* (Sam Wanamaker, 1977) and the two-headed Dioskilos in *Clash of the Titans* (Desmond Davis, 1981) resemble stuffed animals in texture and overall design.[26] Given that Henry Selick considers Harryhausen 'one of his heroes' (as do prominent LAIKA members, notably Travis Knight), it is possible that the Scottie dogs may have a classic stop-motion pedigree.[27]

That taxidermy would become a key visual motif in a film so rich in historical connections is hardly a surprise. After all, this is a practice rooted in the desire to preserve a visual reminder of the past for posterity, to hold on to a certain state of being by freezing it in time – an impulse shared by *Coraline*.[28] However, Selick's feature is not afraid to draw out – and draw upon – the potential for horror inherent to the very act of stuffing an (un)dead (puppet) body. In fact, the film leans into the visceral discomfort associated with the minute details of its craft from the very first moments of its runtime, as the Other Mother empties out a doll in order to refashion its appearance and stuff it anew. This striking image of a (self-)cannibalizing puppet is likely inherited from Czech master Jan Švankmajer.[29] Henry Selick was first introduced to Švankmajer's signature brand of stop-motion surrealism via the short *Jabberwocky* (1971), which he saw during his study at the California Institute of the Arts. *Coraline's* director speaks of this screening as a formative experience, describing the film as a 'life-changer … with stop motion that grabbed hold of you'.[30] Indeed, *Jabberwocky* remains a strongly unsettling work; in one of the film's most palpably self-reflexive scenes, holes appear all over a doll's body as it lays prostrate on the ground, and a mixture of straw and smaller dolls emerge from it. Later on, a doll is seen consuming smaller dolls with a spoon during a sinister tea party. While Selick chooses to structure *Coraline* around the threat of the devouring puppet (rather than, explicitly, the act itself), he nevertheless taps into Švankmajer's vision of domestic space as an uncanny, quietly ominous domain in order to convey the sinister undertones of the family home present at the core of Gaiman's novella.

The Czech director's shadow looms large over *Coraline's* obsession with the fragility of puppets, too. At several points during the film, the grotesque destruction of puppet bodies is used to chilling effect. For example, Coraline's cat companion catches and bites into what, initially, appears to be one of Mr Bobinsky's circus mice. However, as soon as the feline's teeth puncture its skin, the mouse transforms into a large, rubbery rat whose body quickly goes limp as the sawdust filling drains through its open mouth. In the original novella, the rat meets a more gruesome and graphic end: 'It was lying on the brick path at the bottom of the steps, with a surprised look on its face – which was now several centimetres away from the rest of it. … A collar of wet blood glistened at its neck'.[31] While this adaptation change could be attributed to a desire to avoid on-screen bloodshed in a children's film, it is also a self-reflexive gesture highlighting the materiality of puppets. In fact, Selick repeatedly draws attention to the puppet body as a constructed object; in another instance of bloodless body horror, Other Wybie removes his glove and blows on his hand in front of Coraline, making it scatter into particles. This gesture is a poignant moment within the narrative, as it is meant to reinforce his status as a mere shell of his real-world counterpart. It is also, however, a nod to the film's own artifice. For viewers familiar with the history of stop motion, these scenes may recall Švankmajer's 1988 feature film *Něco z Alenky* (*Alice*), in which the White Rabbit (an actual stuffed rabbit) pulls his pocket watch out of his chest and leaks sawdust, resulting in what Ken A. Priebe has described as 'one of the most disturbing and iconic images from the film'.[32]

Still, the Czech filmmaker was not the first to capitalize on the horror potential of puppets revealing their innards to the audience. This particular visual motif can be traced back to earlier classics of the medium, notably Starewicz's *The Mascot*. In this film, a toy puppy finds itself in a sinister realm ruled by a Devil doll and inhabited by all manner of bizarre and revolting creatures. At the end of the scene, the Devil, having been attacked, clawed and ultimately decapitated by a large stuffed cat, crumples into a lifeless heap, his sawdust filling seeping out grotesquely from a puncture in his abdomen.

Thus, what unites *Coraline* with its predecessors is their shared preoccupation with puppet viscera and their capacity to summon terror out of tactility. By exposing the fragility of the crafted body, stop-motion films destroy the illusion of life, underscoring the artifice of the puppet and breaking it down – sometimes literally – into its constituent parts. Birgitta Hosea has argued that such invocations of the physicality of the materials used in animation can have a nostalgic purpose.[33] Indeed, *Coraline*'s foregrounding of stuffing – as both process and material – is not simply an homage to its cinematic lineage but a nostalgic look back at stop motion's analogue past in a time of transition to a hybrid production model.

Coraline and/as personal stop-motion history

Reflecting on why he chose stop motion over other animation techniques, Henry Selick remarked that 'it never seems to age because it's old to begin with. You can't make it new. It's like old magic tricks.'[34] It is fitting – one might say almost inevitable – that someone with a vision of stop motion as a urform that resists modernization would come up with a film as obsessed with tradition as *Coraline*. Indeed, placing this film in the context of Selick's own career trajectory can further illuminate its ties to the medium's institutional memory. After all, while *Coraline* is imbricated in the history of stop motion on a macro level, it also bears traces of a prominent stop-motion animator's personal creative history with the medium.

Several visual motifs in *Coraline* echo Selick's earlier work. A particularly noticeable one is the prominence of insects in many shapes and forms – ornamental (such as the dragonfly hair clip) or alive, harmless or threatening. Stylized bugs have always been part of the director's stop-motion lexicon; *The Nightmare before Christmas*'s memorable antagonist, Oogie Boogie, is a burlap sack filled with insects and spiders. The sticky, unpleasant centipedes Coraline squashes in the shower recall the wriggling mass of his insides. *James and the Giant Peach* (1996), an earlier Selick adaptation of a British children's book, chronicles the adventures of its titular orphan and a band of anthropomorphic insects. One of them, Miss Spider, a brave and nurturing insect lady, is the positive precursor to *Coraline*'s twisted vision of arachnid motherhood. While not retaining any of this character's warmth, the Other Mother has inherited her stark sensuality and elegant, classical fashion sense. One should note that Neil Gaiman had already explicitly tied *Coraline*'s villainess to spider imagery by comparing the world she created to a spider's web[35] and informing the reader that she is 'very pale, the colour of a spider's belly'[36] and she eats 'shiny black beetles'.[37] It was Selick and his team, however, that fully fleshed out the image of a devouring spider-woman. This persistence of insect imagery can – and should – also be tied back to Selick's aforementioned reverence for the masters of stop-motion creature animation. In 2016, the director penned a blog post appealing to fans of the medium to support Jan Švankmajer's crowdfunded film project titled – as perfect coincidence would have it – *Insects* (2018). Appropriately, to help motivate potential donors, Selick offered bug props that were used in the production of *The Nightmare before Christmas*.[38]

Another recognizable facet of Selick's visual signature is the image of a child accessing a fantasy realm through a tunnel. In *James and the Giant Peach*, the young protagonist enters the titular fruit by crawling through a passageway, anticipating Coraline's own journey into the unknown. Notably, there is no such tunnel in Gaiman's novella; the mysterious door opens on a 'dark hallway', and Coraline walks down a carpeted corridor to reach her Other house.[39]

Selick himself has occasionally reflected on resonances between his earlier work and LAIKA's feature. For instance, in his director's commentary for the collector's edition of *Coraline*, he points out that he addressed the challenge of 'coming up with a big white limbo' for the scene in which the Other Mother's world transitions to nothingness by drawing on his late-1980s Pillsbury Doughboy commercials, in which he made similar use of empty space.[40] Another interview highlights Selick's commitment to two stop-motion animation techniques: mechanical armatures and replacement animation. While pointing out that he has 'always used both approaches', the director clarifies that Coraline and most of the other lead characters were animated via replacement animation – a process he describes in both historical terms ('it goes back to George Pal's *Puppetoons*') and in terms of his personal experience applying it to the aforementioned commercials and to Jack Skellington in *The Nightmare before Christmas*.[41]

This consistency in technique goes hand in hand with Selick's stated preference for working with the same collaborators over multiple projects.[42] Industry veterans such as director of photography Pete Kozachik and lead animator Eric

Leighton have repeatedly contributed their talents to Selick's features since the early 1990s, all the while gradually rising through the industry ranks. In that sense, *Coraline* can also be seen as a key intersection in the interconnected career trajectories of a generation (in the creative, if not strictly the temporal sense) of stop-motion artists working in contemporary Hollywood. Even *Coraline*'s Easter eggs can be mined for recent animation history trivia; for example, the film contains a nod to the late Joe Ranft, a Disney/Pixar screenwriter and animator who worked with Selick on *The Nightmare before Christmas* and *James and the Giant Peach*.[43] The Ranft Brothers, who are shown moving Coraline's family into their new home and getting shorted on the tip, are stylized puppet versions of Joe and his brother Jerome, a character sculptor and voice actor for Pixar.[44] While intended as a tribute to a departed friend, this early scene nevertheless sets the stage for the film's preoccupation with broader questions of legacy.

Coraline and the birth of a studio tradition

Coraline's multilayered relationship with its medium is remarkable in its own right, but it has also proven to be a trendsetting phenomenon. Since 2009, LAIKA has maintained a consistent degree of self-reflexivity in all of its feature productions. Following a precedent set by *Coraline*, every one of the studio's titles has featured a mid- or post-credits sequence dedicated to taking the viewer behind the set curtain. At the same time, the films' set and character design has often paid tribute to key figures in stop-motion history, notably Ray Harryhausen. While the entirety of *ParaNorman* (Chris Butler and Sam Fell, 2012) can be read as an extended homage to classic horror films, many of which relied on practical stop-motion effects and animatronic puppetry, *Kubo and the Two Strings* (Travis Knight, 2016) features scenes specifically designed with Harryhausen in mind. For example, *Kubo*'s writer and head of story Chris Butler has revealed that the film's signature origami battle, in which a miniature warrior is self-reflexively animated by the titular character's storytelling powers, was seen by the production team as an 'opportunity to pay homage to the great Harryhausen-animated fantasy epics that entertained us as kids'.[45] In a more direct reference to the legendary model animator's work, the impressive (and much publicized) Hall of Bones scene features an enormous skeleton puppet designed to evoke the celebrated skeleton fight in *Jason and the Argonauts* (Don Chaffey, 1963). As director and producer Travis Knight put it, the scene (which is highlighted in a post-credits behind-the-scenes sequence) is LAIKA's 'attempt at one-upping the master with a pitched battle showcasing a skeleton puppet so immense that it dwarfed the animator bringing it to life'.[46] Knight's assertion that 'Uncle Ray would be proud of us' highlights the studio's preoccupation with notions of legacy and creative lineage, while also betraying a desire to align the LAIKA brand with the craftsmanship of celebrated masters of the medium.[47] Indeed, LAIKA has been eager to insert itself into narratives of historical continuity, as exemplified by a 2019 podcast episode in which several crew members are interviewed as experts on the medium's history.[48]

The studio's latest (as of 2021) feature, *Missing Link* (Chris Butler, 2019), continues the tradition of honouring previous generations of artists. Chris Butler has described his approach to stop-motion monsters in the following terms: 'I figured if I was going to throw all my childhood inspirations into a pot, the stew was going to be seasoned with cool Harryhausen-esque primitive beasts.'[49] In particular, Nessie was designed 'to have the feel of a Harryhausen monster but in the style and look of [this] film'.[50] It is interesting to note, however, that the title and overall concept of this feature are, in fact, more directly tied to Harryhausen's own mentor, stop motion and special effects pioneer Willis O'Brien, who directed the seminal short film *The Dinosaur and the Missing Link: A Prehistoric Tragedy* in 1915.

This persistent attention to institutional history may also be at least in part due to LAIKA's retainment of what Travis Knight has called a 'core team' over the past decade.[51] Thanks to largely the same individuals, many of whom are invested in stop-motion history, working in key production positions over several films, LAIKA's creative ethos has been gradually built on the foundations laid out in *Coraline*. As producer Arianne Sutner explains, this has shaped a studio identity that hinges on the notion of being 'tenaciously and thoroughly devoted to the stewardship of this kind of filmmaking'.[52] In that sense, *Coraline*'s extensive network of stop-motion references not only set the tone for future LAIKA films' tendency to harken back to the medium's classics but also planted the seeds of LAIKA's broader production philosophy.

Conclusion

Coraline embraces traditional and outdated art forms and practices at every turn: the circus, vaudeville and music hall performances, taxidermy, tasseography and even garden catalogues. Deeply nostalgic for older modes of entertainment, including stop motion itself, LAIKA's film is permeated by a longing for the past. Its vision of childhood, too, is quaintly analogue. While Coraline's father owns a computer, she does not seem to possess electronics, aside from her flip phone. Many of her games, activities and toys could very well belong to a child of a previous century. She adopts an old-fashioned doll and plays outside with a dowsing rod. She marvels at the fake snow inside a Detroit Zoo souvenir snow globe. She is offered visibly expired 'hand-pulled taffy from Brighton'.

The idealized domestic space constructed by the Other Mother also seems frozen in time, like the old house itself. The Other World is full of marvellous mechanical objects, such as the mantis tractor, the piano which 'plays' the Other Father and the gravy train at the dinner table. There are no digital screens or buttons to be seen but plenty of pulleys, levers and spring mechanisms. The Beldam, it seems, favours traditional craftsmanship.

However, all of this machinery, while initially wondrous, eventually comes to be associated with danger. The Other World may be a spectacular creation, but it is, ultimately, a prison. This complicates the film's seemingly straightforward nostalgia for a non-digital world. Despite its almost wistful preoccupation with tradition, LAIKA's narrative warns against becoming trapped in the past.

This duality is not as irreconcilable as it may seem, considering that *Coraline* was produced at a time when one of the oldest animation techniques was beginning to adapt to the digital age. As Andrea Comiskey has argued, 'contemporary stop-motion animation is in fact tightly imbricated with digital technologies and aesthetics, but this relationship is contradictory'. She points out that, while 'digital technologies have provided a new set of craft tools', they also '[threaten] to erode what are perceived to be essential tenets of the medium's "analogue" craft practices and aesthetics'.[53] In that sense, the ambivalence highlighted above mirrors LAIKA's own blending of tradition and innovation, exemplified by *Coraline*'s reliance on both classical stop-motion techniques and digital technologies (including 3D printing). In the film's companion volume, Travis Knight 'readily admits that there is something paradoxical in combining an anachronistic film technique such as stop-motion animation with twenty-first century technology'.[54]

Perhaps it is a heightened awareness of this paradox – and a perceived necessity to 'legitimize' the film's status vis-à-vis connections to earlier stop-motion landmarks – that has shaped *Coraline*'s extensive intertextual engagement with its aesthetic roots. Or perhaps it is the transitional moment itself that inspired the film's search for an identity defined in relation to the medium's own canon. Ultimately, as this chapter has shown, LAIKA strives to establish a sense of historical continuity in and through *Coraline*. The studio draws upon a celebrated stop-motion lineage in ways both subtle and overt and inscribes the film within it. In doing so, it presents its hybrid process as the next step in the evolution of stop-motion filmmaking, rather than a radical break in its development.

Notes

1   For an in-depth discussion of the film's relationship with witchcraft, see Kodi Maier's chapter in this volume.

2   Donald Crafton, *Before Mickey: The Animated Film 1898–1928* (Chicago: Chicago University Press, 1993), p. 11.

3   Henry Selick, 'Feature Commentary', *Coraline* (Laika, 2009), DVD.

4   Joe Fordham, '*Coraline:* A Handmade World', *Cinefex*, no. 117 (2009), p. 61.

5   Crafton, *Before Mickey*, p. 11.

6   Dan North, *Performing Illusions: Cinema, Special Effects and the Virtual Actor* (New York: Wallflower Press, 2008), pp. 86–7.

7   Ken A. Priebe, *The Advanced Art of Stop-Motion Animation* (Boston, MA: Cengage Learning, 2010), p. 10.

8   Adrian Danks, 'Ladislaw Starewicz and *The Mascot*', *Senses of Cinema*, no. 31 (2004). http://sensesofcinema.com/2004/cteq/starewicz_mascot/ (accessed 24 July 2020).

9   Neil Gaiman, *Coraline* (New York: HarperCollins, 2015), p. 84.

10 Gaiman, *Coraline*, p. 131.

11 Brian Sibley, 'The Medium', in Peter Lord and Brian Sibley (eds), *Creating 3-D Animation: The Aardman Book of Filmmaking* (New York: Harry N. Abrams, 1998), p. 24.

12 These films are typically attributed to Arthur Melbourne Cooper, although there has been some scholarly disagreement. See David Shepherd, '"Noah's Beasts Were the Stars": Arthur Melbourne Cooper's *Noah's Ark* (1909)', *Journal of Religion & Film*, vol. 20, no. 1 (2016), p. 1. http://digitalcommons.unomaha.edu/jrf/vol20/iss1/20 (accessed 24 July 2020).

13 Paul Wells, '"Picture by Picture, Movement by Movement": Melbourne-Cooper, Shiryaev and the Symbolic Body', *animation: an interdisciplinary journal*, vol. 6, no. 2 (2011), p. 159.

14   Ray Harryhausen and Tony Dalton. *A Century of Stop Motion Animation: From Méliès to Aardman* (New York: Watson-Guptill, 2008), p. 43.

15   Carlos Aguilar, 'Take a Look at the Painstaking Craft behind Laika's "Missing Link"', *Cartoon Brew*, 10 April 2019. https://www.cartoonbrew.com/stop-motion/take-a-look-at-the-painstaking-craft-behind-laikas-missing-link-172509.html (accessed 10 May 2020).

16   Stephen Jones, *Coraline: A Visual Companion* (New York: HarperCollins, 2009), p. 64.

17   Gaiman, *Coraline*, p. 4.

18   Selick, 'Feature Commentary'.

19   Jones, *Coraline: A Visual Companion*, p. 68.

20   Mette Peters, 'George Pal's "Cavalcade of Colours, Music and Dolls": 1930s Advertising Films in Transnational Contexts', in Malcolm Cook and Kirsten Moana Thompson (eds), *Animation and Advertising* (Cham, Switzerland: Palgrave Macmillan, 2019), p. 59.

21   For example, see Rebecca Lloyd, 'Haunting the Grown-Ups: The Borderlands of *Paranorman* and *Coraline*', in Ruth Hehold and Niamh Downing (eds), *Haunted Landscapes: Super-Nature and the Environment* (London: Rowman & Littlefield), p. 205; and Gabi Campanario, 'A Weird, Whimsical – and Somewhat Eerie – "Coraline"', *Seattle Times*, 5 February 2009. https://www.seattletimes.com/entertainment/movies/a-weird-whimsical-8212-and-somewhat-eerie-8212-coraline/ (accessed 10 September 2020).

22   There is no mention of stuffed dogs in the original novella. See Gaiman, *Coraline*, p. 21.

23   Richard Neupert, *French Animation History* (Malden, MA: Wiley-Blackwell, 2011), p. 62.

24   Roy P. Webber, *The Dinosaur Films of Ray Harryhausen: Features, Early 16mm Experiments and Unrealized Projects* (Jefferson, NC: MacFarland, 2004), p. 41.

25   Ibid., p. 133.

26   Harryhausen and Dalton, *A Century of Stop Motion Animation*, p. 24.

27   Jones, *Coraline: A Visual Companion*, p. 68.

28   While Bazin certainly did not have stop-motion animation in mind, one cannot help but be reminded of his famous 'mummy complex'. See André Bazin, *What is Cinema? Vol. 1*, trans. Hugh Gray (Berkeley: University of California Press, 2005), p. 9.

29   For an in-depth discussion of Czech animation's influences on *Coraline*, Selick, and LAIKA, see Miriam Harris's chapter in this volume.

30   Henry Selick, 'Foreword', in Ken A. Priebe (ed.), *The Advanced Art of Stop-Motion Animation* (Boston, MA: Cengage Learning, 2010), p. x.

31 Gaiman, *Coraline*, p. 146.

32 Priebe, *The Advanced Art of Stop-Motion Animation*, p. 33.

33 Birgitta Hosea, 'Made by Hand', in Caroline Ruddell and Paul Ward (eds), *The Crafty Animator: Handmade, Craft-Based Animation and Cultural Value* (Cham, Switzerland: Palgrave Macmillan, 2019), p. 33.

34 Henry Selick, 'Henry Selick Winsor McCay Award Recipient 2020', *YouTube*, 2 February 2020. https://www.youtube.com/watch?v=i5-3I1ly0q8&ab_channel=ASIFAHollywood (accessed 27 September 2020).

35 Gaiman, *Coraline*, p. 88.

36 Ibid., p. 155.

37 Ibid., p. 91.

38 Henry Selick, 'Henry Selick on Why Jan Svankmajer Matters', *Cartoon Brew*, 12 June 2016. https://www.cartoonbrew.com/ideas-commentary/henry-selick-jan-svankmajer-matters-140434.html (accessed 27 September 2020).

39 Gaiman, *Coraline*, p. 33.

40 Selick, 'Feature Commentary'.

41 Fordham, '*Coraline*: A Handmade World', p. 44.

42 Selick, 'Henry Selick Winsor McCay Award Recipient 2020'.

43 Selick paid tribute to his friendship with Ranft in his Winsor McCay Award acceptance speech. See Selick, 'Henry Selick Winsor McCay Award Recipient 2020'.

44 Jerry Beck, 'The Ranft Bros. in *Coraline*', *Cartoon Brew*, 10 February 2009. https://www.cartoonbrew.com/feature-film/the-ranft-bros-in-coraline-11228.html (accessed 23 September 2020).

45 Emily Haynes, *The Art of Kubo and the Two Strings* (San Francisco: Chronicle Books, 2016), p. 51.

46 Ibid., p. 99.

47 Ibid.

48 Holly Frey and Tracy Wilson, 'Stop-Motion Animation History with LAIKA Studios', *Stuff You Missed in History Class*, podcast recording, 10 April 2019. https://www.iheart.com/podcast/stuff-you-missed-in-history-cl-21124503/episode/stop-motion-animation-history-with-laika-studios-30806101/ (accessed 25 September 2020).

49 Chris Butler, 'Introduction', in Ramin Zahed (ed.), *The Art of Missing Link* (San Rafael, CA: Insight Editions, 2019), p. 11.

50 Zahed, *The Art of Missing Link*, p. 55.

51 Caitlin Roper, 'The Man Who Brought Stop-Motion Animation to the 21st Century', *Wired*, 18 September 2014. https://www.wired.com/2014/09/travis-knight-stop-motion-boxtrolls/ (accessed 23 September 2020).

52 Frey and Wilson, "Stop-Motion Animation History with LAIKA Studios'.

53 Andrea Comiskey, 'Special Effects in Contemporary Puppet Animation' in Dan North, Bob Rehak and Michael S. Duffy (eds), *Special Effects: New Histories/ Theories/Contexts* (London: BFI Palgrave, 2015), p. 45.

54 Jones, *Coraline: A Visual Companion*, p. 102.

4

The surprising migrations of 2½ D:
The background to *Coraline*

Norman M. Klein

A great fuss has been made of *Coraline* (2009) being the first stop-motion feature to thoroughly exploit 3D printing, and about 3D animation generally. But this essay will not reinforce that point of view. There is a much broader story that must be understood first, before 3D can take the movie arts any further. We must take stock of what the past five hundred years have taught us about fractures in the animated narrative. *Coraline* is a classic in 2½ D, a far richer category than VR verisimilitude. 2½ D means glitches intentionally slipped into the pulse of a 3D space. Flatness crashing into 3D was the most important of these. It can add layers to the story. These layers refer to a grand old tradition, from carnival to circus, to Baroque Artifice, modernist abstraction – and of course, puppet theatre. This essay is a historical introduction to 2½ D, as a way to launch into *Coraline*'s multiverse.

Many film reviewers spotted how the usual puppet effects of stop motion were enhanced in *Coraline*, how they utterly sublimated the 3D. For example, A. O. Scott wrote,

> The 3-D aspects of *Coraline* are unusually subtle. Now and then stuff is flung off the screen into your face, but the point is not to make you duck or shriek. Instead [the director], Mr. Selick uses the technology to make his world deeper and more intriguing. And of course, the stop-motion technique he uses, based on sculptured figures rather than drawn images, is already a kind of three-dimensional animation. The glasses you put on are thus not a gimmick, but an aid to seeing what's already there.[1]

Henry Selick has this to say in an interview from 2009:

> I found that I was mainly fighting the camera crew who fell in love with 3D and always wanted to crank it up too much. I had a very clear idea of controlling it, minimizing it, in the 'real world' [parts of the story]. Coraline's life is less

dimensional, so there is a muted colour palette [in those early scenes]. The sets are built with less depth because the story is about her dissatisfaction and loneliness at home. I wanted to save 3D for the other world, to draw people from the 3D space as Coraline is thrown into that world herself. I didn't want the 3D to come out and punch you in the eye.[2]

Chris Turnham, an illustrator on *Coraline*, added, 'Everything was still designed as a 2D piece of concept art without too much thought for the 3D aspect of it … The only time we had to think about 3D was when we created matte paintings … It's not unlike a 2D animated production in that regard.'[3]

My second question to Turnham:

Were there any unique animation story disciplines or guiding ideas that you were told to follow?

Turnham answered that

the real and the alternative worlds were designed with visual tricks to switch on and off. For example, in Bobinsky's attic, the table with a lamp and sheet over it became the circus tent in the other world house. Or the armoire in the living room became a giant beetle in the other world. Everything was designed to be a little wonky which worked well with the handmade quality stop-motion animation tends to have.[4]

The guiding model came from concept drawings by illustrator and concept artist Tadahiro Uesugi, whose 'line work had that dirty edge to it'. The spatial layers were impossibly deep, in a very accelerated perspective, as in Uesugi's work. That was how he adapted Neil Gaiman's novel, which he had read in Japanese. To build crazier extremes, he grew increasingly interested in 'more planar graphic designs' for this project, 'with less perspective and therefore less three-dimensional appearance'.[5]

Selick especially admired the way that Uesugi's spaces 'breathe'.[6] Their flow made for impossible (asynchronous) dimensions, suggesting a model of Coraline's mind under threat by a greater will. The space, like a circus version of Expressionism, threatens the puppet figures inside it.[7] CG glitches in dimensionality act like a secret point of view, like a character demanding her obedience. The story is a dimensional arm wrestle. First, there is space itself with a mind of its own, like a blind machine looking for a family. It 'threatens' to erase the touch or tactility of the stop-motion figures. That brings us back to what A. O. Scott may have noticed, when he used the term 'sculptured figures'. Selick wanted to exaggerate the perspective between space and touch – as a give and take into Coraline's alternative states – to make her 'world deeper and more intriguing'.[8] The 3D spaces were enhanced by 'artificial' glitches, to drive the story forward. Like a playful (and finally ruthless) voyeuristic god, 3D incongruities reveal the velvety otherness of data – show Coraline's mind being played with by outside powers (tossed from one world to the next). Finally, she is trapped inside the evil dimensions of *Coraline*'s Other Mother. Even Uesugi's line work in this 'scarier' world tends to be ragged (i.e. frayed, in a state of emotional unfinish).

In the opening scenes, Coraline's hard-working parents are stuck in a flat, gig economy, a start-up for a garden catalogue. Their eyes stay frozen to their work screen. Through a tunnel, however, Coraline finds a charming antidote – at first – a cheerfully psychotic circus that resembles her family and the floating gig-worker types at the Pink Palace apartments. The circus colours tend to spiral like flags in the wind and look extremely handmade. The contrast between the two mothers is meant to stick out like a sore thumb, but elegantly. Eventually, the Other Mother shows itself to be evil. It has been stalking Coraline's family, wants to replace its domesticity. In the final scenes, the visual oppositions intensify as Coraline goes into battle – in brilliant shapeshifting choreography. These sped-up collisions encapsulate what American filmmakers have learned from generations of great battle scenes set in miniature places (like the home). There are withering jump cuts, huge spirals: a cosmic struggle against the yard and its insects. Only a few alienated children are left to fight.

Throughout the film, the engine of the story centres on contrasting dimensions. They oscillate from one extreme to the other. At first, they seem unable to pierce each other. They remain parallel, each with its own skins, or layers (the tunnels, the patterns). At first, Coraline enjoys the antics of her alternative mother. Eventually, the Other Mother loses her cool. She starts to leap out of her spidery skin, like a monster ready to jump down your throat. She is invading from somewhere outside the house itself, from an offscreen underworld. Her colourful antics hide a suicidal impulse about family. The final conflict is both epic and miniaturized. A raggedy Wagnerian outer world trying to swallow a child's world.

That brings me to the clever way that armatures are animated in LAIKA films. Armatures are tiny kinetic sculptures that have movable joints. These can be posed frame by frame. Armatures are impossible skeletons. The characters in *Coraline* tend to look semi-natural in the way that they move; they are almost human toys. I was especially struck by the armature of Coraline's droopy-necked father. His head could slide forward at the neck, like a cash register, for extreme double takes (à la Tex Avery). That allowed him to look endlessly unprepared for what is going on.

Armatures tend to look obviously handmade, but graceful. The handmade aspect is exaggerated, not hidden. The Other Mother moves like exposed tendons or veins made out of wire. It is as if our sense of touch were being removed from the space itself – to deliver a kind of subjunctive physics (or 'cartoon physics', to cite Scott Bukatman).[9] I often call this the 'the strings of the marionette', the tactile loss of will (2½ D). Its vivid place in puppet theatre is well known, another tradition that goes back at least to the fifteenth century. There was also in the 1920s a Puppet Modernism (in cubist dance and agitprop theatre).[10]

Puppets caricature the body – and touch. They are dolls that children hug. But puppets are supposed to have a unique mind of their own. They can go to war with any space they enter. I remember back in the late 1980s, Don Mancini, who rented an apartment from me when he worked on his invention of Chucky for *Child's Play* (Tom Holland, 1988), discussed the tactility of animatronic horror.[11] He was going for an uncanny or *unheimlich* version of touch, more extreme than *Coraline*: by exaggerating the hand of the animator as puppeteer, the 'strings of the marionette'. It is clearly an ageless immersion technique, the materiality of the theatre, going back to Elizabethan masque, medieval carnival, Japanese *bunraku* and masks in theatre since the birth of societies.

In the twentieth century, 2½ D relied more on abstraction. From Oskar Fischinger to Dadaists and Russian constructivists, animated abstractions evolved, through synthetic collages, like El Lissitzky's 'electromagnetic' puppets and in haptic installations from Marcel Duchamp onwards. They tend to abstract space, as a way to comment on representation, within their narrative.

The puppet body in early cinema also remains 2½ D. Its handmade (yet machine-like) nature is comically at war with the human. Students always love the 2½ D sex scenes in Vladislav Starevich's *The Cameraman's Revenge* (1912). Each character has an insect exoskeleton so anatomically detailed, the sex is like Victorian shyness as 2½ D. An oafish beetle, stuffed inside a morning coat (like a Grandville caricature from 1840), engages in boring sex with his dragonfly wife. She, in secret, has feverish sex with an ardent grasshopper.[12] However, when the bodies get down, there are so many extra legs, a weird propriety hides their nakedness – a tactile gag that is perfect for a sex farce. Exaggerated haptic gags always suit 2½ D. In Švankmajer's *Dimensions of Dialogue* (1983), a clay lump gets accidentally born after a graceful but cringeworthy sex scene between clay lovers.[13] Or in the Quays' *Street of Crocodiles* (1986), a slice of blood-soaked liver operates the workings of a pocket watch. Whenever I show these haptic contrasts, the students find them gross, but wonderful. Why gross I ask; I get no answer. A 2½ D haptic shock, like watching surgery online, is more vivid than the fact.

2½ D suggests missing parts, to leave room for the handmade commentary. There must be a figure/ground ambiguity, or spaces between.[14] This is abundantly clear in the opalescent transitions within pinscreen animation by Alexandre Alexeïeff and Claire Parker.[15] They developed pinscreen animation over a period of fifty years; and Jacques Drouin continued with their technique into the 1970s. The sheer morphological stillness of pinscreen movement and staging is hypnotically 2½ D. It requires an entirely different film grammar for intercutting, dissolves. The surface is granular (pointillist, as if with a million gnats). Scenes tend to metamorphose; the usual editing cuts are often abandoned. Living-room walls melt into the next day or into street scenes.

This brings us to how European modernism fits into a poetics of 2½ D. For example, the pioneering Russian literary theorist Viktor Shklovsky had an apt term (1916) that suggests puppets. He called it *ostranenie*, or 'to make objects unfamiliar' – 'to increase the difficulty and length of perception (as) an aesthetic end in itself'.[16] I have always seen that as a cognate to a 2½ D effect – so too Brecht's theories of *Verfrendung* (or "V Effect") as epic theatre. These modes of 2½ D – agitprop about the liberation of the audience – then become vital for video art in the 1970s, for Fluxus; and finally, were applied to digital media.

The digital world is an insane and unstable archive, filled with glitches, hacks, factoids; in other words, a mad chase well suited for animation. Games increasingly caricature the glitching of data – as do media (or database) novels.[17] Memory and history are scrambled into 2½ D effects. The archive becomes as unstable and expressive as *Coraline's* parallel universes. In my digital novels (with accompanying print books), thousands of images (with voice overs) deliver stacks of unfinish to be rummaged through by the viewer (see *Bleeding Through* and *The Imaginary 20th Century*). That is because the narrator refuses to deliver the finished story and relies instead on 2½ D, where erased secrets leave telltale clues.

Bricolage turns into 2½ D, as in Švankmajer's *Punch and Judy* (1960). Two old puppets are thoroughly jaundiced. They only know how to fight to the death. But suddenly, one of them brings in a pet guinea pig. Very soon, they fight to the death for who owns it. In closeup, the guinea pig looks more unreal than the puppets; she is irresistibly supernatural. By contrast, the puppets are chipped and weathered, as they ritualistically destroy themselves. Their concluding death struggle is peppered with a rapid-fire archive about the popular culture dying with them. It is animated bricolage as cultural memory, mostly wood engravings from the nineteenth century. One might compare it to *Coraline*'s archiving of circus choreography. In our datafied culture, 2½ D also grows ever more fractured or granulated, into video maps, and pools of dark data. Even movement has been archived, as video slices take over so many aspects of our civilization. Coraline lives in a datafied household (like a workstation), where life and place are archived into scripted layers.

Like *ostranenie* (defamiliarization), animation is often about slowing down vision. Each step in a morph is slowed down, to violate – or complicate – the persistence of vision. It is an unwinding, a narrative shape-shifting that hides nothing, but exposes voids and seemingly unmotivated acts. Life today, especially in our Trump era, is replete with 2½ D anxieties about the body politic and our own bodies.

In the 1920s, Lissitzky and others in the Soviet avant-garde spoke of the body as 'ideogram'. Sergei Eisenstein defines ideogram as 'the combination of two "depictables"', to represent 'something that is graphically undepictable'.[18] That aptly captures what *Coraline*'s staging does. Two parallel homes coexist, with a wormhole in between. The wormhole is a void that is animated. Think of it as a velvety wheel of data particles that you can jump into, as a detour right through the centre. It is a crawl space, like a secret passage as a leap in time. It conjugates both of Coraline's worlds – back and forth, through a wormhole. 2½ D is graphically very precise. Its mental pictures are solid, like puppets' bodies. No blurry conversations do the trick. To borrow again from Eisenstein, 'a material ideogram' generates a 'transcendental (conceptual) result'.[19]

2½ D animation generates what I call anamorphs.[20] These slow down metamorphoses, until you see the shape-shifting as if in a pencil test (e.g. Cab Calloway singing 'Saint James Infirmary' in Fleischer Studios' *Betty Boop in Snow White*, 1933). The key is to reveal each transposition: slow it down, unwind the gag. As another example, notice 1933 King Kong's brilliant, handmade, sluggish movements.[21] He is a puppet who breathes an alternative kind of air. That makes him more vulnerable, in some ways more alive. In his kingdom on the island, he enjoys a puppet zoology, like bio-organisms who live underneath the Arctic Circle, breathing nitrogen instead of oxygen. 2½ D lets us pause in Kong's posthuman world, as if we were transposed into another species.

Modernist collage fractures into 2½ D, in Leger's (and Man Ray's) *Ballet Mécanique* (1924), but more importantly in Oskar Fischinger's masterpieces. Fischinger's heritage was crucial to training at Cal Arts, where Henry Selick studied (in the program run by Jules Engel, along with classes on Fischinger by Bill Moritz).[22]

2½ D can powerfully index space, like a telescope mapping the space-time continuum. It slows down time while it dissolves into a space. Wile E. Coyote buzzes industriously at the speed of light, then crashes into a stop sign (what I call a hummingbird effect). Alice runs 'across the field after (the rabbit), and was just in time to see it pop down a large rabbit-hole under the hedge'.[23] Coraline has a rabbit hole too – a tunnel. Again, like a wormhole, the tunnel allows for planar leaps. It also leaves blanks for ironic asides, 2½ D ciphers: non-zones, dead spaces, leftovers, clues that used to belong somewhere. Similarly, the rabbit hole in Švankmajer's *Něco z Alenky* (*Alice*, 1988) drops like an elevator to nowhere, through layers of things.

Even voices from outside the screen can be 2½ D. They intrude from nowhere, or are just out of sync – asynchronous sound (to borrow from defenders of Mickey Mouse music in the late 1920s).[24] They operate in a subjunctive tension – between the handmade and illusion of life – that suits animation.

Coraline speaks to me as a 2½ D version of the nineteenth-century fairy tale, a cross between Victorian and modernist aesthetics, like Matthew Arnold's complaint about being trapped between two worlds (in *The Grand Chartreuse*, 1855). Her pilgrimage shares a morbidity so often a part of children's literature since the nineteenth century. Her unstable grip on ad hoc things exists as a ghost trapped inside the digitized present, between childhood and early adulthood, where death has a lot to do with growing up.

The imaginary order is at war with the symbolic order. Kristeva might have compared this type of story to a thin membrane 'threatened with bursting'.[25]

> On close inspection, all literature is probably a version of the apocalypse that seems to me rooted, no matter what its sociohistorical conditions might be, on the fragile border (borderline cases) where identities (subject/object, etc.) do not exist or only barely so – double, fuzzy, heterogeneous, animal, metamorphosed, altered, abject.[26]

No doubt, *Coraline* invites us to apply Freudian theories of the 'uncanny',[27] and of the Double. The most famous examples (beginning with Hoffmann's *The Sandman*) draw from Germany and middle Europe in the nineteenth century and stop-motion masters like Jan Švankmajer, the Brothers Quay and Tim Burton. Indeed, the key text is Hoffmann's short story, *The Sandman* (1816),[28] which is still taught worshipfully from one end of the world to other, especially at CalArts. It speaks directly to the chill of disbelief when parallel worlds do not match.

Gaiman is certainly familiar, even obsessed, with Freud's reading of *The Sandman*. Again, this nexus dates back to 1816 – to the warp of the Baroque into Romanticism and industrialism. The criss-cross between the unearthly and the intimate dominates Gaiman's novels. He is also a parallel worlds storyteller, especially drawing upon H. P. Lovecraft, the Victorian recluse.

That suggests yet another historic connection that is vital here. The automaton craze of the eighteenth century inspired entertainments that led to magic-lantern precinema in the 1790s.[29] And various automata still travelled the vaudeville circuit until about 1850, then were copied by artisans in the industrial era. So, the genealogy of *Coraline* centres on how the late Baroque migrated into industrialism. In the eighteenth century, the automaton was a clockwork device. It was built by artisanal clockmakers, but already pointed toward the earliest industrial technology. Even Watt's original steam engine was treated, at first, as another automaton or philosophical toy. But its practical applications took over quickly. These two worlds – where baroque artifice and early industry met (1780–1850) – were essential to the history of stop motion that leads to *Coraline*.

Today we are witnessing Baroque techniques making a comeback, especially in animation and on the internet. We notice automatons miniaturizing and transforming capitalism. We see the evils of digital capitalism, along with its conveniences. That leads me to ask, is it perhaps relevant to the story that *Coraline* was produced at the time of the 2008 financial crash? Did its stop-motion gags reflect the shocks of the Great Recession? Is the Other Mother an echo of mortgage derivatives, or surveillance capitalism, of the many problems so much in evidence by 2009?

The dark side of animated theatre often satirizes capitalist morbidity and madness. It is always a treat. That was true at the birth of capitalism in Europe. In 1400, the clown and the harlequin were originally corpses running through the village during Carnival, as if stricken by the Black Death. These characters then found their way into commedia dell'arte, as well as circus acts and vaudeville – eventually as stop-motion films about layers of death. For example, pre-Conquest celebrations in Mexico of Day of the Dead enliven the 2½ D in Pixar's animated feature *Coco* (Lee Unkrich and Adrian Molina, 2017).

I have myself been turned into LAIKA 2½ D about the dead. My face (as a 10-year-old boy) was character designer Heidi Smith's model for the design of Norman in *ParaNorman* (Sam Fell and Chris Butler, 2012). My 'gravity-defying hair' was added as a nod (above the forehead) to Norman the old guy. When I see that movie, I get a 2½ D reminder of how many artifices it takes to invent a stop-motion character. I was emailed various incarnations along the way – especially those sculptural little Normans, like pet terriers on a walk. I met myself by accident, so to speak. The feeling is ironic, not dramatic. It is a 2½ D reminder of how many layers the facts can hide. I witnessed my childhood face as stages of production. I was someone else's puppet show. I noticed strings of the marionette about myself. Two puppet Normans collided at the same moment.

Suppose we imagine 2½ D artifice as part of our collective DNA. That means that, in our stage of capitalism, our bodies are frequently invaded by parasites. This condition has generated a pop folklore incredibly familiar to animators (and horror graphic novelists like Gaiman). Artifice is sculptural madness; we are frozen by a wicked smile.[30] And buildings have an archaeological 2½ D smile. Consider the following passage from Neil Gaiman's introduction to *Coraline*. He describes the home where he and his family moved, that inspired the haunted spaces within *Coraline*: 'We were living in a gothic old house in the middle of America, with a turret and a wraparound porch, with steps up to it. It's a house built over a hundred years ago by a German immigrant, a cartographer … and artist [essentially a media engineer for his day].'[31]

Years later, Henry Selick showed Gaiman miniature sets based on this very house. To accentuate the passage from 2D to 2½ D, accelerated perspective was exaggerated, and the face of the miniatures was tilted toward the camera, to make the abrupt shift more immersive, even more violently amazing.[32] This was a trick from the 1990s especially, that was highlighted in fx blockbusters like *Independence Day* (Roland Emmerich, 1996). Gaiman was amazed at how well Selick's toyhouse sets captured the uncanny feel of the house where he had lived.[33]

The key is that buildings come alive as animation, into 'breathing' architecture. Imagine movie sets as an occult order, like the padded interior of a human brain. More than the house is haunted. I keep envisioning this gothic from a German perspective, though Gaiman is more enamoured with Lovecraft's voice (by his 'ellipses') and with Moorcroft and post 1960s science fiction. Selick, I am convinced, is equally obsessed with German set design throughout the 1920s.

What links them both is the psychotropics of the double as a space that breathes. So much of this has nineteenth-century Romantic fittings. Coraline must battle her Victorian 'Other Mother', who has buttons instead of eyes and is a spidery creature snatching human beings on her web. The Other Mother is also thoroughly contemporary – an infernal automaton/cyborg, almost an artificial intelligence (AI) violation of nature. But the references to Hoffmann's *The Sandman* are unmistakable. Like Hoffmann's Coppelius, she efficiently plucks out her victims' eyes. The Other Mother is an evil parasite who lives inside a humble convenience kitchen. She is a cybernetic version of a Singer sewing machine (1850). By 1840, various miniaturized appliances had begun to find their way into rustic American homes, along with dark visions of childhood.

Coraline is a twist on cautionary tales (1815–50) – as they were called back then. They were very sadistic children's stories – horror tales as lessons in citizenship and cleanliness (often set in the kitchen). Some of these tales were known to Tim Burton certainly, and probably to his close friend, Henry Selick. And Neil Gaiman refers to Hilaire Belloc and Edward Gorey's spoofs of these darkly whimsical tales. The most famous American variation was *Slovenly Betsy* (1911),[34] where lazy girls are punished surgically. One even sets herself on fire while playing with matches. The tradition dates from the bestseller, *Struwwelpeter* (1845, Germany, widely translated). Gaiman's *Crazy Hair* (2009) clearly updates this tradition. In *Struwwelpeter* ('Slovenly Peter'), Little Conrad is warned not to suck his thumb.[35] When he does, the Great Tailor visits upon him. With shears as big as a scythe for cutting hay, the tailor snips off his thumbs, as if they were buttons on a jacket.

That brings us to the history of buttons. In the nineteenth century, buttons were considered an accessory item with industrial implications. Button eyes (especially on rag dolls) were not simply eyes to the soul. They suggested haunted toys dating back to Neolithic times. For millennia, buttons were made in simple handcrafted ways, of every imaginable material. This craft was industrialized by the late eighteenth century. In 1776, Adam Smith writes,

> A nail-maker changes postures, blows the bellows, changes tools etc. and therefore the quantity produced cannot be so great as in manufactures of pins and buttons, where the work is reduced to simple operations.[36]

Thus, one of the hallmarks of early industrialism was the production of pins and buttons. That adds a rustic aspect to the machinic evil in *Coraline*. It speaks to the seeds of industrialism, as they entered the frontier American home.

Industrial accessories like buttons invaded the domestic space at the time that Gaiman's nineteenth-century house was built. They were an internet of things (again circa 1850), everyday objects irradiated by industrial methods. One is reminded, of course, of the internet of things today, clearly within *Coraline's* gestalt.

I am reminded of the work-at-home conditions in *Coraline*. They speak to me of farming towns forced to incubate early industrialism. Historically, the loom in the living room suggests gig labour – in cottage industries over the centuries. Labour today is again caught in a kind of precarious indenture. This growing threat of precarity is symbolized by sewing needles automated into evil spiders. By 1800, peasant farmers living in the English countryside were being overwhelmed by the cottage industry. They often had to accept a loom placed in the middle of their cottage by the lord. It was an alien thing from a capitalist/agrarian outsider. It stood blindly, overwhelming their tiny house. The family would then have to weave day and night, like sharecroppers or worker ants.[37]

In *Coraline* of course, the loom has been transformed. It is now a computer workstation invading family life. Coraline's parents are indentured to their screens (their garden catalogue) as peasants were to looms that were owned and leased, by outsiders. Perils from outside are threatening. As in 1850, the home computer – and runaway automation – belong to a crucial seed time in capitalism, still emerging, still blind. An infestation – the Other Mother – is trolling us – slowly, blindly taking over, like something being sewn or knitted, like a moss covering a house. 2½ D suggests an evil infecting the tactility of everyday things.

The Other Mother is therefore a machine possessed by capitalism in grave transition. It shapeshifts in the way capital does. It simulates memories of her family. It interjects evil sewing-needle crabs into very tactile, ordinary things. It is a child's view of digitized indenture growing around her (like those cottage industry families). No one can move or talk much.

After all, this film was made right after the crash of 2008. Its story engine follows the circuitous route that collective memory always takes. The animation industry has been equally infected by precarity. Work at home can alienate one's privacy. Mythically speaking, everyday household objects are infected, as in *Poltergeist* (Tobe Hooper, 1982). Hard surfaces turn soft, as if infected. They sweat out a kind of mucus. It is disgusting, but colourful.

There is also a 2½ D literature about distorted memory and lost intimacy (using ellipses, unreliable narrators, picaresque episodic structure). Its effects are vital to storytelling worldwide, in America, Europe, Asia, in the manifold variations of magic realism in Latin America. Simply tracing all of these could fill another two hundred pages. But I should end with a tangent that fits, as the essay begins to close. I've decided on a factoid about sensory alienation. New research about the effect of data capitalism argues that we are losing our sense of touch.[38] This reminds me of Kracauer's theories about cinematic erasure (between the wars and after) – about fragments inside 'corporeal-material layers', of 'the action below the action'.[39] He was trying to understand how the emotional collapse of Europe was echoed in cinematic glitches.

I will stop here, to allow the reader to fill in a few paragraphs of their own, perhaps something broader, on statuary from Benin animated by imperialism. It's a huge, careening stack – of parallel worlds and dark data. We are off on a picaresque into further dislocation. The next twenty years promise more 2½ D than we can imagine, as film and social networks truly conjoin – while the earth goes through a lapse dissolve.

Notes

1   A. O. Scott, 'Cornered in a Parallel World: Coraline', *New York Times*, 6 February 2009, p. C1.

2   'Henry Selick in Conversation', *Focus Features*, 9 February 2009. https://www.focusfeatures.com/article/henry_selick_in_conversation (accessed 12 December 2019). See also, John Clark, 'Adding Dimension to Storytelling', *New York Times*, 30 January 2009.

3   Email exchange with illustrator Chris Turnham, December 2018.

4   Ibid.

5   Ibid.

6   Bill Desowitz, 'Tadahiro Uesugi Talks "Coraline" Design', *Animation World Network*, 23 January 2009. https://www.awn.com/animationworld/tadahiro-uesugi-talks-coraline-design (accessed 12 December 2019).

7   On materiality and animation: Alexander S. Galloway, 'Polygraphic Photography and the Origins of 3-D Animation', in Karen Beckman (ed.), *Animating Film Theory* (Durham, NC: Duke University Press, 2014), pp. 61–3. On 3D chronomodeling: 'This is a fundamentally anticinematic mode of mediation; likewise, it is antiphenomenological, since complete spatial synchrony is prohibited within the cinematic and phenomenological systems' (p. 63). But what if the

phenomenology of cinema also requires asynchronous mediation at key points, especially those involving 3D, in order to add contour to the immersive experience?

8   Desowitz, 'Tadahiro Uesugi Talks "Coraline" Design'. Uesugi has also said that he has been deeply influenced by 1950s graphic styles, as in UPA; in other words, very much not three dimensional, very much the planar modernist design of mid-century modernism.

9   See Scott Bukatman, *Terminal Identity* (Durham, NC: Duke University Press, 1993); *Matters of Gravity* (Durham, NC: Duke University Press, 2003); *Poetics of Slumberland* (Berkeley: University of California Press, 2012). From the adaptations of 2½ D to cybernetic oscillations in 1980s sci-fi, back to the traditions of cross-fertilized narrative in early animation.

10 Puppet Modernism means the use of puppets in modernist performance: Oskar Schlemmer at the Bauhaus; Soviet public art events circa 1920; agitprop effects for theatre, by Piscator and Brecht in Berlin; the renewed interest in masks for modernist events (Surrealist and Dada 'manifestations'). These tended to be very ludic, influenced by Coney Island – and also highly political, for a decade when politics took to the streets a lot in Europe. In the 1960s, Puppet Modernism reappears in mime theatre, performance art, etc. For a critique of how modernism ignored the implications of 2½ D, see Paul Wells, ' "Picture by Picture, Movement by Movement": Melbourne-Cooper, Shiryaev and the Symbolic Body', *animation: an interdisciplinary journal*, vol. 6, no. 2 (2011), pp. 149–62.

11 Don Mancini interviews by Norman M. Klein, 1987.

12 Grandville's caricatures of animals deeply influenced John Tenniel's work for *Alice in Wonderland*. Grandville's name was Jean Ignace Isidore Gérard (1803–1847). Due to the enduring interest in his fantasy books, he is the pioneer of animal physiognomies in animated form – even before the birth of cinema: an influence as well on Thomas (T. S.) Sullivant (1854–1926) and on Heinrich Kley (1863–1945), who was an influence on Disney in the 1930s). Aspects of this 150-year-old grammar about metamorphosed animal/humans was passed along to Henry Selick, as part of the training at Disney. And it certainly is evident in *The Nightmare before Christmas* (along with Fleischer references to humanoid animals). However, there is not as much animal caricature in *Coraline*. The spirit of that tradition can be seen in the rat circus sequence, most of all.

13 This gag has been called 'gestural marionettes', 'lumpen shapes of clay bearing the rough imprint of their creator's hands'. James Frost, 'Jan Švankmajer: Film as Puppet Theatre', *Animation Studies*, 29 December 2016. https://journal. animationstudies.org/james-frost-jan-svankmajer-film-as-puppet-theatre/ (accessed 8 June 2020).

14   By spaces between, I refer to the blanks where the viewer makes mental pictures. These blanks are very much what is suggested by intellectual montage, for example, or by Rembrandt lighting, or by archival storytelling, or even by the figure-ground ambiguity between a wall and the floor. Without these gaps, the mind has very little room to enter the narrative. Clearly, part of spaces between involves the will of the viewer, the role of the viewer. The more interactive the media, the more that viewers enter as characters (spaces between), the more spaces between, like way stations, are needed. These gaps should distance the viewer from the pleasure of the narrative. The reverse is true, properly handled.

15   The sheer morphological stillness of pinscreen movement and staging is hypnotic. It requires an entirely different film grammar for intercutting, dissolves. The viewer is powerfully aware of the process by which it is made, as a 2½ D overlay that can never quite leave the film.

16   Viktor Shklovsky, "Art as Technique" (1917, though he began the OPOYAZ group a year earlier, where theories of defamiliarization were discussed). Approximately ten pages long, 'Art as Technique (or Device)' appears in many anthologies, like *Theory of Prose* (by Shklovsky, with annotators, Elmwood Park, IL: Dalkey Archive Press, 1990; original 1925) and Alexandra Berlina, ed., *Viktor Schklovsky: A Reader* (London: Bloomsbury, 2016) and in selections online. I excised this from a site, because it perhaps oversimplified that famous passage, but I thought captured the high lucidity in much of Shklovsky's prose. See 'Lecture List: Term 2', *Warwick English and Comparative Literary Studies*, 17 March 2016. https://warwick.ac.uk/ fac/arts/english/currentstudents/undergraduate/modules/fulllist/first/en122/ lecturelist-2015-16-2/shklovsky.pdf (accessed 8 June 2020).

17   Archival media novels about spaces between, and the picaresque of history: Norman M. Klein, *Bleeding Through: The Layers of Los Angeles, 1920–1985* (Los Angeles Labyrinth Projects at USC, Karlsruhe: Center for the Arts and Media, 2003). Also, Norman M. Klein and Margo Bistis, *The imaginary 20th Century* (Karlsruhe: Center for the Arts and Media, 2016).

18   Sergei Eisenstein, *Film Form: Essays in Film Theory*, ed./trans. Jay Leyda (New York: Harcourt, Brace, Jovanovich, 1949), p. 30.

19   Ibid., p. 50.

20   Norman M. Klein, 'Animation and Animorphs: A Brief Disappearing Act', in Vivian Sobchack (ed.), *Metamorphing: Visual Transformation and the Culture of Quick-change* (Minneapolis: University of Minnesota, 2000), pp. 21–41.

21   Jane Shadbolt, 'Parallel Synchronized Randomness: Stop-Motion Animation in Live Action Feature Films', *Animation Studies*, 9 June 2013. https://journal. animationstudies.org/category/volume-8/jane-shadbolt-parallel-synchronised-randomness/ (accessed 9 December 2019). The most cited review of that era: Joe

Bigelow, 'King Kong', *Variety*, 6 March 1933. http://www.variety.com/review/ VE1117792322/ (accessed 9 December 2019). See also Thomas Elsaesser, 'The "Return" of 3-D: On Some of the Logics and Genealogies of the Image in the Twenty-First Century', *Critical Inquiry*, vol. 39, no. 2 (2013), pp. 217–46 (on the new potential of 3D live action cinema), p. 242: '(3-D) may enlarge the scope of perceptual responses, deepen the affective engagement of the spectator, and work towards integrating the originally disruptive effects of stereoptic depth cues with other monocular depth cues, such as resolution, shading, color, and size. Hence, what is being promoted with 3-D is not a special effect as special effect but as the new default value of digital vision, presuming a layered, material, yet also mobile and pliable space.'

22 Fischinger is the grand master of 2½ D space – or spaces between. I remember watching animation students at Cal Arts watching Fischinger animation frame by frame. Some were then hired to work on *Star Wars*. I am convinced that Fischinger's animation of deep space influenced the starship battle scenes. There is no doubt that Fischinger helped inspire Henry Selick's aesthetic.

23 Lewis Carroll, *Alice's Adventures in Wonderland* (Chicago, IL: VolumeOne, 1998), p. 3.

24 Norman M. Klein, *Seven Minutes: The Life and Death of the American Animated Cartoon* (London: Verso, 1993), pp. 8–12.

25 Julia Kristeva, *Powers of Horror: An Essay on Abjection*, trans. Leon S. Roudiez (New York: Columbia University Press 1982; original 1980), p. 141.

26 Ibid., p. 207.

27 Chloé Germaine Buckley, 'Psychoanalysis, "Gothic" Children's Literature, and the Canonization of *Coraline*', *Children's Literature Association Quarterly*, vol. 40, no. 1 (2015), pp. 58–79; Margaret Hartmann, '*Coraline*: A Freudian Fairy Tale That's Not Just for Kids', *Jezebel*, 6 February 2009. https://jezebel.com/5148385/coraline-a-freudian-fairy-tale-thats-not-just-for-kids (accessed 12 December 2019).

28 The nine-minute stop-motion masterpiece by Paul Berry, *The Sandman* (1991) is spectacular 2½ D, clearly in the trajectory that we associate with Tim Burton and Henry Selick. Here, the Sandman itself is an eighteenth century courtly, but evil man-hawk. He always makes his entrance in an iridescent blue (as in the day for night(mare) methods of silent cinema: chrome and glowing blues as the colour of dreams). This birdlike Sandman attacks the sleeping boy, who is a carved wooden puppet. The hapless, sad boy always appears in organic browns to express his peasant woodsy German world (approximating the date of Hoffmann's short story, 1816). Other Sandman adaptations include German director Eckhart Schmidt's brilliant live-action retelling of the tormented original tale, E. T. A. Hoffmann's *Der Sandmann* (1993), Eric Woster's twinning of the Sandman with an Italian

background that suggests *Frankenstein* (1993), J. R. Bookwalter's trailer-park slasher version (1995); also, a little girls' perverse wish fulfilment brings *The Sandman* gruesomely to life, in Peter Sullivan's feature (2017). Finally, of course, Neil Gaiman's cyberpunk graphic-novel series, *The Sandman* (DC Comics, 1989– present), will apparently be adapted to screen.

29 See Richard D. Altick, *The Shows of London* (Cambridge: Harvard University Press, 1978). It remains a model of cultural history that has spawned many variations since.

30 See Norman M. Klein, *The Vatican to Vegas: A History of Special Effects* (London: New Press, 2004).

31 Neil Gaiman, *Coraline* (New York: HarperCollins, 2012; original 2002), p. xiv.

32 Linda Richards, interview with Neil Gaiman, *January Magazine*, August 2001. https://www.januarymagazine.com/profiles/gaiman.html (accessed 8 June 2020). See also Suzanne Buchan, ed. *Pervasive Animation* (London: AFI Reader/ Routledge, 2013). This anthology came out of a conference at the Tate Modern in 2007, where many of these questions about the architectonics of animation were discussed early and at length.

33 Richards, interview with Neil Gaiman. In the interview, Gaiman describes his home in the United States, the model for *Coraline*, as an Addams family house, with a wraparound porch, a big pointy tower and rumours that someone hung themselves in the tower. Also Gavin J. Grant, 'Neil Gaiman Interview', *Indie Bound*. https://www.indiebound.org/author-interviews/gaimanneil (accessed 8 June 2020). He lives in a 'big dark house of uncertain location where he grows exotic pumpkins and accumulates computers and cats'. Also an influence on his writing of the novel *American Gods*.

34 Heidrich Hoffmann, *Slovenly Betsy*, illustrated by Walter Hayn (Bedford, MA: Applewood Books, 2006; reprint from 1911). Also a Project Gutenberg ebook. Many of these morbid, but funny cautionary punishments – chapter by chapter – even predate Heinrich Hoffman, go back to circa 1815, when cautionary children's books first appeared in Germany and Britain. They were a hyper moralistic variation of the fairy tale. There was also a sequel entitled *Slovenly Kate*.

35 Henrich Hoffmann's *Struwwelpeter* (1844) remains part of every German childhood to this day. I should point out also that in the years when Tim Burton was planning or developing *Edward Scissorhands* (1990), Lena Gieseke, his German wife at the time, happened to be a student in my European Studies class. We got around to chats about German Romanticism, and collective folk memory among German children. She pointed out *Struwwelpeter*. One very famous illustration from *Struwwelpete*r shows a wild-haired boy whose hands are outstretched with long fingernails like scissors. In May, 2013, the New York Public Library ran an

exhibition on the fantasy artists and writers directly influenced by *Struwwlepeter*, with special attention given to the costuming of *Edward Scissorhands*. A still from *Edward Scissorhands* was featured, as well as references to Maurice Sendak (clearly an influence on *Coraline*). Culture is often a matter of degrees of separation, with recordings along the way. Available at https://www.nypl.org/blog/2013/05/15/influence-str (accessed 9 December 2019).

36   Adam Smith, *An Inquiry into the Nature and Causes of the Wealth of Nations*, 6th edn, vol. 1 (London: G. Bell and Sons, 1887; original 1776), p. 9.

37   Enclosures, as a model for understanding how feudal land tenure and industrialism took place, are widely studied, even commented on often by Marx and Engels. A recent summary article of the current literature and debates surrounding enclosure: Lisa Tilley, Ashok Kumar and Thomas Cowan, 'Introduction: Enclosures and Discontents', *City*, vol. 21, nos. 3–4 (2017), pp. 420–7. Among the standard histories (pedestrian but earnest): W. E. Tate, *The Enclosure Movement* (New York: Walker, 1967). There is also a renewed interest in enclosures, because they also deal with the Commons and waste, a subject being reoriented into contemporary political and urban theory.

38   Laura U. Marks, *Touch: Sensuous Theory and Multisensory Media* (Minneapolis: University of Minnesota Press, 2002); Barry J. C. Purves, *Stop Motion: Passion, Process and Performance* (Burlington, MA: Focal Press/Routledge, 2008); Ellen Rocha, 'Beyond Materiality in Animation: Sensuous Perception and Touch in the Tactile Existence of "Would a Heart Die?"', *Animation Studies*, 31 December 2016. https://journal.animationstudies.org/category/volume-11/ellen-rocha-beyond-materiality-in-animation-sensuous-perception-and-touch-in-the-tactile-existence-of-would-a-heart-die/ (accessed 9 December 2019).

39   Miriam Hansen, '"With Skin and Hair": Kracauer's Theory of Film, Marseille 1940', *Critical Inquiry*, vol. 19, no. 3 (1993), pp. 437–69. On the early conception by Kracauer of what became his collection of essays *Theory of Film: The Redemption of Physical Reality* (Oxford: Oxford University Press, 1974).

Part Two

Stop-motion technology, process and spectatorship

5

Replacing *Coraline*

Dan Torre

Most of us, when we think of stop-motion puppet animation, think of the manipulation of an individual puppet character being moved incrementally one frame at a time. But what helps to make *Coraline* (Henry Selick, 2009) such a masterpiece of fluid stop-motion animation is its use of *replacement animation*, whereby puppet parts (such as the head) are replaced (one frame at a time) with slightly dissimilar ones. Although replacement animation has been utilized within stop-motion animation productions since at least the 1930s (most notably in the George Pal Puppetoons studio productions), it nevertheless represents a relatively distinctive approach that is worthy of close analysis. Due to recent advances in 3D printing, which have enabled the speedy production of precisely constructed puppet forms, replacement animation is becoming both more prevalent and more complex.

The movie is based on the book *Coraline* by Neil Gaiman and, as with most filmic adaptations, a number of narrative changes were made in order to bring it successfully to the screen; these included adding sequences and introducing new characters. Also, a number of more subtle alterations were made which thematically reflect the handcrafted and labour-intensive process of stop-motion animation and, specifically, the use of the replacement animation technique. Not only is the materiality of stop motion highly visible in *Coraline*, but the use of replacement animation also becomes a kind of metanarrative that permeates the film. That is, the very concept and process of replacement animation is represented thematically throughout the film. This idea is also echoed throughout the primary storyline, for example when the various characters are systematically *replaced* with 'Other characters' (such as the 'Other Mother' and the 'Other Father').

This chapter discusses the use of replacement animation in *Coraline* and considers some of the theoretical, narrative and aesthetic implications that this technique can facilitate.

Replacement animation

Traditionally, there have been two primary methods employed in the creation of animated movement: manipulated animation and replacement animation. Manipulated animation usually involves the moving of a single image or object. Most stop-motion puppet animated films are produced in this way – the animator will incrementally, but directly, move a single puppet form.

By contrast, replacement animation involves the creation of multiple completed images or forms that are then successively replaced (one new image or form at a time), in order to create the illusion of a singular and persistent, yet moving, form. Most examples of traditional cel animation would adhere to this technique. For example, thousands of individual drawings of Mickey Mouse and friends (each slightly different in pose) would be sequentially replaced under the camera in order to produce a seven-minute animated film.

An analogous approach can also be used in the production of stop-motion films. Basically, any movement that requires an elasticity or a distortion of a character's form can be readily achieved through the use of replacements. A notable early example can be found in the work of George Pal's Puppetoons studio which, in the 1940s, regularly used and, in fact, popularized this approach with the advent of its 'replacement animation system'. Although Pal's studio did also animate many of its figures in the traditional stop-motion (manipulated) method, a lot of its animated movement (particularly the more fluid effects of squash and stretch) was achieved through the replacement system. For example, in order to make a figure's arm stretch out to pick up an object, the animators would replace it frame by frame with an incrementally longer arm. Similarly, in order to make a character's jaw appear to drop in surprise, incrementally elongated head-shapes would be replaced onto a character, one frame at a time (see for example, *Jasper and the Haunted House*, George Pal 1942).[1]

Historically, most traditional stop-motion puppet animation could be described as exhibiting somewhat stiff or jerky movements. This aesthetic is partially due to the animator's skill (or lack thereof) – for the more expertly the puppet is animated, the more fluidly it will seem to move. However, this impression also has a great deal to do with the construction of the actual puppet. Most stop-motion puppets are made to endure the rigours of manipulation over many hours of shooting and are therefore constructed out of robust materials and supported with sturdy metal armatures. Often, such constructions tend to resist the more fluid animated movements of, for example, squash and stretch, and metamorphosis.

In order to get truly supple and fluid movement from a stop-motion puppet, there are several different strategies that can be employed. One could work with very malleable materials – for example, the early works of Will Vinton Studios and Aardman Animations took advantage of the supple nature of clay materials and would often showcase intriguing displays of metamorphosis.[2] Alternatively, one can construct a very intricate and nuanced armature structure that can facilitate flexible movements. The feature film *Corpse Bride* (Tim Burton and Mike Johnson, 2005) utilized very intricate puppets whose facial features were controlled by expertly crafted clockwork mechanisms contained within the forms.[3] This allowed for very subtle (and therefore very smooth) changes to facial expressions and articulated mouth movements. Or, as in the case of *Coraline* and other recent LAIKA Studio films, one could make use of the replacement technique.

Of course, *Coraline* does utilize very complex and expertly constructed puppets, but it also makes use of a good deal of replacement animation. For example, a vast number of different facial expressions and mouth shapes were created for each character. In the process of animation, these replacement parts were then fitted to the character's head one after the other in order to create fluid and seamless animated expressions.[4] The animators further employed the use of the replacement animation in order to achieve exaggerated 'squash and stretch' movements, sequentially replacing sections of each puppet with modified elements (such as incrementally longer or stouter torsos). And, as in the 'dancing mice' sequence described below, entire character puppets were replaced one frame at a time in order to achieve dynamic elastic (squashing and stretching) actions as the mice leap from one spot to another.

Replacement cycles

Another outcome that replacement animation can facilitate is animated cycles (or loops). Animated cycles represent a structuring of sequential images that are repeated, at least once, in a consistent order. Because stop-motion animation generally favours a straight-ahead animation approach (in which each new frame of animation is created sequentially), animated cycles are rarely used. It is, after all, very difficult to repeat a series of movements identically when animating in a straight-ahead manner (and generally counterproductive). However, when the replacement technique is employed in stop motion, cycles will often become a more natural occurrence. Not only do they encourage a more economical use of the rather extravagant fabrication of hundreds of parts (that might only be visible on screen for a single frame), but they also allow for a uniquely precise application of animated movement.

There is one extended sequence in *Coraline* in which cyclical replacement animation is heavily utilized: the 'dancing mice' choreographed sequence. This scene, which takes place in the Other World within the apartment of Coraline's neighbour, the Other Mr Bobinsky, is one of the most complexly choreographed sequences in the movie. When the mice first take to the stage, they instantly arrange themselves so as to spell out the main character's name, forming the letters C-O-R-A-L-I-N-E. Then, with their drums and trumpets, the mice take the formation of a marching band; and in a delightful and intricately designed performance they jump, dance and play their music. The approximately fifty individual mice leap and move with absolute precision and with a good deal of animated squash and stretch. It is a performance that absolutely delights the characters of Coraline and Wybie – and it is also a presentation of *animation* that undoubtedly brings joy to the viewer, particularly when one considers the complexity of its production (Figure 5.1).

Henry Selick acknowledged that this sequence was strongly influenced by both the choreographed musicals of Busby Berkeley and, importantly, by the replacement technique of George Pal's Puppetoons.

> They were inspired by the famous George Pal's Puppetoons. ... He wanted the sort of elasticity you get in Disney or Warner Brothers' drawn animation. And in stop-motion, with little joints and so on, you couldn't have that. Characters couldn't stretch or change shape. So, he actually had characters that were hand-carved out of wood, in a series of poses, so they could stretch and squash and deform. It was hundreds and hundreds. That's what we've more or less gone for here with these mice. They are repeating hops, cycles we call them, or runs, and all sort of spit out of our rapid prototype 3D printer machine but based on initially drawn animation that's worked out more carefully with a computer. So, we had hundreds and hundreds of mice all lined up to do these patterns.[5]

Figure 5.1 *Coraline*'s complexly choreographed 'dancing mice' sequence.

In these instances, the sequence utilized carefully pre-planned and prefabricated puppets to allow for very controlled cyclical actions. Significantly, when using replacement puppet forms, most of the animated movement will have been predetermined (and in a sense, pre-animated) long before the production animator has the opportunity to manipulate the forms in front of the camera. This already 'baked-in' movement allowed for the production of a dizzyingly precise and exuberantly dynamic choreographed sequence in *Coraline*.

Replacements: A new metaphysical object

Most animation can be thought of as, at least in part, a metaphysical construct because it really only becomes visible when it is presented (i.e. played back through a device of some sort). Replacement animation, because of its unique production process, represents an exceptional variant of the metaphysical form of animation.

Manipulated animation (where a single object is moved incrementally over time) can be thought of as essentially a *time-lapse* method of animation – in that it represents intermittent grabs from a normal time-duration. As the animator proceeds to manipulate the puppet, he or she will take discontinuous photographs of the proceedings and these photographs are then compressed into a new and concise sequence of animation. The result comprises a series of lapses of time, or a *time-lapse* sequence. But, of course, because there is an animator involved in the process of manipulated animation – one who is deliberately imbuing the form with movement – the result constitutes more than a mere time-lapse of a natural event. So, to highlight this deliberate manipulation, we can designate it as being an *animated* time-lapse sequence.

However, replacement animation goes a step further, as it also represents an amalgamation of many different images or objects. So, rather than having a single puppet that is moved frame by frame, one might have potentially hundreds of different puppets that are placed in front of the camera one at a time in order to give the illusion of a single moving puppet. Therefore, in addition to animated lapses in time, we can also think of replacement animation as being comprised of 'lapses of objects', or an *object-lapse*. The result of the replacement animation process affords both lapses of time and lapses of objects, which all coalesce in the guise of a unified animated form.

Replacements can therefore be conceived of as an embodiment of a *multiplicity* because they are the amalgamation of many things over time and space (conflated time, conflated objects). In his book *Bergsonism*, Deleuze points out that Henri Bergson considers there to be two types of multiplicity; one can be thought of as that which makes up a concrete object (in space). He notes that if such a spatial multiplicity were to be cut up, the resulting elements would still be similar to that *of* the original multiplicity (if you cut up a watermelon, the slices are still watermelon). Deleuze, while further referencing Bergson, notes that when this multiplicity is in *duration* it must be considered to be a 'continuous multiplicity'. However, if a continuous multiplicity were to be cut up, the resulting elements would be 'changed in kind'.[6] This raises the important idea that animation which utilizes replacements results in a form that is composed of many elements which are not necessarily of the same thing; therefore, it is not any singular 'thing'. And, if you were to cut up a replacement animation sequence (into individual frames) you would find that, not only is the movement no longer visibly expressed, but each particular frame (or 'slice') is comprised of a radically different object.

Thus, in *Coraline*, each puppet head is actually an amalgamation of potentially thousands of replacement parts all sutured together (through the process of animation) to represent *a single form*. It is simultaneously one head (as we watch it through duration) – but it is also many different heads from many different periods of time. It seems very appropriate that a movie like *Coraline*, which expresses shifting realities and ambiguous events, would involve this particular approach.

3D-printed replacements

Literally, thousands of 3D-printed faces were used in the making of *Coraline*, in addition to the many other puppet parts that were also 3D-printed.[7] Prior to the advent of 3D-printing, replacement stop-motion animation would comprise a very tedious undertaking. For example, the previously mentioned George Pal Puppetoons studio would first work out the timing and placement of an animated sequence (sometimes this would be planned using traditional 2D animation drawings); then each replacement form would need to be expertly crafted in wood or clay. These would be tested, then perhaps modified, or re-crafted if necessary, in order to ensure a smooth and fluid animated effect.[8] Similarly, in the more recent feature *The Nightmare before Christmas* (Henry Selick, 1993), nearly seven hundred individual replacement heads for the character Jack Skellington were handcrafted.[9] With the aid of 3D printing, this process becomes much more streamlined. Although the animated movement is again worked out beforehand (in this case using 3D software), the process of translating these replacement forms into the physical world is expedited, becoming more precise and more automated. As *Coraline* lead animator Travis Knight observed,

> we were modelling and sculpting in the computer, printing them out on these wacky 3-D printers, painting them all by hand, and then fitting them and putting them on the puppets. That was how we got this really incredible, subtle, beautiful, and expressive facial animation.[10]

Thus, a very interesting transformative process occurs, one in which the virtual (digital) animation can become actuality – part of the physical world. Once the digital animation sequence is completed, each individual frame of the character's movements will be 3D-printed. This might involve simply the mouth shapes of a character or, increasingly, the entire character. The resulting 'printed' plastic sculptures can then be photographed one at a time using the replacement stop-motion technique. This process has become increasingly frequent in other recent LAIKA features such as *The Boxtrolls* (Graham Annable and Anthony

Stacchi, 2014) and *Kubo and the Two Strings* (Travis Knight, 2016), where a wide range of character movements were achieved through the replacement of 3D printed forms.[11]

What makes the translation process of moving from the 3D digital realm into the traditional stop-motion world so fascinating is that traces of the 3D digital animation process remain quite evident even in the final stop-motion film. For example, the somewhat 'spliney' (or unnaturally smooth) nature of the computer-generated (CG) character movement is frequently transmitted into the stop-motion replacement forms, which is a phenomenon that becomes increasingly evident in LAIKA's more recent films.[12] Thus, we might see a stop-motion production that has much of the movement aesthetic of CG animation (and, in fact, some have confused more recent LAIKA productions, including *The Boxtrolls* and *Kubo and the Two Strings*, with CG productions).[13]

Simultaneously, traces of the material nature of the 3D printed pieces also tend to persist. Though these traces can be quite subtle, the 3D-printed plastic forms will often exhibit a number of slight imperfections that can be perceived as flickering rough patches, oscillating etched lines and irregular dimples and protrusions (which become most pronounced in *Coraline*, during close-up shots of lip-synched facial animation). Thus, two alternating visual traces emerge in the finished product of *Coraline* – one is the spliney (very fluid) animated movement which is associated with CG animation; the other is the textured and tactile qualities associated with stop-motion puppet animation.

Dreaming of replacements

The movie's Other World displays a distinctly uncanny and dream-like atmosphere, which is not surprising given that Coraline first enters the Other World *through* what appears to be a dream. Undoubtedly, the use of stop-motion (and replacement) animation also helps to add to this dream-like aesthetic. Stop-motion has been regarded by some to be a particularly appropriate method for the expression of the surreal or the uncanny.[14] This is due, at least in part, to its fundamental production processes; that is, the physical puppet forms (and other objects) will invariably have had external movement applied to them (and, when we stop to think about it, this added movement is seemingly quite incongruous and alien). As a result, the viewer will normally (and comfortably) recognize the inanimate real-world objects but will simultaneously be surprised by the *movement* of those objects. In her discussion of the Quays' *Street of Crocodiles* (1986), Suzanne Buchan similarly makes note of the 'apprehension' that emerges between our awareness of the material construct of the puppets and the 'fallacy of anthropomorphisation, in the moment when these materials are reified and attributed with senses, feelings, and cognizance'.[15] Ultimately, stop-motion animation represents real-world forms, yet the movement that they exhibit is decidedly other-worldly.

Such dichotomies also seem to be commonly found in dream-scenarios; the people and settings within a dream will often appear to be simultaneously familiar and unfamiliar. This is certainly something that Coraline experiences upon first entering the Other World – she quickly observes that everything is very similar to her own world.[16] However, as she soon discovers, things tend to *move* differently to how they do in her own world. For example, Coraline's Other Father has better posture and moves in a more upright manner. Her Other Mother also looks generally healthier and moves more expressively and with a more confident flourish. The Other Wybie is decidedly less awkward in his overall movement as well. Another noticeable difference between the real world and Other World is that many of the items that Coraline encounters are actually *animated*. The chairs actively move into place; at dinner, the gravy is delivered on a moving miniature 'gravy train'; and all the toys in Coraline's Other World room are equally full of life. Even the photograph of the two friends she left behind in her old hometown displays movement. Importantly, in a dream, it is not merely the *look* of things that can seem surreal but also the incongruous *movement* of things that can provoke a sense of the uncanny.

An intriguing conceptual link can be made between the process of animation and the mechanism by which we create mental dream images.[17] Most animation involves considering movement and form separately. That is, the animator will generally add movement to a character or an object (this is most evident in the case of motion-capture animation, where movement is usually captured from an actor's performance and then applied as a distinct layer to a digital form). Similarly, our brain normally handles movement and images separately within our visuo-spatial working memory system. So, when we view the real world, we do not simply record events and store them as little QuickTime movies in our head; in most cases, our brain separately stores observed movement and observed images in two distinct cognitive systems. And then when we recall or dream about an event, our brain essentially *re-animates* these, that is, it brings the stored movement and the stored imagery back together to play for us in our mind's eye.[18] However, similar to the process of animation, the movement will not necessarily be derived from a congruous real-world event. It is quite possible that the movement will have derived from another time and in fact from another person. To illustrate this point, imagine that you had observed someone that you have never seen before, sitting on a train. And then suppose you had a dream a few nights later in which that person appeared – but in your dream, rather than simply sitting down, that person was walking around gesturing wildly and even speaking. Obviously, the image of the person would have been recalled from a real-life moment – but where did the new dream-movement come from? It could have come from any number of external sources – probably from movement that you had mentally captured previously, perhaps of your best friend or from some other random person that you saw walking on the street.

The ability to recombine together separate movements and separate images is one of the great strengths of our visual cognitive abilities, and it is one of the things that allows us to be so creative. Similarly, a great strength of animation derives from its capacity to amalgamate separate movement and separate images in new and intriguing ways. And ultimately, as in the case of stop-motion animation, adding incongruous movement to a form allows for both the fantastic and the disquietingly uncanny.

Arguably, the use of *replacement* stop-motion animation can add a further layer of dream-like uncanniness to an animated film. Not only are the inanimate forms given incongruous movement, but they are also given incongruous *formations*. That is, the apparently single animated form will be comprised of *numerous* different real-world forms – one form (or part of a form) replaced after the other. The multiplicity that is inherent within the replacement animated object is also akin to the multiplicity that is sometimes inherent in our own cognitive dream imagery. Quite often the figures and spaces in our dreams will exhibit a certain degree of instability – and this is also a result of a sort of mental replacement animation that we engage in. The characters and spaces within our dream imagery are often the result of an amalgamation of many disparate elements that we have cognitively sutured together (both in terms of imagery and of movement).

Not surprisingly, it is within the production of the Other World sequences that the greatest amount of replacement animation was used – for example, in the abovementioned dancing mice sequence. Additionally, due to the use of replacement animation, the fundamental forms of many of the Other characters also prove to be very fluid. Thus, as the movie progresses, the Other Mother becomes more insect-like (or perhaps more stop-motion-puppet-armature like) and the Other Father becomes much more floppy and flabby. Notably, the overall edifice of the Other World also degrades over time (signifying the Other Mother's lessening influence). Although such changes and variations are driven by the narrative, they are facilitated through the use of replacement animation, which enables the characters to dramatically (and seamlessly) alter their forms. Such transformations also seem to emulate how we experience certain degrees of fluidity in the characters and settings that occupy our own dreamscapes.

Replacing characters

In his review of *Coraline*, film critic Roger Ebert noted that 'the ideal audience for this film would be admirers of film art itself'.[19] However, one could also argue that, because the film acts as essentially a metaphor for the stop-motion animation process, it is possible to declare that the film caters particularly to admirers of the art of stop-motion animation. The materiality of stop-motion animation and specifically the use of replacement animation is thematically reflected throughout a number of the film's sequences. This is overtly expressed in the 'Other' World, where many allusions to the process of stop-motion animation emerge. It is also thematically expressed in the Other Mother's scheming and systematic replacement of original characters with 'Other' characters.

During the film's opening sequence, we witness the first occurrence of a character replacement. In this instance, a rather anonymous-looking doll is transformed into a doll that looks exactly like Coraline. During this transformation, the puppet-making process is vividly visualized. We see mechanical armature-like hands working on the doll with absolute precision. The fluffy wool stuffing of the old doll is removed and is replaced with a sawdust filling. Then a number of unique features are added to the doll in order to transform it into a 'mini-Coraline' – including her characteristic blue hair and yellow raincoat. The resemblance of the transformed toy to Coraline (except for the button eyes) is uncanny. In fact, the first line that we hear from Coraline's work-weary dad is '(sigh) Hello Coraline'. And then, upon noticing the doll that she holds, he adds, 'And … hello … Coraline … *doll?*'

We soon learn that it is the villainous witch character who made this doll and who is ultimately behind the character replacement scheme, which she employs in order to lure and trap her victims. In this way, Coraline's real mother is replaced by a character (the witch in disguise), that is referred to as 'Other Mother', who is (unlike her real mother) kind, attentive and an excellent cook. Her real father is replaced by a form that is referred to as 'Other Father', who is (unlike her real father) funny, talented and an excellent gardener. Her real friend Wybie is replaced with 'Other Wybie' who, instead of being excessively chatty, merely nods and smiles, never saying a word. Similarly, Coraline's neighbours are replaced with more impressive 'Other' versions.

In the Other World, the characters look much more like puppets. In fact, it is here that their believability as living creatures becomes less convincing, as we become increasingly aware that they are fundamentally *animated puppets*. That is, the true-material nature of the stop-motion puppet form becomes almost as significant as the character that the puppet form is intended to represent. Most noticeably, the characters display buttons for eyes, rather than ones that move, blink and appear to *see*. In this realm, the characters are also filled with sawdust and occasionally their armature constructs become visible. For example, when the Other Mother begins to perceive that Coraline is putting up too much resistance to her demands, she begins to become much more aggressive both in manner and particularly in her appearance. She gradually begins to look more and more insect-like – but also more and more like an exposed stop-motion armature device. There are even sequences in which what could be described as external stop-motion rigging devices are also sometimes visible. For example, in one sequence, Coraline discovers that the Other Father is an excellent pianist. When she exclaims, 'I didn't know you could play the piano!' he murmurs back, 'I don't play the piano, the piano plays me.' It is then revealed that he is adorned with Mickey Mouse-style gloves which are supported and controlled by an elaborate array of external rigs.[20] Notably, this rigging apparatus is somewhat similar to the manner in which such a scene would have been animated in a typical stop-motion shoot.

At one point, we see that Other Wybie is actually made of sawdust – which he demonstrates to Coraline by blowing on his fingers, which disintegrate into dust particles. Later in the film, his clothes can be seen flapping in the wind like a banner – after he has presumably had all of his stuffing removed by the witch. Similarly, Coraline's neighbours, Miss Spink and Miss Forcible, exist in both the real world and the Other World. In the real world, whenever one of their pet dogs die, they have them stuffed. Thus, they have a rather macabre collection of a half-dozen stuffed (and puppet-like) Scottie dogs. However, in the Other World, there are 450 of these stuffed dogs (presumably created by the Other Mother) which comprise the audience when the two women put on their stunning stage performances.[21] This extraordinary collection of nearly identical dog puppets mirrors and alludes to the process of replacement animation and its frequent use in *Coraline*.

When Coraline first attempts to escape from the Other World, she soon encounters an empty void of pure whiteness. 'Nothing's out here', explains the cat. 'It's the empty part of this world. She only made what she knew would impress you.' This is perhaps the movie's most poignant reference to the process of stop-motion animation, for when designing a stop-motion set, only that which will be seen by the camera needs to be built. Everything else is superfluous and therefore not constructed. In that sense, we can think of the Other World as being one big stop-motion set and the Other Mother as being the powerful animator behind it all.

Animated gardens

Although the Coraline character ultimately resists being replaced by another form, there are two proxy-Coralines that do get replaced. The first example, as previously discussed, is when a doll is transformed into a Coraline lookalike. The second, and perhaps more important, proxy-Coraline replacement occurs when the large garden that surrounds her house is replaced in the Other World.

Significantly, the garden is not merely a place where plants grow but a metaphorical space which represents the manner in which Coraline's parents habitually neglect her. In the real world, Coraline's mother and father 'get paid to write about plants', but they are so busy *writing* about plants that they never actually do any gardening. One would expect most plant enthusiasts to be very happy upon moving into a new house with a large established garden at their disposal. But Coraline's parents simply regard the garden as a burden and, rather than actually gardening, they spend their time in front of computer screens, typing away. Her parents, in a sense, spend much of the film's duration replacing real plants with words and pictures of plants, which they hope will soon be published in a garden catalogue. Similarly, one would think that most parents would be very pleased to have a daughter like Coraline (creative, self-sufficient and generally good-hearted); unfortunately, her parents also seem to regard her as a burden. They almost completely ignore her, stopping work only in order to chide her and tell her to go away. Her parents neglect the garden and are only gardeners in title. Similarly, her parents neglect Coraline and are only really parents in title.

Although her mother drinks her coffee from a cup that proclaims, 'I (love) Mulch', it is clearly a throw-away sentiment that she does not really embrace. Her parents also have stockpiled a wide range of plant and vegetable seeds – but do nothing with them. In a display of utter boredom, Coraline arranges these seed packets upon the window sill, while being thoroughly ignored by her mother. Her mother also does not like to get her hands dirty; 'Mud is messy,' she asserts when Coraline asks if she can explore the new garden. Later, when Coraline does go wandering, she inadvertently contracts a poison oak rash on her hand. Her real mother ignores her plight. However, that night, in stark contrast, the Other Mother shows concern and applies a mud-cream (something the real mother would never touch) to heal Coraline.

In the Other World, Coraline soon discovers the wondrous new garden that her Other Father has created. In fact, her Other Father spends much of his time in the Other Garden; even at night he can be found planting row after row of colourful flowers and exotic plants. These plants also include spectacularly *animated* plants, such as tickling snapdragons, and beautiful pitcher plants (*Nepenthes sp.*) that, rather than being carnivorous, open their lids to provide a sanctuary for frogs. But what becomes the most spectacular aspect of the Other Garden is that her Other Father has planted it in such a formation as to create an enormous image of Coraline's face. This is revealed to her when the Other Father flies her up into the air on his flying garden tractor. From their airborne perspective, the entire garden can be seen to form a remarkable image of Coraline (which constituted a massive and elaborate stop-motion set comprising thousands of illuminated flowers) (see Figure 5.2).[22]

Later, when Coraline begins to fight back against the witch, the garden plants are soon replaced by ones that are much more menacing. For example, the 'tickling' snapdragons become killer-snapping-dragons. The once passive carnivorous pitcher plants also become much more aggressive.[23] Similarly, the once beautiful pollinating hummingbirds are replaced with large stinging wasps (which, like most forms in the Other World, are later revealed to be merely filled with sawdust – clearly illustrating their artifice). Although the witch is able to animate inanimate forms within the garden, she is unable to create or nurture *life*, which is what a true gardener would aspire to do. Thus, the entire garden is incrementally replaced (and thus transformed) into a

Figure 5.2 The old garden is replaced with another more beautiful and colourful one, specifically designed with Coraline in mind and ultimately in Coraline's image.

most insidious, yet artificial, botanical nightmare, revealing the truly horrific underpinnings of the Other World.

Conclusion

Henry Selick had to work strategically in order to ensure that *Coraline* would be made using the technique of stop-motion animation.[24] Selick's love for the medium comes through clearly in the film and, in a sense, becomes an essential aspect of the film. The movie ultimately reflects the handcrafted and labour-intensive process of stop-motion animation and the replacement animation technique. Arguably, a deeper understanding of the process of stop-motion animation and in particular of replacement animation can afford an enhanced appreciation of this film.

Not only did the process of replacement animation play a significant role in realizing the very fluid and masterful animated movement (particularly with regard to facial animation), but it also allowed for a compelling sequence of dancing circus mice, engaged in expertly choreographed animated cycles. But in addition, replacement animation functions as an important metanarrative in *Coraline*. As this chapter has shown, replacement animation can be thought of as a multiplicity that fosters a unique metaphysical formation which gives solid real-world forms a unique plasticity. Such a technique has conceivable parallels to our own visual cognitive processes. Ultimately, the use of replacement animation helped to make *Coraline* an irreplaceable masterwork of animation.

Notes

1 Neil Pettigrew, *The Stop-motion Filmography – A Critical Guide to 297 Features Using Puppet Animation*, vol. 2 (Jefferson: McFarland, 1999), p. 566.
2 For example, the clay-animated short film, *The Great Cognito* (Will Vinton, 1982) from Will Vinton Studios (which later became LAIKA) contains an extensive use of metamorphosis; the clay-animated series *The Amazing Adventures of Morph* (Peter Lord, David Sproxton, 1980–1) by Aardman Animations also features recurring sequences of metamorphosis.
3 Bill Desowitz, 'Corpse Bride: Stop Motion Goes Digital', *Animation News Network*, 16 September 2005. www.awn.com/vfxworld/corpse-bride-stop-motion-goes-digital (accessed 21 October 2018).
4 Stephen Jones, *Coraline: A Visual Companion* (New York: HarperCollins, 2009), p. 107.
5 Henry Selick, Coraline DVD extras, Henry Selick Audio Commentary, 2009.
6 Gilles Deleuze, *Bergsonism* (New York: Zone Books, 1991), pp. 41–2.
7 Jones, *Coraline: A Visual Companion*, pp. 107–8.
8 Rolf Giesen, *Puppetry, Puppet Animation and the Digital Age* (New York: CRC Press, 2018), p. 36.
9 Simon Braund, 'Through the Looking Glass', *Empire*, no. 239 (2009), p. 67.
10 Jones, *Coraline: A Visual Companion*, p. 107.
11 C. Edwards, 'How Laika Pushed 3D Printing to New Heights with "The Boxtrolls"', *Cartoon Brew*, 13 August 2014. https://www.cartoonbrew.com/feature-film/how-laika-pushed-3d-printing-to-new-heights-with-the-boxtrolls-101512.html (accessed 10 June 2019).
12 This is particularly evident in the movement of hair, fur and cloth in *Kubo and the Two Strings* (2016).
13 See Jason Bailey, 'The Stop-motion Animation Studio That Created Coraline Is Still Toiling Away', *Vulture*, 9 April 2019. https://www.vulture.com/2019/04/inside-laika-stop-motion-studio-that-made-missing-link.html (accessed 10 June 2019); Amid Amidi, ' "Missing Link" Bombs at the Box Office', *Cartoon Brew*, 14 April 2019. https://www.cartoonbrew.com/box-office-report/

missing-link-bombs-at-the-box-office-172729.html (accessed 10 June 2019); Matt Kamen, 'How Boxtrolls Studio Revolutionised Stop Motion Animation', *Wired*, 8 September 2014. https://www.wired.co.uk/article/boxtrolls-travis-knight-interview (accessed 10 June 2019). Each of these articles allude to the general public's uncertainty over which animation techniques were used in the production of several of the more recent LAIKA productions.

14 See Suzanne Buchan, *The Quay Brothers: Into a Metaphysical Playroom* (Minneapolis: University of Minnesota Press, 2011); Dan Torre, *Animation - Process, Cognition and Actuality* (New York: Bloomsbury, 2017); Paul Wells, *Understanding Animation* (London: Routledge, 1998).

15 Buchan, *The Quay Brothers*, p. 125.

16 Darren Harris-Fain, 'Putting the Graphic in Graphic Novel: P. Craig Russell's Adaptation of Neil Gaiman's Coraline', *Studies in the Novel*, vol. 47, no. 3 (2015), p. 344.

17 For a great deal more on comparisons between the process of animation and the process of human cognitive processes see Torre, *Animation – Process, Cognition and Actuality*.

18 See for example Robert H. Logie, *Visuo-Spatial Working Memory* (Hove: Lawrence Erlbaum Associates, 1995), p. 2; Stephen M. Kosslyn, William L. Thompson and Giorgio Ganis, *The Case for Mental Imagery* (Oxford: Oxford University Press, 2006), p. 137.

19 Roger Ebert, 'Coraline (2009)'. RogerEbert.com, 4 February 2009. https://www.rogerebert.com/reviews/coraline-2009 (accessed 21 October 2018).

20 External rigs are essentially mechanical structures that are used on a set, in order to prop up and support a puppet, and which are then digitally removed in post-production.

21 Jones, *Coraline: A Visual Companion*, p. 113.

22 Ibid., pp. 96–102.

23 For more on carnivorous plants and their representation in art, literature, animation and popular culture see Dan Torre, *Carnivorous Plants* (London: Reaktion Books, 2019).

24 Braund, 'Through the Looking Glass', p. 65.

6

Coraline's 'Other World': The animated camera in stop-motion feature films

Jane Shadbolt

Coraline (Henry Selick, 2009) opens in storm clouds with a high sweeping exterior shot that cranes down from a grey Ashland sky, past foggy evergreen forest mountains, sweeping over a large Queen Anne mansion and gently coming to rest framing a softly swaying sign that reads 'Pink Palace Apartments' (see Figure 6.1). A mover's van pulls up with a hiss of hydraulic brakes and a jaunty little VW Beetle scoots around to the back of the house bearing a teetering pile of suitcases. Apart from Mr Bobinsky's enthusiastic calisthenics performance on the ridge of the mansion roof, it could be the opening scene for any number of teen movies where a heroine's journey starts with a reluctant forced move to the countryside.[1] The camera moves on, floating through a montage of furniture, curious neighbours and disgruntled movers, before travelling around to the back of the house and crashing into a young girl. We watch her from afar as she explores the gardens and beyond until, startled by a cat, she runs headlong into an unfamiliar and threatening landscape. She turns, confronts the cat angrily and we, as the audience, are introduced to Coraline.

This opening, which lasts approximately two and a half minutes, is a filmic introduction to place and character that walks the audience through the plot (a move to the country), a location (creepy, lonely house with a strange Russian acrobat on the roof), a heroine who is a curious, independent girl (one who sets out exploring alone) and a cat with uncertain motives (we watch it watching Coraline). We travel through abandoned Victorian ornamental gardens and into an autumnal landscape that is as beautiful as it is bleak, and it almost comes as a surprise to think of all these elements as puppets in miniature-scaled sets because the visual storytelling style is so familiar. Much of what creates this intimate understanding of the narrative is the effortless, gravity-defying way in which the camera moves. There are no locked off and static shots here; the camera glides as

Figure 6.1 The opening shot of *Coraline*: the family arrives at the Pink Palace Apartments.

if floating through space, taking the viewer through the air with it – a technique which echoes the familiar conventions of contemporary commercial live-action filmmaking. Equipment, such as cranes, jibs and Steadicams gives live-action directors a broader range of camera motion to use in visual storytelling, and one of the remarkable things about *Coraline* is the way in which the film draws from the vocabulary of live-action cinema to make puppet animation that looks markedly different from previous generations of stop-motion films, where the camera was often still and moving shots were mostly limited to linear tracks and pans.

This chapter explores how the stop-motion camera paired with digital technology to reinvent the stop-motion animated feature with a broader storytelling vocabulary of animated camera motion. *Coraline* marked a particular point in a near two-decade-long[2] watershed in technical developments in US mainstream stop-motion production. It was a period launched by the extensive use of computer-controlled camera rigs, known as 'motion control' in *The Nightmare before Christmas* (Tim Burton, 1993), and subsequently expanded by the replacement of film-based cine cameras with off the shelf consumer grade digital still cameras in the *Corpse Bride* (Tim Burton and Mike Johnson, 2005). A few years later, *Coraline* (2009) used both of these techniques extensively and, additionally, was designed and filmed for screening in stereoscopic 3D.[3] This is not to suggest that technical developments in stop-motion animation have ceased since *Coraline*, only that the major features of digital stop-motion shooting (motion control, digital cameras, frame grabbers, 3D printing and 3D stereoscopic cinematography) had reached a point of technical maturity, becoming ubiquitous on future productions worldwide. A decade on from *Coraline*, each one of these technologies (with the possible exception of 3D cinematography) is easily available to independent filmmakers and students outside of specialized studio expertise and budgets. By the time *Coraline*'s production studio, LAIKA, began shooting its next stop-motion feature *ParaNorman* (Sam Fell and Chris Butler, 2012), the tools of stop-motion filmmaking had become accessible in a way that was completely new to the stop-motion form. Travis Knight, *Coraline* lead animator and CEO of LAIKA, explained:

> You know you just go to a camera shop and get a prosumer camera and you can shoot a stop-motion feature. That's what we did. We're using stuff that you can download off the internet, software like *Dragonframe* or a camera you buy from a camera shop. It's that good. That's one of the wonderful things, a democratizing thing with technology.[4]

The digital workflow is now an indivisible part of the stop-motion process. The painstaking, hand-winched camera track movements of the twentieth century have been replaced by the precision of repeatable motion-controlled camera rigs, and shooting with 35mm celluloid film has been unceremoniously discarded for the immediacy offered by digital cameras.[5] There has been an expansion of digital and computer-controlled tools for production use that have enabled analogue filmmaking techniques to become more sophisticated and more complex, while borrowing more heavily from the cinematic language of live-action filmmaking. Ironically, for stop-motion animation, a type of filmmaking wedded to handmade miniatures, tactile surfaces and the sequence of the celluloid frame, the same digital processes that threatened to make stop motion redundant as a special effect have propelled this very analogue style into the feature film mainstream.

Digital transitions

Technological advances don't always progress in a straightforward linear fashion, and while *Coraline* might neatly mark an endpoint of a period of intense innovation and rejuvenation of the stop-motion form, the future of stop motion didn't appear quite so clear in the early 1990s, when it looked to be overtaken by computer-generated imagery (CGI). *Jurassic Park* (Steven Spielberg, 1993) is widely regarded as a turning point in the commercial viability of CGI and has been described by Stephen Prince as the film that 'demonstrated [CGI blockbusters'] dramatic and economic potential more vividly than any previous film'.[6] Despite being a CGI effects film, *Jurassic Park* still used an underlying stop-motion animation method through an innovative hybrid digital/analogue system where stop-motion animators manipulated sensor-equipped physical armatures to feed positioning information to their digital counterparts at the CGI end of the animation.[7] The stop-motion side of the process was led by Phil Tippett, the award-winning stop-motion effects animator. While the dinosaurs' animated performance was created by stop-motion animators manipulating physical puppets, the quality of the CGI that the system produced signalled the end of traditional stop-motion animation to Tippett. When he saw an early *Jurassic Park* test of the dinosaur CGI footage, he turned to Steven Spielberg and said, 'I'm extinct.' He described experiencing a kind of personal crisis around the transition:

> I felt like Georges Méliès, that was a real low point. I actually got physically ill with pneumonia and had to go to bed during that period. It was definitely a big change of life for me, because when something new is replacing something old, there's a kind of trashing of what's gone on before.[8]

The change Tippett felt so bodily was a paradigm shift in visual effects and filmmaking aesthetics. The visual approximations of analogue special effects, where the integration of puppet and live-action elements was always apparent by a mismatch of scale or texture or movement, were being replaced with new digital ideas that pursued the potential for invisible visual integration into a photorealistic cinematic vision. Stop motion appeared to be dying; it no longer had a place in visual effects, and as a stand-alone filmmaking technique, it was regarded as quaintly old-fashioned. 'In this dawning digital age', trade magazine *Cinefex* opened on its 1993 technical review of *Nightmare before Christmas*, 'the art of stop-motion animation seems wonderfully archaic'.[9] Only two years later, the release of Pixar's CG box office hit *Toy Story* (John Lasseter, 1995) made the idea of making puppet films at all seem wilfully old-fashioned.

Even before the death knell of digital production, stop-motion animation was losing its place as a special effects technique. By the early 1980s animators were exploring tactics to keep stop-motion effects in the mainstream cinema vocabulary by attempting to embed similar visual cues to that of live-action films by using a technique called Go Motion. Go Motion, pioneered by ILM visual effects supervisors Dennis Muren and Phil Tippett, is a mechanical system of computer-controlled rods that vibrated the puppet while the camera shutter was open to introduce film-like motion blur into the stop-motion frame. The technique won Muren (with Stuart Ziff) a Technical Achievement Award at the 1981 Academy Awards, but it wasn't photorealistic enough to compete with digital effects. According to Muren, analogue visual effects had 'hit a dead end', and he was instrumental in leading the transition to digital effects as the visual effects supervisor of both *Terminator 2: Judgement Day* (James Cameron, 1991) and *Jurassic Park*.[10] Go Motion has never been revived; not only was it quickly swept away by digital techniques, but it also sought to erase one of stop motion's visual strengths by removing the way it represents movement, the element that makes stop motion so powerful as both a visual effect and as a standalone filmmaking technique.

By the time *Jurassic Park* dominated the box office, commercial mainstream cinema wanted diegetic photorealism or the immersive digital worlds of *Toy Story*, not the aesthetic friction of stop-motion models and animated motion inside the live-action frame. Julie Turnock discusses the impact of Industrial Light and Magic (ILM) on the aesthetics of visual effects in Hollywood in the late 1970s and early 1980s, pointing out how influential ILM became in setting the visual agenda for the visual effects (VFX) industry as a whole. ILM championed a set of visual conventions that coalesced into a dominant style that had photorealism at its core. As Turnock described, 'the ideal ILM aesthetic would start with a perfectly executed, seamless photorealism, where live-action and effects material are composited together to look as if filmed at the same time by the same camera'.[11]

Stop-motion effects in live-action films don't work towards a diegetic whole because the combination of the two types of filmmaking creates a point of difference between the visual space occupied by the live action and the visual space occupied by the stop motion. The visual markers of this difference include disparate rates of motion, lack of motion blur and contrasts in scale and materials. In turn each of these aspects combine to create a visual space that Ray Harryhausen termed 'a dream world rather than a fake reality'.[12] It was this 'dream world' that was made redundant by the new aesthetic developing in digital effects, one that could bring together photorealistic elements and combine them with increasingly seamless levels of accuracy. And in the 1990s, if CGI wasn't being blended into live action, it was proving its own as a fully featured animation form, as Pixar's *Toy Story* franchise or DreamWorks' *Antz* (Eric Darnell and Tim Johnson, 1998) demonstrates.

This could have been the end of stop motion, as a specialized technique that solved a particular problem being simply replaced by newer more flexible technology, in much the same way three-strip Technicolor was displaced by colour film. Rather, the change began to work in its favour, as the advent of digital effects not only brought a slew of production technologies that make creating stop motion easier and cheaper, but it also helped uncouple stop-motion animation from its dominant role in Hollywood as a special effect in live-action productions, opening a different path for stop motion in contemporary cinema. Since *Coraline*, stop motion has re-established its place in the mainstream as a stand-alone animated filmmaking technique and is having something of a renaissance with filmmakers and audiences. The journalist Steve Rose, reviewing Charlie Kaufman and Duke Johnson's *Anomalisa* (2015), wrote of popular interest in feature-length stop-motion animation despite the seismic cultural shift to CGI:

> Few people would have put money on old-fashioned stop-motion animation surviving this far into the digital age. … But stop-motion has not just prevailed, it has moved into new territories. Once associated with children's entertainment, it has somehow found a new lease of life among 'grown-up' film-makers – be they live-action auteurs, or animators dealing in darker, child-unfriendlier content. *Anomalisa* ticks both boxes, and it's the tip of an iceberg that's still growing.[13]

In the timeline of stop motion's post-CGI development, *Coraline* was a distinct part of that cultural transformation, where a series of technological advances coalesced to create a new brand of digitally enabled stop-motion animation. This hybrid style brought together an analogue form (the tactility of sets, puppets and miniatures) with the advantages of digital production (faster, instant and repeatable). Travis Knight credits the production development on *Coraline* as a turning point for the form:

> I thought at the time that *Coraline* really did represent a systemic shift in what we did with the medium. It had been kind of creaky and hadn't evolved too much. When we decided to bring technology into the mix, it opened up a whole new world for us that allowed us to do really interesting things with an old art form.[14]

The world that opened up for LAIKA through *Coraline* was one that allowed for more ambitious creative scope in the way stop motion is made and a distinct, technology fuelled path to the future.

The animated camera

A large part of stop-motion animation's 'new lease of life for grown-up film makers' has been facilitated by an enthusiastic embrace of digital technologies. The advent of shooting animation with digital cameras brought no lamentations from the industry about the loss of film as a shooting medium. *Corpse Bride* cinematographer Pete Kozachik (who later worked on *Coraline*) was asked by the production company (Motion Picture Co) if he wanted to add film grain. He responded with, 'I don't see why. I could see why they would want it to look more like the shots around it. But I don't miss [film]. It still feels like a movie and not a fancy video.' He added that, compared to film, the digital creative process 'allows easier choices to make'.[15]

Kozachik's work on Tim Burton's *Corpse Bride* in 2005 demonstrated the possibilities of the digital path. It was the first commercial stop-motion feature film shot on a digital single lens reflex (DSLR) camera,[16] marking a turning point for stop-motion animation because it produced cinema-quality film – which at that time meant 2K (2048 × 1080 pixels) for cinema projection[17] – using off-the-shelf stills cameras, rather than expensive modified movie cameras shooting 35mm film. This adoption of digital cameras was the most significant shift in the production of stop-motion animation film, but the path towards digital production techniques had begun over a decade before, with the use of motion control on *The Nightmare before Christmas*. While *Nightmare* can be considered an analogue film, shot on traditional film stock using 35mm Mitchell film cameras, the production made extensive use of digital motion control rigs from the then industry leader, Bill Tondreau's Kuper Controls.[18] Motion control is a robotic movement system that makes repeatable and programmable camera moves possible by utilizing stepper motors, the same as used in CNC routers or 3D printers. Driven by a computer-control system, the technology leverages the stepper motor's capacity for extremely precise incremental rotations to move the cameras, lights or set pieces through complex movements for shooting or special effects. Motion control was embraced by the film industry in the late 1970s, and had a profound effect on both the visual styles and performances of all modern stop-motion features.[19] For camera operation, motion control gives the possibility of smooth multi-axis camera control and automated lighting rig movements, and it can shift a camera to different intraocular positions for 3D stereoscopic shooting. Motion control rigs can even move the camera completely out of the way between shooting frames, allowing an animator to access the puppet. Once they have set the pose and cleared the set, the camera can return precisely to a pre-assigned position to take the next frame. On a performance level, motion control for stop-motion animation allows for more ambitious, multilayered and complex camera work by automating the process, allowing the animator to focus entirely on the puppet performances instead of advancing an additional slew of technical camera and lighting actions as they progress each frame. *Coraline* made extensive use of the technology, and the spectacular opening sequence of the film is an example of the type of roving, mobile camera work that is simply not possible with manual or analogue techniques.

Digital technology slowly began to solve the technical challenges inherent in shooting stop-motion animation. One of its most important advantages was the ability to review an animated sequence as it was shot. Before the introduction of video and digital capture, the playback of filmed animation during shooting was impossible because the film had to be developed as a negative filmstrip, if not additionally printed as a positive filmstrip, to be viewed. Even seeing through the lens of the camera (rather than through the side-mounted parallax corrected viewfinder attached to the side, common in film cameras) required a specialized mechanism called a 'rack over' which moved the lens to allow the operator to see through it for focusing and viewing. The mechanism was manual and required repositioning when taking a shot, the operator sliding the lens across the camera body and back over the film strip to expose the frame.[20] Animators once used articulated devices called surface gauges to pinpoint key positions and move the puppets relative to the gauge. The gauge, like the racking, required constant attention while filming, as it needed to be removed from the frame after each use so as not to appear in the final shot.[21] Even when video split systems became available in the 1960s, there was no way of seeing both the captured frames and the current frame together. By the mid-1990s video cameras' capacity for immediate review and instant access to stored images led to the development of tools like the *Video Lunchbox* by Animation Toolworks.[22] This was a revolutionary video frame grabber system that digitized video images and at last allowed the animator to compare the image they had just taken with the image they were about to take. This was the three-dimensional equivalent of a traditional 2D animator using a light box to trace a new drawing over an existing one. The process of referring to a previous image while viewing the current image is called onion skinning and allows for precise registration and consistency between drawings. The transfer of that concept to stop-motion animations through frame grabber technology had a profound effect on the production and style of animation. It was the crucial technological advancement that has since determined key elements of the visual qualities of stop motion; the complexity, quality and sheer volume of contemporary stop-motion animation is made possible by the simple digital act of overlaying semi-transparent images over each other to compare frames before committing to capturing a frame.

Animators who worked with film cameras and could not review their work had to rely on timing charts, surface gauges and the muscle memory of experience to make their puppets move. The work of the film animator is an embodied experience of tactile skill, and the rippling fur of King Kong in 1933 or the clipped deathly movements of the skeletons in the fight scene in *Jason and the Argonauts* (Don Chaffey, 1963) are all the more remarkable for being animated by their creators almost blindfolded. Using a digital camera as an animation tool brought the immediate technical advantages of instant playback of footage, previewing frames before shooting and increased manoeuvrability around the set. The progression towards full onion skinning review tools was incremental over the decades. Video feeds allowed the 35mm film cameras used on *The Nightmare before Christmas* to have a supplementary frame grabber that could store a couple of frames for reference, but the animators could still choose to use old-fashioned surface gauges to keep track of their puppets.[23] On *Corpse Bride*, despite the innovative use of DSLRs, there was still no preview feed through the camera lens, so their rigs needed a separate camera set-up (in this case a tiny security camera attached to the flash mount of the DSLR) to capture a live preview.[24] This only approximated the DSLR's view, but it could save many more frames for animators to review. *Coraline* went digital but used specialist industrial cameras, with an in-house LAIKA frame grabber for previewing.[25] Miniaturization also led to more nimble approaches to shot planning and access to a film vocabulary that had previously been the preserve of live-action cinema. Cinematographer Pete Kozachik, who shot *The Nightmare before Christmas* and *James and the Giant Peach* (Henry Selick, 1996) using 35mm cameras and *Corpse Bride* and *Coraline* with DSLRs, compared the two types of production:

The SLRs allowed for things that were unheard of back when we used those 30-pound [35mm] Mitchell cameras. With those, you really had to consider how much the camera weighed, how you were going to support it, and how the animator would get their head around it. Suddenly, when the cameras were tiny, we were more on par with what live-action could do. If live-action film had to mimic how stop-motion used to be shot, the camera would be the size of a Volkswagen.[26]

The sort of changes brought about by digital processes are not just related to the reproducible digital image; every aspect of the filming workflow changed with smaller, more agile cameras and immediate image review. Changes in production processes are not simply systems made more efficient or practices modernized; they also affect the way creative works are conceived and produced. For stop motion, the animation becomes smoother with visual review tools, and the camera moves become more complex because of motion control. This led to a shift in the way stop motion was considered as a filmmaking form and a pursuit for a type of equivalence with live-action cinema. Even as early as *The Nightmare before Christmas*, industry magazines feature interviews with crew members positively comparing their work to live-action filmmaking. Eric Leighton, supervising animator on *Nightmare*, describes how the camera and animation work towards a live-action aesthetic:

One of the things that we are pushing the barrier with is a lot of motion-controlled camera moves, so that means big sweeping camera moves going through the scenes the characters act out, particularly during songs. It's a lot of fun as an animator to be able to work on stuff like that because it makes your shots look more like live action, more fun.[27]

Their enthusiasm is easy to understand, as prior to motion control the camera movement in stop-motion animation was mostly shot from a locked off camera position. Camera moves could only be achieved using hand-winched geared camera heads or other types of mechanical tracks. For instance, all of the camera shots in the famous skeleton fight scene animated by Ray Harryhausen in *Jason and the Argonauts* are static. It was a real point of difference for later animated films to move the camera using motion control technology, as Henry Selick said of *The Nightmare before Christmas*:

The tradition in stop-motion is the locked off camera but we were moving over sets, through windows, around characters. The camera was alive. We were moving cameras on better than eighty or ninety percent of the shots.[28]

The push towards complex 'live-action' camera moves is a feature of the modern Hollywood stop-motion animated film. In much the same way that Turnock identified ILM as a driving force in digital aesthetics, the creative crews that have worked together on contemporary stop-motion shoots have also formulated particular aesthetic goals and aspirations in animation, many around the idea of fluid animated movement and flowing camera moves. The films discussed in this chapter were made by different production companies, but many crew members worked on more than one of them. Some of the key creative crew, like cinematographer/visual effects director Pete Kozachik, have worked on all of them, including *Coraline*. The small community of stop-motion technicians and animators featured in trade and enthusiast magazines like *Stop Motion Magazine* and *Cinefex* routinely refer to improvements and advances across several of the productions they were involved in. This is a significant marker in the development of a specific cultural direction for stop-motion animation. Selick, talking about the visual characteristics of *Nightmare* and *Coraline*, could see the relationship between a creative process that evolved over multiple productions with the same crew:

> You build on what you know, so that there are no doubt some similarities between the two projects. I also have many of the original *Nightmare* team members working on *Coraline*. We've all grown and the visual aesthetic is ultimately a very different one [compared to *Nightmare*].[29]

The two productions may differ in overall design and aesthetics, but they shared a push towards a type of polished, frictionless movement that in many ways mimics the digital 3D animation that was threatening to replace them. As early as 1993, filmmakers expressed concerns that stop motion struggles in comparison to live-action movie making, as Mark Cotta Vaz, writing about *The Nightmare before Christmas* in trade magazine *Cinefex*, reported:

> Because of the growing sophistication of technically cognizant audiences, the films' creators were convinced that moviegoers would not accept a feature full of the pops and pixelations and other technical glitches prevalent in conventional stop-motion.[30]

In this analysis, 'sophistication' is a move towards an audience expectation of live-action fluidity. Selick also felt that using performance and camera styles that echoed live action was, in some ways, 'fixing' the problems of stop-motion animation: 'In the past, some people have thought of stop-motion as an inherently flawed effect; but [*Nightmare*] allowed people to suspend their disbelief and really believe these characters were alive.'[31]

The idea that stop motion can have a shared cinematic language with live-action films has become deeply embedded in mainstream animated productions as a filmmaking aim. *Coraline* shared that ambition and continued the refinement of that production process. From *Coraline* onwards, the industry-standard stop-motion tools have remained relatively stable in their development, and they all support the goal of live-action equivalence through digitally enabled processes embedded in both the equipment and production workflows. Although the production used an in-house LAIKA software system to shoot *Coraline*, it also used a pre-release version of the now-ubiquitous frame grabber software, *Dragonframe*, for some early tests.[32] Additionally, LAIKA implemented workflows that have become quite standard for contemporary stop-motion feature production. Those processes leverage all of the inherent advantages of digital cameras by utilizing live preview technology to shoot 4k footage, currently a cinema standard.[33] Elaborate, frame-by-frame camera moves are made possible using affordable motion control rigs which can also be controlled as an animated element using *Dragonframe*. Frame preview is instant and total, and includes the ability to compare, delete, reverse or reorder frames during a shot or to use an underlying layer as a visual guide for motion or timing. Using these tools, stop-motion animation is more controllable, allowing movement of all the elements in the shoot (cameras, puppets, props, lights and sets) to be more finely tuned. The tools that support digital imagery allow for sophisticated post-production manipulation so the creative scope of shots can be enhanced beyond that which can be captured on set, but most importantly, the digital frame is affordable, malleable and instant. *Coraline* was the film that started to pull all the pieces of the previous twenty years of stop-motion technical development into a recognizable contemporary workflow, and one of the main creative visual outcomes was a camera style that echoed live-action cinema.

The other animated camera

The smooth-flowing live-action quality that the filmmakers were aiming for is illustrated in the final shots of *Coraline*. Pete Kozachik described the last crane shot, in which the camera snakes alongside Coraline and a tray of drinks as she offers refreshments to all the major characters in the film, as 'monumental' and 'one of our most complicated shots'. This seemingly straightforward narrative closure was made using five separate stages (model set ups) with matched motion control movements, greenscreen and matte painting, all stitched together in post-production to make a continuous narrative space.[34]

The elegant simplicity in camera motion the *Coraline* crew achieved with digital tools is not the only way in which the stop-motion animated camera can be used as a narrative device. Some animators, like the Quay Brothers, have actively engaged with other visual qualities of frame-by-frame filmmaking and have exploited and celebrated the ways in which it differs from live-action camera moves. Susan Buchan's extensive analysis of the animated whip-pan camera moves in the Quay Brothers' *Street of Crocodiles* (1986) describes how they frequently use the device as a blurred, space-smashing technique to 'meld two phenomenally independent spaces into a continuous perceptual flow'. According to her, the Quays create shots that highlight the essential and embedded visual qualities of stop-motion filmmaking where 'the visual result is not a convention of live-action film, it self-reflexively draws the viewer's attention to how animation's formal technical means expand those of live-action cinema'.[35] The Quays consider the camera integral to the narrative itself and refer to it as 'the third puppet'.[36]

Engaging the camera as an additional stop-motion element is also employed by Jan Švankmajer in his early short films like *Et Cetera* (1966) or *Rakvičkárna* (*Punch and Judy*, 1966), where intercut sequences of objects, sets, graphics and animated motion happen so fast that the distinction between animated stop-motion action and cutting between shots becomes almost immaterial. In these films, it is the exploration of stop-motion animation's frame-by-frame process that draws constant attention to the structure of the medium itself. It is a visual loop of self-reference that reminds the viewer of the camera work, the artificiality of the animated motion and the impossibility of the motion of inanimate objects.

In *Coraline*, the camera work is engaged with a more invisible type of motion; the camera constantly travels with Coraline, and the majority of shots in the film have some sort of movement. The camera moves range from a subtle push into or out of a shot to convey a sense of spatial depth by introducing the gentlest of parallax effects, to huge crane shots that echo the dramatic camera work of an action film. Rather than drawing attention to themselves and referring to the process of frame-by-frame shooting, the shots use familiar cinematic language to help structure the film's narrative. The shots that show Coraline escaping the final web of the Other Mother at the film's end could easily be a live-action sequence. The camera work is dramatic, swift and mobile: from the moment Coraline flings the cat at the Other Mother, the camera barely pauses as the two characters engage in a fast-moving chase scene. The exaggerated point of view of the Other Mother plummeting towards a stunned Coraline as the latter lies at the bottom of the web, followed by a time-expanding reverse shot showing Coraline's point of view of the same action, are the stuff of action films everywhere. The action just after this point is as dramatic, but perhaps in the context of *Coraline* as a stop-motion film, it is the most interesting, as this is the sequence with the most self-referential stop-motion camera work in the film. As Coraline escapes from the Other Mother's web and rushes to the tiny door at the end of the tunnel to return to her own world, she is chased by the just-closed door that appears closer and closer in a choppy series of quick shots. The shots, staccato, abrupt and crisp without motion blur, are undeniably stop motion in their movement and very different to the smooth, sweeping, controlled camera work of the rest of the film. It is a point where the two worlds, that of Coraline and that of Coraline's 'Other World' could potentially unite, and it is here where these two types of camera work, the stop-motion animation as live action and the stop-motion animation as simply stop motion, also combine for a brief hybrid moment.

It is interesting that Selick chose this point of high drama to briefly utilize the inherent visual affect of the stop-motion camera and the way discontinuous frames can be used as a denaturalization device, as if the raw aspects of stop-motion animation are too outlandish for the other, more conventionally shot scenes in *Coraline*. The use of these compressed jump cuts highlights the visual distinction between the two ways of shooting. Animated motion cannot exist without the camera and the act of shooting the frame. Although the stop-motion camera and live-action camera processes both record real objects in a physical space, the stop-motion camera cannot simply record the movement of inanimate objects because the camera itself is an integral part of making the inanimate move.

This is one of only two points in *Coraline* where there is even a hint of exploring those built-in aspects of the stop-motion form. Instead, the production embraces the digital push for diegetic seamlessness and largely rejects the self-referential nature of stop-motion animation in the way it uses the camera. The artifice that shapes the reflexive element of the aesthetic of the stop-motion form is distilled by the technical labour of dozens of highly skilled people working tirelessly to reduce the visual differences between the look of live action and animation. This effort is visible not just in the camera work but also in the set dressing and props; Coraline's sweaters, for example, were knitted by a miniature knitting specialist who could keep the stitches of Coraline's tiny gloves to an incredible small scale.[37] As cinematographer Kozachik explained, this was all part of a deliberate visual strategy to keep the puppet world of *Coraline* as much like a live-action film as possible:

> The thing we have been trying to do, with all of the crews I have worked with, is to emulate the same film language and techniques as are used in live-action. Most of the time it can be done, in terms of lighting, composition, lens choices, colour, contrast, camera movement, and things like that.[38]

This is not to say *Coraline* was seeking to erase all aspects of stop-motion animation from an animated feature. In fact, the film celebrates the playful nature of creating a tiny and complete world that exists nowhere else except in front of the camera. The feature was designed, from the outset, with 3D stereoscopic projection and viewing in mind, and as Scott Higgins points out, *Coraline* is a perfect vehicle for 3D effects because it allowed Selick to 'embrace the shoebox diorama effect as an aesthetic choice rather than a deficiency'.[39] Selick also positioned the 3D aspect of the production as a type of homage to the stop-motion filmmaking process and a way to help convey some of the pleasure of creating these films:

> There was often a longing when we had these beautiful setups [and] we wish we could capture that little world completely. Shooting traditionally flattens things out and you never really get a sense of what we filmmakers [see, and that] we could touch these things, walk around them [and] that they really existed. So there was a longing to show that difference between the two worlds.[40]

Selick is referring to a deliberate creative strategy to make Coraline's 'Other World' more stereoscopic and more dimensional as a location, but he's also referencing the deeply self-reflexive nature of stop-motion animation. It's what Donald Crafton termed the 'self-figuration' of the animator, a kind of compulsion to share the incredible nature of the process of filmmaking through the film itself.[41] This compulsion infuses the entire production process, from the camera work to the props to the design. *Coraline*'s knitting specialist Althea Crome, who made all of Coraline's immaculate miniature sweaters, saw this as being self-evident in the animated objects themselves: 'When one shrinks a craft or a skill into something so tiny, it asks the viewer to imagine how it was done.'[42]

The animators' desire to represent themselves in the work bleeds through in all sorts of ways. Travis Knight described how he and the crew 'bring so much of ourselves to it that it ends up filtering into the show, to the point that businesses on the sets are named after people who worked on the film. We name props after people.'[43] In *Coraline*, this type of homage to the animated process is most pronounced in the final shot that closes the credits. It is a beautiful sequence that is entirely raw, with the studio blue screen untouched and all the rigging and wires visible, propelled by unseen hands controlling a host of dancing mice. The fragile fabric rodents curl around their ribbon-like tails, and the whole rig elegantly retreats from the camera to give the appearance of the mice disappearing into a distant swirling whirlpool (see Figure 6.2). The shot was a sequence that was never used in the film, but Selick liked it so much that it appears after the credits, an unexpected, unexplained and silent homage to the skill and dedication required to create stop-motion animation.[44] It is also a final reveal of the complicated nature of the filmmaking process itself and a glimpse into the complex multilayered methods needed to make stop-motion appear seamless. It is as if the filmmakers want to remind us that making something look this effortless requires an almost superhuman amount of effort.

The advent of CGI marked the end of a certain type of animation. Stop-motion special effects and creature features are no longer part of mainstream live-action

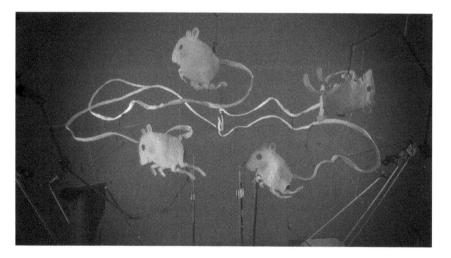

Figure 6.2 The *Coraline* post-credits scene showing an untreated blue screen shot of receding dream mice, a sequence that was dropped from the final film.

film. However, that end marked a type of new beginning and, in abandoning film for digital technology stop-motion animation, created a new type of mainstream production. The contemporary tools of stop motion are cheaper, faster and more instantaneous than anything possible with film, and the style and aesthetics of the form have evolved in lockstep with these advances. *Coraline* was a moment of completion, in that it marked the end of one technical era for stop-motion animation and was an instrumental part of creating the beginning of another way of viewing style, form and the contemporary animated camera.

Notes

1   This is a popular trope in both films and books. In film adaptations, see any version of C. S. Lewis's *The Lion, the Witch and the Wardrobe*. Other examples include *How I Live Now* (Kevin Macdonald, 2013), Lemony Snicket's *A Series of Unfortunate Events* (Brad Siberling, 2004), *The Spiderwick Chronicles* (Mark Waters, 2008) or, for an animated example, *Spirited Away* (Hayao Miayzaki, 2001).

2   All aspects of stop-motion animation are slow.

3   Robin Rowe, '"Bride" Stripped Bare', *Editors Guild Magazine*, vol. 26, no. 4 (2005), pp. 1–8.

4   John Ikuma, 'Interview with Lead Animator/CEO Travis Knight', *Stop Motion Magazine*, no. 16 (2012), p. 23.

5   Since *Corpse Bride* (2005), all large-scale Hollywood productions have used some form of digital shooting. Aardman Animations in the UK moved to an all-digital workflow in 2010 to shoot *The Pirates! In an Adventure with Scientists* (also known as *The Pirates! Band of Misfits*, Peter Lord, 2012).

6   Stephen Prince, *Digital Visual Effects in Cinema: The Seduction of Reality* (New Brunswick, NJ: Rutgers University Press, 2012), p. 25.

7   Ray Harryhausen and Tony Dalton, *A Century of Stop Motion Animation: From Méliès to Aardman* (New York: Watson-Guptill, 2008), p. 188.

8   Lawrence French, 'Phil Tippet: Stop-Motion May be Going Extinct, but the Former Animator Is Alive and Well', *Cinefantastique*, vol. 31, no. 1/2 (1999), p. 40.

9   Mark Cotta Vaz, '*The Nightmare before Christmas*: Animation in the Third Dimension', *Cinefex*, no. 56 (1993), p. 32.

10   Harryhausen and Dalton, *A Century of Stop Motion Animation*, p. 188.

11   Julie Turnock, *Plastic Reality: Special Effects, Technology, and the Emergence of 1970s Blockbuster Aesthetics* (New York: Columbia University Press, 2015), p. 68.

12   Harryhausen and Dalton, *A Century of Stop Motion Animation*, p. 113.

13   Steve Rose, 'Masters of Puppets: Charlie Kaufman and the Subversive Allure of Stop-Motion', *The Guardian*, 7 January 2016. https://www.theguardian.com/film/2016/jan/07/subversive-allure-stop-motion-anomalisa-tim-burton (accessed 1 March 2020).

14   Ikuma, 'Interview with Lead Animator/CEO Travis Knight', p. 28.

15   Bill Desowitz, "'Corpse Bride: Stop Motion Goes Digital', *Animation World Network*, 16 September 2005. https://www.awn.com/vfxworld/corpse-bride-stop-motion-goes-digital (accessed 1 May 2020).

16   Rowe, ' "Bride" Stripped Bare'.

17   Digital projection standards are set by a consortium of studios represented by the Digital Cinema Initiative. See 'Digital Cinema System Specification'. https://www.dcimovies.com/archives/spec_v1/DCI_Digital_Cinema_System_Spec_v1.pdf, p. 12 (accessed 20 April 2020).

18   Vaz, '*The Nightmare before Christmas*: Animation in the Third Dimension', p. 49.

19   Motion control was first utilized by *Star Wars* (1977). See Turnock, *Plastic Reality* for a full overview of the early uses of motion control technology.

20   Harryhausen and Dalton, *A Century of Stop Motion Animation*, p. 27.

21   A good overview of the use of the surface gauge by *The Nightmare before Christmas* animator Anthony Scott can be found at Anthony Scott, 'The Importance of Using Gages', *Stop Motion Animation*. http://www.stopmotionanimation.com/page/the-importance-of-using-gages (accessed 1 May 2020). He also details how the development of the frame grabber changed his animation practice.

22   The LunchBox was made redundant by digital camera technologies because a digitizing intermediary (converting video information to digital information) was no longer required in a wholly digital pipeline. The system can be seen in internet archives at 'LunchBox DV: Summary', *Animation Tool Works*, 10 August 2006. https://web.archive.org/web/20060810022321/http://www.animationtoolworks.com/products/lbdv_summ.html (accessed 30 April 2020).

23   Vaz, '*The Nightmare before Christmas*: Animation in the Third Dimension', p. 45.

24   Rowe, ' "Bride" Stripped Bare'.

25   'Machine Vision Enables Stop-Motion Animation, *Vision Systems Design*, vol. 14, no. 2 (2009), p. 9.

26   Ken A. Priebe and Henry Selick, *The Advanced Art of Stop-Motion Animation* (Boston, MA: Course Technology, 2011), p. 191.

27   TV is OK Productions, 'The Making of The Nightmare before Christmas', in *The Nightmare Before Christmas Special Edition Dvd* (Buena Vista Home Entertainment, 2000).

28   Vaz, '*The Nightmare before Christmas*: Animation in the Third Dimension', p. 45.

29   'Henry Selick Interview: the Director of *The Nightmare before Christmas* Reflects on His Biggest Hit and Discusses Next Film *Coraline*', *DVDizzy*, 26 August 2008. https://www.dvdizzy.com/henryselick-interview.html (accessed 13 November 2018).

30   Vaz, '*The Nightmare before Christmas*: Animation in the Third Dimension', p. 33.

31   Ibid., p. 53.

32   'Coraline in 3D: The *Dragon* Stop Motion Connection', *Dragonframe*, 21 February 2009. https://www.dragonframe.com/blog/coraline-in-3d-the-dragon-connection/ (accessed 21 April 2020).

33   'Digital Cinema System Specification', p. 12

34   Joe Fordham, '*Coraline*: A Handmade World', *Cinefex*, no. 117 (2009), p. 61.

35   Suzanne Buchan, *The Quay Brothers: Into a Metaphysical Playroom* (Minneapolis: University of Minnesota Press, 2011), p. 161.

36   Michael Atkinson, 'The Night Countries of the Brothers Quay', *Film Comment*, vol. 30, no. 5 (1994), p. 37.

37   'Coraline – Tiny Knitting', Focus Features/LAIKA, YouTube, 28 January 2009. https://www.youtube.com/watch?v=7wADZBNvA_s (accessed 10 October 2018).

38   Priebe and Selick, *The Advanced Art of Stop-Motion Animation*, p. 192.

39   Scott Higgins, '3D in Depth: *Coraline, Hugo*, and a Sustainable Aesthetic', *Film History: An International Journal*, vol. 24, no. 2 (2012), p. 200.

40   Joshua Foster, 'Special Feature: Director's Commentary', in *Coraline 2-Disc Collector's Edition* (Leg Productions, 2009).

41   Donald Crafton, *Before Mickey: The Animated Film, 1898–1928* (Chicago: University of Chicago Press, 1993), p. 12.

42   'Coraline – Tiny Knitting'.

43   Ikuma, 'Interview with Lead Animator/CEO Travis Knight', p. 21.

44   Foster, 'Special Feature: Director's Commentary'.

7

A world within reach: A neuroanimatic perspective on themes of threat in the miniature world of *Coraline*

Ann Owen

In 2009 studio LAIKA's much anticipated adaptation of Neil Gaiman's book *Coraline* premiered at the Portland International Film Festival.[1] The excitement surrounding the film's release was due, in part, to the digital renaissance of 3D stereoscopic film that was taking place at the time and which saw its stop-motion feature debut in *Coraline*. However, this was not the only emerging technology to be showcased in the film: *Coraline*'s use of digital design and printing to produce facial animation, seen by many for the first time in this film, was arguably of more interest. Replacement animation was not new, having been used decades earlier by animators such as George Pal and more recently by Henry Selick for facial animation in *The Nightmare before Christmas* (1993). However, by 2009 advances in digital technology allowed animators to design and animate the puppets' replacement face pieces digitally and print them using a 3D rapid prototyping printer. This resulted in incredibly smooth facial movement that could at first sight be mistaken for computer-generated (CG) animation. Additionally, the film's miniature costumes, props and sets were constructed with accurate scaled-down detail. Many were created using the same 3D printing technology while others were painstakingly crafted by hand, such as Coraline's sweater and gloves, which were hand-knitted on tiny sewing needles. In the 'making of' material that accompanies the DVD, Georgina Hayns, character fabrication supervisor on *Coraline*, emphasizes the importance of making sure that the puppets and props are perfectly and accurately scaled down versions of their real-word equivalents, saying, 'It's all about making sure that nothing gives away the scale.'[2]

While the makers of *Coraline* focused on creating a perfectly animated and scaled-down world, two other stop-motion films released in the same year, *Mary and Max* (Adam Eliott, 2009) and *Fantastic Mr. Fox* (Wes Anderson, 2009), took a different approach. Rather than trying to hide the method of production and the inaccuracies of scale that often accompany stop motion, both films allow these things to remain obvious. Max's tracksuit, for example, is very clearly sculpted from clay, utilizing the same visible finger-print approach that has been made famous by Aardman Animation's claymation films. The bubbles in Max's bubble bath are visibly made from white beads or balls with only a passing resemblance to real bubbles. Similarly, *Fantastic Mr. Fox* celebrates rather than disguises the method of its production, using sets that are often sparse in detail and slightly mis-scaled, reminding the spectator of a child's farmyard toy or model railway. The film does not try to hide the slight movement of the character's fur that is produced accidentally when the animator touches the puppet in order to manipulate it. This was common in animation created prior to the introduction of video assist technology in the 1990s.[3] Used in *Fantastic Mr. Fox*, it not only references earlier animation but is also a visual reminder of the actions of the animator and the stop-motion method of production.

The words 'handmade' and 'handcrafted' are regularly used in relation to stop-motion animation.[4] Indeed, the handmade aesthetic is arguably one of the most important and defining aspects of the medium. Yet many of the techniques used to create *Coraline*'s perfectly scaled replica of the real world, such as the jumper knitted on tiny needles or the perfectly scaled digitally printed props, render the method of production less visible than its 2009 competitors. Despite this, the film still contains unmissable references to its miniature real-world existence. The most notable of these, and most central to the original narrative, are the expressionless button eyes of the Other Mother and Father. Another clue is present in the visible inner skeleton of the Other Mother, the fingers of which are made from fine sewing needles. What is particularly interesting is that while the button eyes were provided by Gaiman's original story and are intrinsic to the narrative, the visible armature and its needle fingers are unique to the animated film. They are not without narrative purpose of course; alongside the button eyes, the needle fingers act as visual signifiers of the jeopardy that Coraline faces in the story. However, these needles are not scaled down; each finger is made from a single needle, which indicates that the puppet is small and doll-sized, appearing to act *against* the apparent desire of the filmmakers to render the real-world scale of the puppets invisible.

This raises an interesting conundrum: on the one hand there is an apparent desire to disguise the scale, and so the method of production; yet on the other hand there seems to be a realization that making the scale and the method of production visible is important to the way that stop-motion film communicates to its audiences. Neuroscientists V. S. Ramachandran and W. Hirstein assert that artists are, in a sense, neuroscientists who unconsciously deploy an intuitive understanding of the workings of the human brain when creating art.[5] For example, a caricaturist knows instinctively how to exaggerate certain aspects of a face or body to create an image that reveals something of the 'essence' of the subject. A landscape artist knows how to manipulate paint so as to not only replicate the scene but also to tell the viewer something about the 'essence' of the scene, something that cannot be seen in the real world.[6] Both caricaturist and landscape artist are able to do this because they have an understanding of the way that human beings read images and have skill in manipulating this through their art. If Ramachandran and Hirstein's hypothesis is correct, might this not also be true of stop-motion filmmakers? Could the makers of *Coraline* be innately picking up on some neural process that links artifact, medium and content, and that benefits from some elements of the stop-motion technique remaining visible? This chapter will take a neuroanimatic approach to this question. That is to say that it will apply neuroscientific and neuroaesthetic knowledge of the human visual processes and will seek to unravel the relationship between the visual signifiers in *Coraline*, the stop-motion method and the narrative needs of Gaiman's story.

Neuroscience can be a contentious method when it comes to studying what is essentially a cultural artifact. Although the use of neuroscience in arts research is becoming more widespread, there is still the potential for valid criticism.[7] It is therefore prudent to establish the limitations, as well as the benefits, of neuroanimatics. Developments in fMRI and PET scanning have meant that researchers have been able to make significant advances over recent decades, but there is still a great deal about the functioning of the brain that we do not yet understand. The neuroscientific avenues explored in this chapter are therefore similarly limited; neuroanimatics is not by any means the be-all and end-all of the study of stop-motion animation spectatorship.

Not only is the brain an extremely complex organ, but it has also been found to be incredibly plastic. What this means is that it has the ability to adapt to the conditions that it finds itself in, such as particular environmental, social and cultural conditions and, to an extent, to physical injuries. Genes provide the brain with a blueprint, just as they do for the rest of the body, but experience dictates how that blueprint develops.[8] There are, however, sufficient similarities to be able to draw valid conclusions about the nature of visual perception, which are due in part to the genetic blueprint and in part to basic consistencies in the physical world that all newborn infants find themselves in. For example, light usually comes from above, which creates consistencies in the behaviour of light and shadow and causes the related visual processes of different humans to develop in a largely consistent way. Sharp objects pierce the skin, regardless of culture or an individual's situation, leading humans to have broadly similar responses to the threat of injury. So, while there may be many differences in the way that individuals perceive a film or an artwork, there are also considerable similarities that allow valid generalizations to be made. Where it is possible within the confines of this chapter, the issue of individual experience and difference will be addressed; otherwise, the reader should assume that the things being discussed here are not likely to apply in equal measure to all human spectators.

Animation is ostensibly a non-realist film medium. Although animation can, and often does, imitate the conventions of live action-film production, most animation does not possess the indexical reality of live-action film; that is to say there is no direct link between the representation and the thing that is being represented. Stop motion is unique in this respect. Although the characters of Coraline and Wybie are not real people, and the house where Coraline lives is not a real house, they are real miniature objects that exist in the real physical world. The world of Coraline can be walked around, explored and perhaps most importantly of all it can be touched. It is this unique quality, and its potential effect on the brain, that is at the core of the issue being investigated in this chapter.

The haptic nature of stop-motion animation has been commented upon by animators and scholars alike. Jan Švankmajer was fascinated with the tactile nature of objects and with what he referred to as the 'tactile imagination'.[9] This can be seen in many of his animated films such as *The Fall of the House of Usher* (1980) and *Dimensions of Dialogue* (1982) and is something that Švankmajer wrote about at length.[10] Aardman Animations similarly created a visual trademark out of the visible fingerprints that animators leave on the clay puppets. The tactile quality of stop-motion animation has also been noted by Ellen Rocha.[11] Rocha describes it as 'embodied' spectatorship; audiences are not only looking with their eyes but are also *feeling* the animation via memory and previous experiences of touch. This use of the word 'embodied' is apt as the term 'embodied brain' is often used in neuroscience to stress the brain's connectedness to, and reliance on, the body and its experiences.[12] One area where this connection is especially relevant, and which is related to the issue addressed in this chapter, is the neuroscientific theory of 'simulation'.

Neural simulation

Prior to the word being adopted by neuroscience, 'simulation' was used to refer to theories from philosophy of mind that sought to explain how it is that human beings are able to read the intentions of other people.[13] More recently it has been used to describe the neural processes that scientists believe underpin not only the ability to read intentions but also our ability to empathize with, bond with and learn from other people.[14]

Our understanding of the neural activity involved with these abilities first came to light via the research of Italian neuroscientist Giacomo Rizzolatti, who had been conducting experiments with macaque monkeys. Rizzolatti's researchers found that when one monkey watched another monkey carry out a goal-oriented action (an action driven by an intention), the active parts of the brain of the observing monkey were almost identical to the active parts of the brain of the monkey carrying out the action. Rizzolatti and his team went on to identify the specific neurons that were involved in this process and named them 'mirror neurons': the observer's brain *mirrors* that of the observed subject.[15]

Science has not identified specific 'mirror neurons' in human beings, and it is not yet known exactly how this process works in our own brains. However, there is a compelling amount of evidence indicating that a similar, but more sophisticated, system does exist in humans.[16] Human brains not only simulate goal-related actions but can also simulate the separate movements that make up a goal-related action. Furthermore, we can simulate complete actions based on the observation of only a part of the action. For example, if we watch someone moving their arm as if to reach for an object but do not see the object being grasped, our brain simulates the entire action of reaching and grasping. We also simulate when we *imagine* carrying out actions.[17] There is additional evidence to suggest that we are able to simulate the actions involved in chewing and eating.[18] These simulations largely take place in the motor control areas of the brain; this is the bit of the brain that controls our muscles. It is as if we were doing the action ourselves, but without the neural activity that creates the actual physical movement. The evidence also indicates that our body's experiences of carrying out actions ourselves play a key role in this ability, hence the emphasis on *embodied* simulation.[19]

Our ability to understand the emotions of others is also rooted in simulation, as is our ability to imagine emotions.[20] Again it is the motor control area of the brain that is activated. We simulate the facial expressions and posture of those we observe, and we are able to simulate the associated emotion from our own brain's experiences of muscle activity and matching emotions. Our brains can also simulate the senses of the flesh, such as touch and pain.[21] We do not actually *feel* the pain, but experience a keen sense of it. Once again it is our own body's experiences that facilitate the simulation. Perhaps unsurprisingly, neural simulations have been found to be stronger if the person who is watching or imagining an act has experience of having previously carried out that same act.[22] The uniqueness of individual experience of course means that there are variations in the extent to which the process works in individuals.

Neural simulation is thought to serve several important functions such as facilitating the learning of motor skills and emotional bonding between humans, both of which have implications for stop-motion animation and the phenomena that are apparent in *Coraline*.[23]

Simulation and animation spectatorship

Animated characters are, of course, neither human nor real living beings. This raises the issue of how effectively our brains can create neural simulations of things that only imitate real life. Non-human characters can without doubt elicit strong human emotions, as can be seen in films such as *Mary and Max* or *Bambi* (James Algar et al., 1942). It could be argued that this is due to the human voice actors, or our conscious knowledge of the narrative; it would therefore be untrue to claim that the ability of these to elicit emotional reactions is entirely down to empathetic responses triggered by vision. However, there is evidence showing that neural simulation can be provoked by the observation of non-human and non-real bodies. For example, it has been found that we are able to simulate the actions of animals, providing that our own anatomical structure can carry out the actions that we observe in the animal.[24] We are also able to effectively simulate the actions of an illustrated animated walk cycle[25] and of a human represented by only a few moving pinpoints of light.[26] It is therefore reasonable to assume that human beings are able to simulate the actions and emotions that are apparent in non-real stop-motion characters.

Where this research becomes particularly pertinent to *Coraline*, however, is not simply in the human ability to simulate movement and emotion but in our ability to also simulate the sensations of the flesh. Freedberg and Gallese use the example of Caravaggio's painting of *The Incredulity of St Thomas* (1601–2) to demonstrate this.[27] The painting depicts Thomas inserting his finger into a wound in Jesus's torso; looking at this picture causes the observer to become acutely aware of the sensations in the corresponding parts of their own body. Animators such as Robert Morgan, the Quay Brothers and Jan Švankmajer have explored this potential to great effect in their stop-motion films, creating a strong sense of threat to the body through scenes that invoke an awareness of our own flesh (see Figure 7.1). While *Coraline* does not utilize this technique to the same extent, there are similar themes of bodily threat present that are key to successfully portraying the film's narrative, and which will be discussed in detail in the final section of this chapter.

A second way in which the neuroscientific research is particularly pertinent to *Coraline* is through our ability to simulate *implied* actions; these are actions that we do not see, but that leave behind some kind of visible evidence. Freedberg and Gallese argue that marks such as the brushstrokes on a van

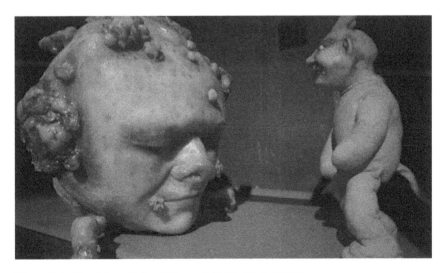

Figure 7.1 'Face', from Robert Morgan's *Bobby Yeah* (2011).

Gogh painting or the paint splatters of a Pollock painting *imply* the movement that created the artwork and provoke a simulation of that action.[28] There is compelling evidence to support this idea; research has found that the observers of handwritten letter forms simulate the movements associated with creating the letter forms.[29]

Again, this is something that animators such as Švankmajer and Nick Park have made effective use of by purposefully showing the fingerprints of the animator.[30] It is unlikely that these animators would have been familiar with the neuroscience involved, but they were no doubt aware of the strengths of the medium and the effect that leaving these marks would have on the audience. In view of our ability to simulate implied gestures, it is perhaps not surprising that Ellen Rocha notes that stop-motion spectatorship is a particularly 'haptic' and 'embodied' experience.[31]

A further aspect of implied gesture that is highly relevant to stop-motion animation is the way that the human brain simulates grasping and manipulation actions. Studies have found that when we watch another person grasping an object, or when we imagine grasping an object, a simulation of the motor neuron activity involved in grasping takes place.[32] This also occurs when we look at photographs of hands carrying out, or about to carry out, grasping actions.[33] Furthermore, it has been found that our brain simulates grasping and manipulating actions simply by observing graspable or manipulatable objects such as tools.[34] The visible indication of the potential of an object to be grasped or manipulated provokes a simulation of that action.

A film like *Coraline*, therefore, could trigger simulation in three ways: firstly, by provoking simulation of the actions and emotions of the characters; secondly, by provoking simulation of the sensations of the flesh of those characters; and thirdly, by provoking simulation of the implied actions of the animators. Each of these simulations is dependent on the audience being able to identify the things that they see on screen as real-world miniature objects. On the surface it appears that this kind of technique is something that the makers of *Coraline* strove to avoid, preferring to hide signs of the scale and real-world existence of the puppets and animators. However, a closer examination of the film will reveal that the filmmakers, perhaps unconsciously, replaced obvious visual clues with subtler references to the real-world nature and scale of the animated world.

Simulation and themes of threat in *Coraline*

The opening section of this chapter identified two key elements that provide *Coraline*'s audience with clues to the real-world scale of the objects that we see on screen. These are the button eyes of the Other Mother and Father and the visible armature of the Other Mother puppet with its sewing-needle fingers. This last section of the chapter will examine the ways that Henry Selick and his production team, through a keen understanding of their medium, have used these elements to tap into stop motion's unique embodied spectatorship qualities.

The button eyes of the Other Mother and Father are one of the most important elements of Gaiman's original story. They function both as a literal threat of physical harm and as a symbolic threat of the dehumanizing, or de-souling, of Coraline. Due to the size and scale of real buttons and their common use as eyes on children's toys, stop motion was perhaps the only medium that could bring a visual logic to their presence in the narrative. Indeed, Ken A. Priebe suggests that the book may have been written with stop motion in mind.[35] However, in the light of the visual processes discussed above, the button eyes in the film take on additional significance. The scale of the buttons, together with the audience's past experiences of handling toys, shows us that the puppets are likely to be toy-like in their proportions. This allows our brain to identify the world of Coraline as a miniature space that exists within our real world, within reach of our grasping hands. Once the puppets have registered as graspable, the animated movement and the implied movement of the animator indicates to our brains that these puppets are also *manipulatable*. Bearing in mind that the identification of graspable and manipulatable objects provokes simulations of grasping and manipulating, the animated puppets in *Coraline* are likely to provoke similar simulations. While the perfectly scaled down clothing and the computer-generated face pieces might hide the real-world scale of the puppets, other elements, such as the button eyes, re-establish it. It is not surprising that Peter Lord once said of stop-motion animation that it is like watching an 'invisible spirit transforming the puppet into a living being'.[36]

The button eyes are of course a key part of Gaiman's original narrative and are not unique to the film. However, Selick and his production team have added a host of additional reminders of the miniature scale of the puppets, which cannot be attributed to the original narrative. During a scene in which the

Other Father attempts to help Coraline, the Other Mother pulls a string coming from his ear; this string deactivates his ability to speak. The scene alludes to the type of child's doll that plays a short piece of pre-recorded speech when a string is pulled and draws attention to the possibility that the things on screen can likewise be manipulated. A similar effect is created by the Coraline lookalike doll; in one scene Coraline holds and manipulates the doll, mimicking its imagined responses to her questions and drawing attention to the fact that Coraline herself is manipulatable. The most significant added indicator of the real-world scale and nature of the film is the visibility of the Other Mother's armature. This is seen in the opening sequence and again towards the end of the film as the true nature of the Other Mother becomes apparent. The needle fingers of the armature are not scaled down, as with other elements of the film; they are a size appropriate to a real-world armature. This design, unique to the film, appears to go against the desire of the filmmakers to hide the scale of the puppets, instead reminding us of their graspable and manipulatable nature.

This last reminder, and its potential to encourage simulations of grasping, also has significance regarding the simulation of bodily sensation and pain. If we can imagine grasping the Other Mother's armature, we can also imagine being injured by its sharp needle fingers, and we can then simulate the sensation of damage to the flesh that this would cause. This in turn echoes and amplifies the threat that the needle fingers represent to Coraline within the narrative: that is, the threat of having her flesh pierced by needles in order for the buttons to be sewn to her face. There are several further portents of this threat. During the opening scene in which we see the hands of the armature refashion the doll to resemble Coraline, we see the seams of the old doll sliced open, its innards/ stuffing removed and replaced (see Figure 7.2), the threads attaching the old eyes cut, and the eyes removed. Of particular significance is a shot of the replacement buttons being attached to the repurposed doll. In this shot a needle threads the cotton through the button from behind, pointing outwardly towards the camera and the audience. In the 3D stereoscopic version of the film, the needle protrudes into the space in front of the screen; but even without the 3D effect the threat of piercing is clearly established, and also felt by the audience. This threat is then repeated via shots of the buttons that the Other Mother has presented to Coraline. In the animated film, these sit in a box on the kitchen table together with a reel of cotton and a needle. The Other Father reinforces the threat with the words 'so sharp you won't feel a thing'.

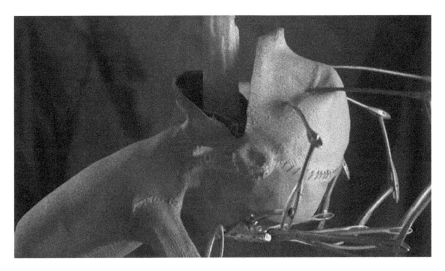

Figure 7.2 The Coraline lookalike doll gets filled with sawdust in the film's opening sequence.

Following the opening sequence, we don't see the Other Mother's armature again until much later in the film when her true form is fully revealed. There are, however, occasional reminders of the threat to the flesh, some of which are very subtle and some of which are more obvious. For example, when leaving Mr Bobinsky's house, Coraline picks up a pair of garden shears that are embedded point downwards in the wooden decking, using them to cut the rope that ties her suitcase to the roof of the family car. In a later scene we see that the Other Mother has sewn Wybie's mouth into a fake smile. The secateurs and indeed the entire gardening theme, together with the character of Wybie, are present only in the film, as are the needle fingers of the Other Mother. All of these elements have the potential to stimulate an awareness of our own flesh through simulation, reinforcing the threat to the characters.

A further element involving bodily harm, present in the book and expanded upon in the film, is the severing of the Other Mother's hand. This takes place towards the end of the film as Coraline escapes, trapping and riving the hand as she closes the door to the Other World. As with the threat of the buttons, this narrative element is foreshadowed and reinforced with additional visual references that are unique to the film. During the scene in which Miss Forcible and Miss Spink read Coraline's tea leaves, we see the shape of a clawed hand in the bottom of her cup. Similarly, one of the garden scenes ends with a shot of wispy clouds in front of the moon, ominously forming the shape of two severed hands. During the scene in which the Other Father sings to Coraline, the piano takes control of his arms and hands by the use of mechanical gloves. In a later scene the Other Father prises a similar controlling glove off his hand, and it flies away from him, looking very much like a severed hand. In another sequence we see the Other Mr Bobinsky bend over backwards and walk on all fours like a crab, resembling the way that the Other Mother's hand moves during the final scenes of the film.

These shots not only foreshadow the severed hand's role as the antagonist in Coraline's final battle, but create a triangle of visual indicators provoking simulations that enhance the narrative. The visible grasping hands provoke simulations of grasping gestures, adding to our awareness of our own hands and simulations of grasping the puppets. This awareness, as well as the proliferation of piercing tools on screen, including the needle fingers of the Other Mother, makes us mindful of the sensations of our own flesh and the threat of damage to that flesh. The simulation of grasping the Other Mother's armature and being pierced by its needles similarly creates an unconsciously felt threat of injury to our own flesh. This in turn reinforces the central narrative theme of physical threat to Coraline's flesh.

It has to be acknowledged that these scenes probably don't provoke the same tangible simulation and awareness of our own flesh that some scenes in *Street of Crocodiles* (Stephen and Timothy Quay, 1986) or *Bobby Yeah* (Robert Morgan, 2011) might provoke. Bearing in mind that all human brains simulate slightly differently due to our differing experiences, the unconscious sensations that one audience member experiences might not be the same, or as strong, as those of another. Nevertheless, the scenes referred to above, at the very least, allude to the more tangible simulations of threat found in independent shorts and arguably reproduce them in full in some scenes.

One last narrative trope that is relevant to the adaptation of *Coraline* from book to screen involves the theme of eating and of internal bodily sensations. Both stop motion and live-action film have explored tropes of eating and the subversion of eating in order to create discomfort in the spectator. In Charlie Chaplin's *Modern Times* (1936), The Tramp is fed metal bolts by a mechanical feeding machine. The sense of internal discomfort that this scene provokes is quite disturbing, which is not surprising when you consider our brain's ability to simulate the things that we watch. Švankmajer has also used the theme of eating, and in particular of eating non-food items, to similar effect in his stop-motion animation *Jabberwocky* (1971), in which we see dolls eating the body parts of smaller dolls. As we are able to recognize the objects on screen as real things that we could eat in the real world, even if doing so would be quite unpleasant, the potential for simulation is palpable.

The importance of food in Gaiman's original story is established when Coraline expresses dislike of her father's 'recipes', preferring to eat pizza and microwave chips.[37] The Other Mother then uses an array of appetizing food in an attempt to entice Coraline to remain in the Other World. Once the Other Mother's true intentions are revealed, the theme of eating becomes less pleasant as Gaiman describes the Other Mother eating live and wriggling beetles.[38] In the animation these become 'cocoa beetles from Zanzibar', which has the effect of making them seem slightly more palatable while maintaining the sense of discomfort that the neural simulation creates. This technique of using eating to create both pleasant and unpleasant sensations is developed further in Selick's animation. During the mouse circus scene, Coraline eats candyfloss, which shoots out of a cannon. Miss Forcible and Miss Spink repeatedly offer Coraline pastel-coloured sweets, both of which are pleasant forms of eating. Later in the film, as the world that the Other Mother has created begins to break down and disintegrate, the sensations of eating that the film provokes become less enjoyable. Coraline finds the Other Spink and Forcible wrapped in a giant sweet wrapper hanging above the stage in the theatre, looking very much like two entwined pieces of candy. In another scene Wybie teases Coraline by pretending to eat a somewhat slimy and stretchy slug. When Coraline is looking for the eyes of the children in the garden, the 'dragon-snapper' plants attempt to bite her. A low garden wall then opens up like a mouth and tree roots attempt to drag Coraline inside. The dragon-snapper flowers appear once again as cut flowers in a vase that are being hand fed by the Other Mother. The idea of ingestion is also alluded to by the presence of the tunnel that Coraline crawls through in order to get to the Other World. In Gaiman's book this tunnel is simply a corridor, but in Selick's film it has the appearance of an organic internal space, such as an intestine.[39]

As with the other narrative tropes, the theme of eating provides a metaphor for the peril that Coraline is in; she is in danger of being swallowed up and digested by the Other Mother's world. However, in a stop-motion film in which we can see that the things being eaten and the things that are doing the eating are real objects, if not real digestible food, this theme also creates a powerful sense of ingestion and of the insides of our own bodies via the simulation of the things we see on screen. This is useful to a film in which a key narrative threat is one of harm to the body.

As with the threats of damage to the flesh, most of these visual indicators don't create the same level of simulation of eating and internal bodily discomfort that Chaplin's *Modern Times* or Švankmajer's *Jabberwocky* invoke. Selick and his production team needed to create a family-friendly film that would be palatable to the general public and that would not be classified as animation horror. While children may not have the range of experiences to enable them to fully empathize with every situation, they will almost certainly have had some experiences that would allow them to simulate harm to the flesh. Due to this potential, a full and unrestrained use of stop motion's abilities to provoke simulation would not have been appropriate. With this in mind, the steps taken to hide some of the more obvious signifiers of the real-world existence of *Coraline's* puppets, props and sets become understandable. Selick could not have used all of the methods discussed above with their potential to stimulate neural simulations without also taking steps to temper their effect. Michael Frierson describes Tim Burton's film *Vincent* (1982) as a kind of pastiche of B-horror movies.[40] In much the same way, Selick has created a kind of pastiche of the techniques used in the tactile animations of Morgan, Švankmajer and the Quays and in so doing has been able to subtly invoke and allude to the same mechanisms without overly frightening or disgusting his audience.

The commonalities between the work of Morgan, Švankmajer and the Quays, and the feature animations of directors such as Selick and Burton indicate that stop motion has a predilection for content that involves threat to the body and might be described as either horror or pastiche horror. The neuroscientific research discussed in this chapter offers a neuroanimatic explanation as to why this might be. It demonstrates that stop motion's unique potential can only be fully realized if audiences are able to identify that what they are seeing on screen exists in miniature form in the real world, whether that be through obvious indicators or through more subtle and tempered ones. However, this is by no means intended to be an all-encompassing and complete explanation of stop motion's particular properties. The research discussed in this chapter also does not imply that themes of harm to the flesh are the only themes that are well suited to stop-motion animation. Nevertheless, the threat of bodily harm is an important element in Gaiman's narrative that has been cleverly adapted to animation by Selick and his production team, providing just the right level of menace for the film's target audience.

To conclude this chapter, I would like to return to Ramachandran and Hirstein's assertion that artists are, in a sense, neuroscientists.[41] They are people who have a profound awareness of the relationship between their medium and the human spectators of their work, as well as a sophisticated understanding of how to use this relationship to communicate to an audience. Rather than saying that stop motion has a tendency towards certain content, it might be more accurate to say that it is the directors, animators, designers, puppet makers and prop makers, with their expert knowledge of medium and audience, who are drawn to and able to fully exploit narrative content, such as that which is found within Gaiman's *Coraline*.

Notes

1 Neil Gaiman, *Coraline* (London: Bloomsbury, [2002] 2012).

2 Georgina Haynes, 'Coraline's Closet' [DVD] (USA: Universal Pictures, 2009).

3   Orville Goldner and George E. Turner, *The Making of King Kong* (New York: Ballantine Books, 1976), p. 131.

4 Joe Fordham, '*Coraline*: A Handmade World', *Cinefex*, no. 117 (2009), pp. 41–61; Andrea Comiskey, '(Stop)Motion Control: Special Effects in Contemporary Puppet Animation', in Dan North, Bob Rehak and Michael S. Duffy (eds), *Special Effects: New Histories/Theories/Contexts* (London: Palgrave, 2015), pp. 45–61; Ken A. Priebe, *The Advanced Art of Stop-Motion Animation* (Boston, MA: Cengage Learning, 2010), p. xvii.

5 V. S. Ramachandran and William Hirstein, 'The Science of Art: A Neurological Theory of Aesthetic Experience', *Journal of Consciousness Studies: Controversies in Science and the Humanities*, vol. 6, no. 6–7 (1999), pp. 15–51.

6 Ibid., p. 8.

7 Ramachandran and Hirstein, 'The Science of Art: A Neurological Theory of Aesthetic Experience'; David Freedberg and Vittorio Gallese, 'Motion, Emotion and Empathy in Esthetic Experience', *Trends in Cognitive Science*, vol. 11, no. 5 (2007), pp. 197–203; Semir Zeki, 'Art and the Brain', *Journal of Consciousness Studies: Controversies in Science and the Humanities*, vol. 10, no. 3 (1999), pp. 76–96; Marcos Nadal and Anjan Chatterjee, 'Neuroaesthetics and Art's Diversity and Universality', *Wiley Interdisciplinary Reviews: Cognitive Science*, vol. 10, no. 6 (2019).

8 Mark F. Bear, Barry W. Connors and Michael A. Paradiso, *Neuroscience: Exploring the Brain* (Philadelphia: Lippincott Williams & Wilkins, 2007), p. 167.

9   Jan Švankmajer, *Touching and Imagining: An Introduction to Tactile Art* (London: I.B. Tauris, 2014), pp. 26–81.

10 Ibid., pp. 26–81.

11 Ellen Rocha, 'Beyond Materiality in Animation: Sensuous Perception and Touch in the Tactile Existence of "Would a Heart Die?"', *Animation Studies*, vol. 11 (2016). https://journal.animationstudies.org (accessed 17 March 2020).

12 Jean Decety and Julie Grèzes, 'The Power of Simulation: Imagining One's Own and Other's Behavior', *Brain Research*, vol. 1079, no. 1 (2006), p. 4; Freedberg and Gallese, 'Motion, Emotion and Empathy in Esthetic Experience', p. 197.

13 Vittorio Gallese and Alvin Goldman, 'Mirror Neurons and the Simulation Theory of Mind-Reading', *Trends in Cognitive Science*, vol. 2, no. 12 (1998), p. 496.

14 Decety and Grèzes, 'The Power of Simulation: Imagining One's Own and Other's Behavior', pp. 4–14; Gallese and Goldman, 'Mirror Neurons and the Simulation Theory of Mind-Reading', pp. 493–501; Giacomo Rizzolatti and Laila Craighero, 'The Mirror-Neuron System', *Annual Review of Neuroscience*, vol. 27 (2004), pp. 169–92.

15 Rizzolatti and Craighero, 'The Mirror-Neuron System', p. 169.

16 Decety and Grèzes, 'The Power of Simulation: Imagining One's Own and Other's Behavior'; Gallese and Goldman, 'Mirror Neurons and the Simulation Theory of Mind-Reading'; Rizzolatti and Craighero, 'The Mirror-Neuron System', p. 174.

17 I. G. Meister, T. Krings, H. Foltys, B. Boroojerdi, M. Muller, R. Topper and A. Thron, 'Playing Piano in the Mind – an fMRI Study on Music Imagery and Performance in Pianists', *Cognitive Brain Research*, vol. 19, no. 3 (2004), pp. 219–28.

18 P. F. Ferrari, C. Maiolini, E. Addessi, L. Fogassi and E. Visalberghi, 'The Observation and Hearing of Eating Actions Activates Motor Programs Related to Eating in Macaque Monkeys', *Behavioral Brain Research*, vol. 161, no. 1 (2005), pp. 95–101; Rizzolatti and Craighero, 'The Mirror-Neuron System', p. 171.

19 Decety and Grèzes, 'The Power of Simulation: Imagining One's Own and Other's Behavior', p. 4; Freedberg and Gallese, 'Motion, Emotion and Empathy in Esthetic Experience', p. 197.

20 Decety and Grèzes, 'The Power of Simulation: Imagining One's Own and Other's Behavior', pp. 7–8; Meister, Krings, Foltys, Boroojerdi, Muller, Topper and Thron, 'Playing Piano in the Mind – an fMRI Study on Music Imagery and Performance in Pianists'.

21 Decety and Grèzes, 'The Power of Simulation: Imagining One's Own and Other's Behavior', p. 8; Freedberg and Gallese, 'Motion, Emotion and Empathy in Esthetic Experience', p. 201; Tania Singer, Ben Seymour, John O'Doherty, Holgar Kaube, Raymond J. Dolan and Chris D. Frith, 'Empathy for Pain Involves the Affective but Not Sensory Components of Pain', *Science*, vol. 303, no. 20 (2004), pp. 1157–62.

22 Decety and Grèzes, 'The Power of Simulation: Imagining One's Own and Other's Behavior', p. 7; Rizzolatti and Craighero, 'The Mirror-Neuron System', p. 180.

23 Decety and Grèzes, 'The Power of Simulation: Imagining One's Own and Other's Behavior', pp. 4–14; Gallese and Goldman, 'Mirror Neurons and the Simulation Theory of Mind-Reading', pp. 493–501; Rizzolatti and Craighero, 'The Mirror-Neuron System', pp. 169–92.

24 Giovanni Buccino, Lui Fausta, Nicola Canessa, Ilaria Patteri, Giovanna Lagravinese, Francesca Benuzzi, Carlo A. Porro and Giacomo Rizzolatti, 'Neuroal Circuits Involved in the Recognition of Actions Performed by Nonconspecifics: An Fmri Study', *Journal of Cognitive Neuroscience*, vol. 16, no. 1 (2004), pp. 114–26.

25 Kevin A. Pelphrey, Teresa V. Mitchell, Martin J. KcKeown, Jeremy Goldstein, Truett Allison and Gregory McCarthy, 'Brain Activity Evoked by the Perception of Human Walking: Controlling for Meaningful Coherent Motion', *Journal of Neuroscience*, vol. 23, no. 17 (2003), pp. 6819–25.

26 Ayse Pinar Saygin, Stephen M. Wilson, Donald J. Hagler Jr, Elizabeth Bates and Martin I. Sereno, 'Point-Light Biological Motion Perception Activates Human Premotor Cortex', *Journal of Neuroscience*, vol. 24, no. 27 (2004), pp. 6181–8.

27 Freedberg and Gallese, 'Motion, Emotion and Empathy in Esthetic Experience', p. 201.

28 Freedberg and Gallese, 'Motion, Emotion and Empathy in Esthetic Experience', p. 199.

29 Günther Knoblich, Eva Seigerschmidt, Rüdiger Flach and Wolfgang Prinz, 'Authorship Effects in the Prediction of Handwriting Strokes: Evidence for Action Simulation During Action Perception', *Quarterly Journal of Experimental Psychology*, vol. 55, no. 3 (2002), pp. 1027–46.

30 Sean Wilson, 'Exclusive Interview: Early Man Director Nick Park Talks Aardman, Bristol and Eddie Redmayne', *Cineworld*, 31 January 2018. http://www.cineworld.co.uk/blog/early-man-aardman-nick-park-interview (accessed 17 March 2020); Caroline Briggs, 'Gromit Film "a Force for Britishness"', *BBC News*, 9 October 2005. http://news.bbc.co.uk/1/hi/entertainment/4309544.stm (accessed 17 March 2020).

31 Ellen Rocha, 'Beyond Materiality in Animation: Sensuous Perception and Touch in the Tactile Existence of "Would a Heart Die?"'

32 Decety and Grèzes, 'The Power of Simulation: Imagining One's Own and Other's Behavior', p. 7.

33 Scott H. Johnson-Frey, Farah R. Maloof, Roger Newman-Norlund, Chloe Farrer Souheil Inati and Scott T. Grafton, 'Actions or Hand-Object Interactions? Human Inferior Frontal Cortex and Action Observation', *Neuron*, vol. 39, no. 11 (2011), pp. 1053–8.

34 Freedberg and Gallese, 'Motion, Emotion and Empathy in Esthetic Experience', p. 200.

35 Priebe, *The Advanced Art of Stop-Motion Animation*, p. 56.

36 Peter Lord, 'Foreword', in Ray Harryhausen and Tony Dalton (eds), *A Century of Stop Motion Animation: From Méliès to Aardman* (New York: Random House, 2008), p. 9.

37 Gaiman, *Coraline*, p. 10.

38 Ibid., p. 91.

39 Ibid., p. 31.

40 Michael Frierson, 'Tim Burton's "Vincent" – a Matter of Pastiche', *Animation World Network Magazine*, vol. 1, no. 9 (1996). https://www.awn.com/mag/issue1.9/articles/frierson1.9.html (accessed 9 August 2019).

41 Ramachandran and Hirstein, 'The Science of Art: A Neurological Theory of Aesthetic Experience', pp. 15–51.

8

Darkness and delight: The reception of *Coraline* in the United States and the UK

Rayna Denison

The title for this chapter is borrowed from a *New York Post* review of *Coraline* (2009), written by Lou Lumenick, which captures the essence of the discourses swirling around Henry Selick's film on its release. Lumenick remarks that *Coraline* is 'wonderfully creepy', filled with Selick's 'dark sensibilities', and offering an adaptation of Neil Gaiman's 'twisted variation of "Alice in Wonderland"', which Lumenick claims is

> perhaps the most effective 3-D movie I have ever seen, with a sophisticated, involving story that will appeal to many adults. The only reservation I have is with the PG rating, which seems too lenient for a story that may give very young children – particularly if they are sensitive – nightmares.[1]

Lumenick's assessment of *Coraline* rehearses the main debate residing at the heart of the film's reception: a darkness that delights but refuses to sit comfortably within the Parental Guidance (PG) ratings category. This chapter investigates the contradictions between darkness and delight as they played out in the news, magazine and trade reception for *Coraline* in the United States and the UK. I argue that the conflict was born of the commingling of two sets of discourses: first, concerns about increasing amounts of horror and violence in children's films enabled by a 'ratings creep' in both the United States and the UK in the late 2000s;[2] and second, a debate that centred on the film's innovations in stop motion and 3D animation techniques. When combined, these two discourses created a near-paradox within *Coraline*'s reception – with positive appraisals of this 'dark' modern fairy tale's animation contrasting sharply with concerns about its potential negative impact on child audiences. Journalists in the United States and the UK have questioned the extent to which children's horror is desirable, while at the same time lauding the animation techniques that make it so. *Coraline* is, therefore, a useful case study for thinking about the role of critics in negotiating and interpreting the meanings of ratings systems, and the film also provides a window onto a set of debates about the place of animation within culture.

In order to examine how the reception of *Coraline* solidified, I adopt the historical materialist reception method laid out by Janet Staiger.[3] My use of this approach is tempered by Barbara Klinger's variation on reception studies, particularly her concerns about the lack of scope, and sometimes generalizability, found in synchronic reception case studies.[4] Time is, however, only a single contextualizing valence, and we might also consider many others, including nation, language, age, gender or sexuality. In my study of *Coraline*, therefore, I have chosen to expand the 'case study' parameters of Staiger's method along three vectors. Firstly, I draw a comparison between two national reception contexts: the United States and the UK. This transnational approach has been taken in part because the promotional materials created for *Coraline* placed heavy emphasis on the transnational as a key part of the film's development and production, most especially contrasting the work of British author Neil Gaiman and the US-production team at LAIKA, under director Henry Selick.[5] Secondly, the United States and the UK have similar histories of news, magazine and trade press coverage, they share a common language and, additionally, the UK acts as a significant secondary market for US film releases. Consequently, the UK's reception of US-produced films can be read dialogically, with the UK's critics sometimes responding to the work of their US-based counterparts. Finally, in the case of *Coraline*, choosing these two contexts also allows me to expand the temporal dimension of the study. There was a temporal lag of three months between the United States and the UK releases that turns this potentially synchronic study of *Coraline*'s release into an – albeit relatively short – diachronic study.[6] This transnational reception study revealed the existence of critical consternation about the film's PG rating in both the United States and the UK and in both this was juxtaposed with *Coraline*'s innovative uses of old and new animation technologies.[7]

Censors, critics, ratings and suitability; or, how *Coraline* means taking PG seriously

The ratings systems in the United States and the UK are somewhat similar but have developed independently of one another, and in different periods.

The UK's is the older of the two systems, beginning in 1912, whereas the current US ratings system was introduced in 1968.[8] A report by the UK's British Board of Film Classification (BBFC), outlining the similarities and differences, notes that the 'unrestricted' parts of each system (from the G for General in the United States and U for Universal in the UK, to PG) are similar and that in each country decisions about ratings are made by a small board of non-experts (sixteen in the UK and twelve in the United States), following a set of guidelines in each case. However, the similarities in ratings categories do not necessarily indicate that these ratings are universally applied, and their basic starting points are also different. In the UK, the basis for the guidelines is the Human Rights Act of 1998, which places emphasis on allowing adult viewers to access films whenever possible. In the United States, by contrast, greater emphasis is placed on parental expectations of films, and examiners have to be parents whose children may be affected by the ratings they apply.[9] The language of the Motion Picture Association of America's (MPAA) Classification and Rating Administration (CARA) is, perhaps as a consequence, more overt about who its ratings are for: 'Today's voluntary movie rating system is aimed at giving parents the information they need to decide whether a film is appropriate for their family.'[10] In the UK, by contrast, the BBFC claims that their ratings categories were set up 'to provide guidance to the UK's local authorities' who have the legal power to enforce the BBFC's recommendations.[11]

As this suggests, the purposes and roles of the ratings systems in the United States and the UK differ substantially, despite resulting in similar outcomes for *Coraline*: a Parental Guidance (PG) rating. Within academic debates about the ratings systems, Noel Brown and Bruce Babington have argued that ratings systems tend to be child-focused, rather than adult-focused as the BBFC report suggests. Taking a global view, Brown and Babington argue that 'acting on the need to protect children from too-early exposure to disturbing content (e.g. physical and psychological violence; overt sexuality) has been a constant in the history of film, contingent on shifting societal norms and expectations'.[12] Their assessment cleaves closely to the 'media effects' tradition, which is often rehearsed by a wide variety of commentators worrying about the effect media texts can have on 'vulnerable' audiences. Martin Barker and Julian Petley have roundly criticized this stance, noting that part of the problem resides in attempts to conceptualize childhood as an unchanging and universal constant. As Barker and Petley note, many critics' assessments of what childhood is and how it operates efface the experiences and opinions of real children, in favour of adult interpretations of children and childhood.[13]

Heather Hendershot argues that children's media are firmly ensconced in these debates, and her approach informs how I have assessed the critical responses to *Coraline*. Hendershot contends that 'adults both produce and censor TV for children, and they speak to and for children through such activities'.[14] As with television, so too with films aimed at children. Hendershot's example is useful in that its discursive, historical focus is not dissimilar to the study proposed here. But, more importantly, her focus on adults and their accounts about children's imagined reception are vital to understanding the roles film journalists play in making sense of a film like *Coraline*. Nor is Hendershot's the only account to adopt this position. Filipa Antunes, for example, argues that the creation of the PG-13 category of filmmaking was the result of several PG-rated films pushing at the boundaries of critical conceptions of childhood, pointing to 'an alteration of the structure of childhood in Western society in its distinction between early childhood (before the age of 13) and late childhood (adolescence)'.[15] Both authors demonstrate the range of ways adults, including film critics, shape and police the borders of children's media cultures, which is the focus of my own investigation into *Coraline*.

Coraline offers a particularly notable instance where newspaper critics' debates about 'ratings creep' coalesced into warnings to parents about taking *Coraline*'s PG rating seriously. In the UK, *Coraline* became so controversial that the BBFC did its own 'case study' report on the film, defending its decision to award the film a PG rating. The BBFC claims that

> despite the scariness, the film features a number of 'mitigating factors' – elements which lessen the intensity of the more frightening scenes ... Not all parents agreed with the PG classification for *Coraline*, however, and some wrote to the BBFC to complain that their children had been scared by the film – some to the point of having to leave the cinema.[16]

The image of traumatized children fleeing cinemas was one that repeated in the discourse on *Coraline*'s release, especially in the UK. For example, Graham Young, writing for the *Birmingham Evening Mail*, declared *Coraline* 'the first "X-Certificate" PG-rated movie for children', going on to claim that 'during last weekend's preview screening at the Odeon New Street, some children were leaving before half-way and some of those were in tears'.[17]

However, in the United States, extreme reviews were more likely to claim that *Coraline* had the power to psychologically damage children, rather than temporarily traumatizing them:

> Good news for family psychiatrists across the land: 'Coraline' is opening today, which means on Monday they'll have a whole new clientele of traumatized young children whose parents saw the PG rating and thought this was the latest 'Kung Fu Panda'.[18]

In both cases, the ratings system sits at the crux of the debate. In the first instance, the critic's response is to push for an adults-only rating for the film, whereas the second, Ty Burr's account in the *Boston Globe*, suggests that the problem with *Coraline* is that the film does not compare easily to other animated films of the period. Each response demonstrates how fiercely critics in both countries police the boundaries between ratings categories. They both also present the critic-as-moral-guardian, a role that film critics frequently adopt for films that sit on the border between adult and children's media.

Gary Thompson, writing for the *Philadelphia Daily News*, explains the critic's gatekeeper role in relation to children's films:

> I was once accosted by a parent who wanted to know why I didn't warn people that 'Finding Nemo' was 'dark'.
>
> Lesson learned: You never know what's going to frighten some children. Given that, I'd say that if 'Nemo' were too dark for your kids, or the post-apocalyptic 'Wall-E' too bleak, then stay far away from the 3-D 'Coraline', the most unnerving kids movie in many a full moon, and one of the best.[19]

As Thompson's anecdote shows, critics have developed a nuanced contextual set of recommendations for parents that goes beyond the ratings system. Here, Thompson uses a comparative, film-centred formula, which places Pixar's animated films at the heart of the meanings and expectations for contemporary animation. This is part of a nuanced and highly developed alternative ratings system that operates within professional critical reviews. Sometimes, as in this example, critics use comparative analysis, while at other times, they refer to children's ages, or simply repeat, exaggerate or add to the language used by the ratings bodies themselves.

This loosely formulated alternative ratings system comes in a variety of forms. For example, the *New York Observer*'s review ends with the following statement: 'Who should see it: Young girls who shop in Hot Topic.'[20] This assessment is both dismissive and a complex commentary on *Coraline*'s perceived audience. The Hot Topic retail chain in the United States sells merchandise and clothing aimed at a general teen market, focusing on licensed items from films and television, including a range based on Selick's previous success *The Nightmare before Christmas* (1993). Therefore, this judgement doubly categorizes *Coraline*'s potential audiences, asserting that it is the exclusive province of girls' culture, whilst also suggesting that it will become a popular or cult teen text.

In more generic examples of this alternative ratings system, critics often assessed *Coraline* not just for its potential impact on children but for its impact on adults and children alike. For example, one reviewer for the UK's *Sunday Business Post* claimed that '*Coraline* might be too much for sensitive members of the pre-teen audience. It was almost too much for me',[21] and George Lange from the *Oklahoman* declared that 'while this is not for small children, adults who never fully grew up will relish every moment inside the Other world of "Coraline".'[22] Again, these reviews read as extremes, on the one hand suggesting that *Coraline* is almost too frightening for some adults, while on the other hand implying that it is a film for immature adults incapable of growing up. From girls to infantilized adults, the variety seen in these attempts to pin down the nature of the 'correct' audiences for *Coraline* in the United States and the UK suggests that critics found the film consternatingly resistant to categorization.

In answer to this problem, reviewers tended to relate their assessments of *Coraline* to an imagined family audience. In these cases, the language in both countries tends to be more proscriptive, taking on a warning tone. For instance, the *Atlanta Journal-Constitution*'s review of *Coraline* concludes with the following: 'Parents Guide: The film revels in the nightmarish elements of classic fairy tales that scare and delight kids. Exciting fare for most kids 8 and older, but with the strong caveat that some easily spooked kids as old as 10 or 12 may find the film upsetting.'[23] *Time Out London*'s Tom Huddleston likewise concluded that *Coraline*'s 'dark edge will be the biggest test of the film as a commercial prospect: it may be too terrifying for the target audiences. But for braver kids – and parents – this is a thrilling, even challenging ride.'[24] These kinds of family-oriented commentaries return us to questions about the PG category in the United States and the UK.

Critics' questions about the applicability of the PG rating for *Coraline* worked in contradistinction to the promotional interviews with the film's cast and crew. Selick, in particular, was repeatedly quoted dismissing claims that the film was too scary for children. Selick makes the case that the film should be seen as 'a PG movie for brave children from 8 to 88. It's ludicrous to pretend that kids don't like a good scare.' In the same interview, he goes on to state that *Coraline* suffers from the tendency of adults to read it from their own perspective:

> Kids identify with Coraline ... We found that they see her story as an adventure. So they're not worried about it in the way a parent is. Parents are hard-wired to want to protect their children. But I think it's the kids who will be holding their parents' hand to reassure them in the theatre.[25]

Roger Ebert, one of the United States' more famous film critics, countered by stating that 'the director of "Coraline" has suggested it is for brave children of any age. That's putting it mildly. This is nightmare fodder for children, however brave, under a certain age.'[26] Ebert's challenge to Selick's promotional discourse echoes the way critics took up advisory positions throughout *Coraline*'s reception, pushing back against its PG rating and promotional discourse alike.

As a result, a split in the meanings of the PG rating becomes visible. For the ratings boards, PG indicates that parents should attend to the warnings and cautions provided in detail; but, for parents and critics, PG seems to have become a marker of a film's unchallenging content. *Coraline* seems to have caused controversy because it met the letter of the PG rating, but not the essence of what that category meant to critics and parents in the United States and the UK. This would explain why critics in both the United States and the UK were enjoining parents to take *Coraline*'s PG rating more seriously than normal.

The controversies within *Coraline*'s reception align the film with other academic studies on the way film ratings were being renegotiated in the late 2000s. The boundaries appear to have been blurring between U/G, PG and PG-13/12A in the United States and the UK, and critics were working to find new age ranges and comparative methods to ensure that parents were satisfied with their reviews. As a consequence, when *Coraline* was released in the United States and the UK, the film was pulled between the desires of industry (for a low and non-restricted rating), ratings institutions (who want to inform parents or government about film content) and critics (who want to intervene between parents, industry and ratings bodies). The debates about how to categorize *Coraline* reflect a perpetual process of negotiation at work in ratings systems, wherein the reception of films consistently works as pressure for the redefinition of ratings categories in relation to new types of content.

Sucked into the darkness: 3D and stop motion as the 'perfect' medium for the scary fairy tale

In both Antunes's account of the PG-13 rating, and Catherine Lester's analysis of the children's horror genre, animation has played key roles in testing the boundaries between ratings categories.[27] Perhaps the most obvious example of animation's brushes with rating controversies can be found in the case of anime's encounters with ratings boards. Emma Pett's study of the controversial *Urotsukidōji* anime films' releases in the UK, for example, demonstrates the way adult-oriented animation can split examiners. In the case of *Urotsukidōji* – a series of pornographic science fiction and horror anime Original Video Animations – Pett finds that the medium of animation allowed some examiners to see the films as fantastical and divorced from reality, while others 'argued that the animation medium made the film potentially more harmful' because of the medium's association with children's media.[28] *Coraline*'s assessment by film critics as children's horror animation similarly calls into question the stop-motion animation medium's association with horror aesthetics.

The production team and film critics for *Coraline* were keen to draw parallels between the way their film flirts with the horror genre, and the way past animated classics also draw upon the darker side of fairy-tale storytelling.[29] Selick and Gaiman both repeatedly invoked early Disney films as 'scary' counterpoints to *Coraline*, with Gaiman claiming in one interview that, 'if you have a kid who can cope with Disney's "Snow White," they will have no problem with "Coraline." It's just the same amount of scary, possibly less brutal than that.'[30] Selick also regularly compared *Coraline* with *Pinocchio* (Norman Ferguson et al., 1940) and *Fantasia* (Samuel Armstrong et al., 1940) and stated that 'we're still in tune with that, we just haven't made those sort [*sic*] of animated films in this country since the early Disney, but there is a tradition. We're just reviving that.'[31] Critics picked up on this strand of defensive comparison, with one US journalist echoing the production team's claims directly: 'Selick – who wrote the screenplay, directed and was the production designer – follows the classic Walt Disney model, which says even fairy tales have some dark scares at their core.'[32] Working to offset concerns about *Coraline*'s associations with the horror genre, these allusions to Disney act as a reminder to parents that children's horror is part of classic animation culture in the United States and the UK. In turn, they also associate *Coraline* with some of US animation's earliest and most innovative feature films.[33]

However, journalists' comparison points for *Coraline* were inventively wide. On the one hand, the film's association with Gaiman's novel seems to have inspired literary comparisons, especially comparisons to film versions of classic genre storytelling and children's literature. For example, Dana Stevens, writing for *Slate*, argues that *Coraline*'s comparators include classic children's literature from *The Lion, the Witch and the Wardrobe* to *The Wizard of Oz* and even classic horror films like *Invasion of the Body Snatchers* (Don Siegel, 1956).[34] The range of touchstones used to describe *Coraline*'s content helps to position the new film as part of a long-standing tradition of adaptation from children's literature to film. By contrast, the shift in register to *Invasion of the Body Snatchers* uses an adult-oriented science fiction-horror hybrid to once again suggest a slippage between categories for *Coraline*.

Such slippages were frequent, with *Coraline* compared to everything from *Child's Play* (Tom Holland, 1988) to more recent horror films like *The Haunting in Connecticut* (Peter Cornwell, 2009).[35] *Coraline* was even used in one review as an example of horror more frightening than the newly released *Drag Me to Hell* (Sam Raimi, 2009): '*Coraline*, with its very particular brand of dark weirdness and parents with buttons for eyes, is bizarrely far more psychologically disturbing.'[36] Even though the production team sought to align *Coraline* with animated classics, journalists seemed more interested in making connections to fantasy literature and horror films. This may simply be because *Coraline*'s PG status is easier to call into question by comparison to adult horror films. What emerges from the reception of *Coraline* is a critical hierarchy of horror in which psychological forms of horror in children's animation are seen as more 'disturbing' than effects-heavy, gory and ostensibly adult horror fare.

Coraline's stop-motion animation played a vital role in the horror perceived by critics. Dann Gire of the *Chicago Daily Herald* proclaims,

> The stop-motion animation works its magic, sucking us into a vortex of horrifically exaggerated proportions, inventive transitional shots and frightening, phantasmagorical spectacles, among them anime-inspired ghost children and a spidery monstrosity that easily rivals the best/worst of Disney villains. Digital animation would look too sterile; hand-drawn 2-D animation would look too flat. Selick's medium of choice – old-fashioned stop motion like the kind used in

1933's 'King Kong' – proves to be the ideal way to tell *Coraline*'s scarifying lesson in getting what you wish for.[37]

Here, as elsewhere in *Coraline*'s US and UK reviews, Selick's reputation within the world of stop-motion animation dominates Gire's response to the film, and in this instance, the existence of the computer-generated (CG) augmentations used in many of the sequences cited in the review is elided from the conversation. This privileges not just Selick's position in the stop-motion medium but also the medium's own long industrial history in US cinema.

The attention to detail required by stop-motion animation and its radical potential were also frequently commented upon by critics. The UK's *Daily Telegraph*, for example, takes *Coraline*'s detailed mise-en-scène as a benchmark for undefined notions of 'quality' animation:

> Any animated film with a credit for 'facial structure supervisor' has its eye reassuringly on the small things. Henry Selick's *Coraline*, whose 11-year-old heroine has saucer eyes, a sceptical mouth, and a blue curtain of hair from which ears quizzically protrude, is a gorgeously hand-crafted and pleasurably detailed piece of work.[38]

Here, as in Gire's previous comment, stop motion is seen as reassuringly old-fashioned and as a craft or even 'artist's' medium and *Coraline*'s CG animation is elided. Ty Burr assesses *Coraline*'s use of stop motion similarly, but also claims that the medium itself offsets some of the more horror-oriented content of the film. He argues that

> because the technique here is stop-motion clay [*sic*] animation – an old-world, hands-on craft with none of the eerie smoothness of computer rendering – the film feels warm and fussed over. It's the product of humans instead of machines. Like its heroine and like its audience, it has a soul.[39]

Here, in contrast to some of the earlier reviews, we can see how the traditions of stop-motion animation become a cipher for 'old-world' animation craft, privileged in the face of what Burr perceives as a CG animation onslaught. Stop-motion animation, then, is accorded numerous roles in *Coraline*: it is a way of generating horror, while also infusing the film with a sense of 'traditional' animation that makes the film feel 'warm and fussed over'. While seemingly paradoxical, the unease generated by the uncanny potential of *Coraline*'s stop-motion animation also acts as evidence for its handmade, detail-oriented craft aesthetic. As a production of 'hands-on craft', *Coraline* is made simultaneously appreciable as a known art form and an uncanny terror.

If stop motion made *Coraline* a 'product of humans', its innovative uses of 3D sealed its reception as high calibre children's horror. Notably, in one of the first accounts of the history of film ratings, Stephen Vaughn argues that technology plays crucial roles in how films are assessed.[40] Echoing this assessment, the critical discourse around *Coraline* was centred on the marriage of 'traditional' stop motion with Real 3D. In the UK, the race to install new 3D projectors was even blamed for a delay in releasing *Coraline*, not least because the more expensive 3D screens had been so central to the film's box office takings in the United States.[41] Most reviewers in both countries also noted that *Coraline* was the first stop-motion film to be shot in digital 3D, perhaps making it unsurprising that discussions of stop motion and 3D came to dominate the assessments about the film's quality, often eliding the other hybridizations in technique the filmmakers employed when making *Coraline*, such as CG animation of backgrounds and special effects sequences.

Journalists worked hard to make claims about the subtlety, quality and unusual uses of 3D in their reviews of *Coraline*. Their comments often made a point to distinguish *Coraline*'s deployment of 3D from the more common spectacle-oriented uses to which the technique has been put.[42] For example, Dana Stevens argues,

> Unlike CGI, stop-motion animation is a tactile medium, its textures and volumes vividly palpable. The pink, gabled house in which Coraline and her parents live looks and feels like a dollhouse full of marvelous small objects (a tiny stuffed toy, a hand-stitched sweater) that the viewer wants to reach in and touch – and the subtly realized 3-D effects make that interaction with the image seem almost possible.[43]

3D, in this instance, adds a near-haptic dimension to *Coraline*, encouraging the viewer to reach in and touch the characters and emphasizing depth in the image rather than the more common screen extrusions for which 3D is famed.

This was a common refrain in the reviews, with A. O. Scott from the *New York Times* claiming that 'the 3-D aspects of "Coraline" are unusually subtle. Now and then stuff is flung off the screen into your face, but the point is not to make you duck or shriek … The glasses you put on are thus not a gimmick but an aid to seeing what's already there.'[44] Scott's interpretation sees stop motion fused with 3D in *Coraline*, and his assessment that this fusion helps the viewer to 'see what is already there' extends the metaphor. In these debates, concerns about the content of *Coraline* nearly disappear, replaced by a discourse of technological mastery, craft and wonder. The positive tenor of these reviews comes, therefore, from a marriage of technologies wherein the new 3D reveals more about the older stop motion, allowing the audience greater perceived access to the animated imagery.

As these examples indicate, stop motion ran the gamut in reviews, becoming a hallmark of *Coraline*'s quality while at the same time an inherent generator of problematic children's horror content. The marriage with 3D offset some of these critical concerns by generating a competing discourse that, at times, allayed critical debates about ratings. The fact that Selick and his team used 3D as a way to pull audiences into their stop-motion animated world created a critical context for journalists, who seem to have been sucked in, and were also emotionally responding to what they saw.

Conclusion

The two strands of discourse analysed within this chapter have shown the varied roles that critics take upon themselves. On the one hand, journalists tend to amplify industrial promotional discourses, while on the other – and in the case of *Coraline* – being critical of industry and other gatekeeping institutions when films push against cultural norms. Journalists, as this study reveals, have their own systems for rating and assessing films that can wildly disagree with ratings systems. Able to build upon wider cultural understandings of films, reviews deploy generically indiscrete comparators to make sense of films and to advise those who may choose to watch them. In this respect, at least, the function of critics is significant as a mechanism for negotiating and interpreting ratings institutions and systems. That so many of the reviews for *Coraline* made reference to the correct age at which children (or indeed adults) would be safe to watch the feature, further suggests residual tensions around both its medium of production and its generic identity.

One of the remarkable things about the critical reception of *Coraline* was the transnational consensus about what made this film more (and less) acceptable for children in a moment of both industrial change (with Real 3D) and renegotiation of ratings systems in the United States and the UK (following in the aftermath of introducing new PG-13 and 12 ratings that competed with the PG rating in the United States and the UK, respectively). The traditional becomes the counterpoint to these changes, making stop-motion animation a key discussion topic for critics. This was often carried out at the expense of recognizing LAIKA's CG animation augmentations of Henry Selick's stop-motion techniques. Indeed, stop motion was credited with the creation of an already notionally three-dimensional world that the new 3D techniques could augment in a way that writes out other kinds of animation from the discourse around *Coraline*.

Furthermore, and perhaps most tellingly, these accounts repeated and became exaggerated over time as *Coraline* shifted from its US to UK release context. The time lag between releases seems to have engendered a doubling-down on ratings debates by critics in this instance. In these ways, the reception of *Coraline* in the United States and the UK worked to police the boundaries between children's horror and adult horror, while simultaneously and repeatedly reinforcing the importance of stop-motion animation to the history of horror filmmaking. On the one hand, then, darkness lingered around perceptions of genre and concerns about shifting cultural standards in US filmmaking, while delight was to be had from the craftsmanship on display in *Coraline*. The result was reception that both suggested audiences should be cautious about and embrace *Coraline* by turns, never presenting a consensus view on the film. On its release, therefore, *Coraline* was a set of confounding contradictions for critics: it was full of new spectacle, but prized for traditional animation techniques; it was steeped in genre traditions that were seen as adult and child-oriented by turns, and that is how *Coraline* became a darkness that delights.

Notes

1   Lou Lumenick, 'Darkness & Delight', *New York Post*, 6 February 2009, p. 38.
2   Filipa Antunes, 'Rethinking PG-13: Ratings and the Boundaries of Childhood and Horror', *Journal of Film and Video*, vol. 69, no. 1 (2017), pp. 27–43; Ron Leone and Lauri Barowski, 'MPAA Ratings Creep: A Longitudinal Analysis of the PG-13 Rating Category in US Movies', *Journal of Children and Media*, vol. 5, no. 1 (2011), pp. 53–68.
3   Janet Staiger, *Perverse Spectators: The Practices of Film Reception* (New York: New York University Press, 2000), pp. 161–4; Janet Staiger, *Interpreting*

Films: Studies in the Historical Reception of American Cinema (Princeton: Princeton University Press, 1992).

4 Barbara Klinger, *Melodrama and Meaning: History, Culture, and the Films of Douglas Sirk* (Bloomington: University of Indiana Press, 1994), p. xvii.

5 Stephen Jones, *Coraline: A Visual Companion* (New York: William Morrow for HarperCollins, 2009).

6 Barbara Klinger, 'Film History Terminable and Interminable: Recovering the Past in Reception Studies', *Screen*, vol. 38, no. 2 (1997), pp. 107–28.

7 Clusters of discourse were sought in both contexts, following Staiger's method, and no notable differences in the national reviewing cultures emerged. Staiger, *Perverse Spectators*, p. 163.

8 British Board of Film Classification (BBFC), 'Same Difference? – A Comparison of the British and American Film and DVD Rating Systems', British Board of Film Classification. https://forum.blu-ray.com/showthread.php?t=309139 (accessed 8 September 2018).

9 Ibid.

10 The Classification and Rating Administration (CARA), 'History of the Ratings', filmratings.com. https://filmratings.com/History (accessed 9 September 2018).

11 BBFC, 'Same Difference?'

12 Noel Brown and Bruce Babington, 'Introduction: Children's Films and Family Films', in Noel Brown and Bruce Babington (eds), *Family Film in Global Cinema: The World Beyond Disney* (London: I.B. Tauris, 2015), p. 5.

13 Martin Barker and Julian Petley, 'Introduction', in Martin Barker and Julian Petley (eds), *Ill-Effects: The Media/Violence Debate* (London: Routledge, 1997), p. 6.

14 Heather Hendershot, *Saturday Morning Censors: Television Regulation before the V-Chip* (Durham, NC: Duke University Press, 1998), pp. 6–7.

15 Antunes, 'Rethinking PG-13: Ratings and the Boundaries of Childhood and Horror', p. 29.

16 BBFC, 'Case Studies: Coraline', British Board of Film Classification. http://www.bbfc.co.uk/case-studies/coraline (accessed 1 September 2018).

17 Graham Young, 'Animation May be the First X-Certificate', *Birmingham Evening Mail*, 8 May 2009, p. 31.

18 Ty Burr, '*Coraline*: Alice in Freudland', *Boston Globe*, 6 February 2009. http://archive.boston.com/ae/movies/articles/2009/02/06/alice_in_freudland/ (accessed 1 September 2018).

19 Gary Thompson, '"Coraline" May be Unnerving for the Kids', *Philadelphia Daily News*, 6 February 2009, p. 38.

20 Anon., 'Opening this Weekend', *New York Observer*, 6 February 2009.

21 Anon., 'Abrams Boldly goes to Trekkie Heights', *Sunday Business Post*, 10 May 2009.

22 George Lang, 'World of "Coraline" Worth a Visit', *The Oklahoman*, 6 February 2009, p. 5D.

23 Anonymous, 'Movies: New This Week', *Atlanta Journal-Constitution*, 6 February 2009, p. 8E.

24 Tom Huddleston, '*Coraline*', *Time Out*, 5 May 2009. https://www.timeout.com/london/film/coraline (accessed 1 September 2018).

25 Selick, quoted in Paul Liberator, 'Movie Director Animates his "Weird Imagination"', *Marin Independent Journal*, 4 February 2009.

26 Roger Ebert, '*Coraline* (2009)', Roger Ebert.com, 4 February 2009. https://www.rogerebert.com/reviews/coraline-2009 (accessed 9 September 2018).

27 Catherine Lester, 'The Children's Horror Film: Characterizing an "Impossible" Subgenre', *Velvet Light Trap*, no. 78 (2016), p. 23.

28 Emma Pett, '"Blood, Guts and Bambi Eyes": *Urotsukidōji* and the Transcultural Reception and Regulation of Anime', *Journal of British Cinema and Television*, vol. 13, no. 3 (2016), p. 400.

29 Lester, 'The Children's Horror Film'.

30 Barbara Vancheri, 'PG-Rated Movies with More Kick are Catching Parents Off-Guard', *Pittsburgh Post-Gazette*, 6 February 2009. https://www.post-gazette.com/ae/movies/2009/02/06/PG-rated-movies-with-more-kick-are-catching-parents-off-guard/stories/200902060205 (accessed 9 September 2018).

31 Steven Rea, 'On Movies: "*Coraline*" Animator Started with the Story', *Philadelphia Inquirer*, 1 February 2009, p. H02.

32 Sean P. Means, 'Movie Review: Take a Trip to the Dark Side with "*Coraline*"', *Salt Lake Tribune*, 5 February 2009.

33 Chris Pallant, *Demystifying Disney: A History of Disney Feature Animation* (London: Bloomsbury, 2013).

34 Dana Stevens, 'Button Eyes', *Slate*, 5 February 2009. http://www.slate.com/articles/arts/movies/2009/02/button_eyes.html?via=gdpr-consent (accessed 9 September 2018).

35 Young, 'Animation May be First X-Certificate'.

36 Grant Lauchlans, 'A Hell of a Movie', *Daily Record*, 29 May 2009, pp. 50–1.

37 Dann Gire, 'Creepy Stop-Motion Animation Highlights "*Coraline*"', *Chicago Daily Herald*, 5 February 2009, p. 19.

38 Tim Robey, '*Coraline*', *Daily Telegraph*, 8 May 2009, p. 31.

39 Burr, '*Coraline*: Alice in Freudland'.

40 Stephen Vaughn, *Freedom and Entertainment: Rating the Movies in an Age of New Media* (Cambridge: Cambridge University Press, 2006), p. 3.

41 James Tully, 'The Future is Here!', *The Argus*, 26 March 2009.

42 Keith Johnston, '"Three Times as Thrilling!": The Lost History of 3-D Trailer Production, 1953–54', *Journal of Popular Film and Television*, vol. 36, no. 3 (2008), pp. 152–3.

43 Stevens, 'Button Eyes'.

44 A. O. Scott, 'Cornered in a Parallel World', *New York Times*, 6 February 2009, p. C1.

Part Three

Puppet politics: Ideology, identity, representation

9

The Other Maiden, Mother, Crone(s): Witchcraft, queer identity and political resistance in LAIKA's *Coraline*

Kodi Maier

Introduction

Science fiction and fantasy author Neil Gaiman once wrote, 'Fairy tales are more than true: not because they tell us that dragons exist, but because they tell us that dragons can be beaten.'[1] There are plenty of dragons to be fought: fascism, white supremacy, sexism, homophobia, transphobia, xenophobia, ableism and countless other institutional systems of oppression. The task of resisting, disrupting and dismantling these structures can be overwhelming, if not outright terrifying. Yet such work is necessary to create more equitable, inclusive societies. Where can a person find the inspiration and strength to continue to fight for social justice? One source is in works of fiction and fantasy – which is to say, modern fairy tales. In discussing his motivation for writing the young adult fantasy novella, *Coraline*, Gaiman notes that 'the point of it was to write a story for my daughters to tell them that being brave didn't mean that you weren't scared, it meant that you were scared but you did the right thing anyway'.[2]

Gaiman's message to his daughters holds true in LAIKA's *Coraline* (2009), a stop-motion adaption of Gaiman's book. Directed by *The Nightmare before Christmas*'s Henry Selick, *Coraline* is about a young girl, Coraline Jones, who moves into a new home and is lured into a fantastical, magical realm created and ruled by a creature who calls herself Coraline's 'Other Mother'. At first this alternate realm seems like a dream come true: the Other Mother showers Coraline with affection and love, making all of her favourite foods, fashioning her stylish new clothes, creating new friends for her to play with and populating the world with wonders to delight and dazzle the senses. When the Other Mother kidnaps her real parents, however, Coraline realizes this dream is actually a nightmare. It is only through her wits and a little bit of magic that she is able to defeat the Other Mother and bring her parents home. Indeed, elements of magic and witchcraft – in the form of black cats, magical stones and clairvoyant witches, not to mention the Other Mother herself – are threaded throughout the film.[3]

Just as witchcraft is an integral part of Coraline's world, so, too, is it important among the disenfranchised in ours. Members of the LGBTQIA+ community have embraced witchcraft in a variety of circumstances, from the women-only covens of 1970s America to the queer activists who organize nationwide rituals and spells to resist former President Donald Trump's oppressive policies.[4] In light of these movements, the film's use of magic and witchcraft opens *Coraline* up to being both a source of inspiration for and an allegory of queer resistance. By modelling Coraline, the Other Mother, and Coraline's neighbours, Miss Forcible and Miss Spink, on the Craft's primary female deity, the Triple Goddess, one can trace Coraline's journey of self-discovery and queer empowerment. For it is through her encounters with these characters that Coraline unearths her own latent power and finds the strength to become a formidable witch/queer.[5]

Witchcraft, outcasts, queers and activists

Witchcraft has long been the realm of the outcast, the deviant and the queer, especially women. Historically, any woman who was not silent and pliant and who did not abide by the numerous, contradictory, misogynist rules set down by patriarchal Western society was considered wayward enough to be labelled a witch. Yet this was not always the case. In 1487, Heinrich Kramer, a German Dominican monk, printed the *Malleus Maleficarum* and effectively forged the link between 'women' and 'witch'. The *Malleus* was a highly influential handbook meant to help priests and other inquisitors identify and neutralize witches. As Sigrid Brauner notes, it was with the *Malleus* that 'witches came to be defined as primarily female, and all women were seen as prone to become witches'.[6] Specifically, it was female sexuality, amalgamated into the figure of the witch, that was to be tried, condemned and ultimately destroyed: Kramer writes in the *Malleus* that 'all witchcraft comes from carnal lust, which is in women insatiable'.[7] Moira Smith further explains that 'many of the crimes (*maleficia*) attributed to witches concerned sexuality: copulation with incubus devils, procuring abortions, causing sterility and stillbirth, and impeding sexual relations between husbands and wives'.[8] Kramer's influence was so widespread that by the nineteenth century his idea of the witch as a terrifying, sexual, supernatural woman had become firmly established in the Western world. American suffragette Matilda Joslyn Gage wrote that 'the persecution of witches ... was simply entrenched misogyny, the goal of which was to repress the intellect of women'.[9] Pagan journalist and author Margot Adler would echo Gage a century later, writing, 'the Witch, after all, is an extraordinary symbol – independent, anti-establishment, strong, and proud. She is political, yet spiritual and magical. The Witch is woman as martyr; she is persecuted by the ignorant; she is the woman who lives outside society and outside society's definition of women'.[10] Thus, the witch ruptures that which is considered 'normal', and her very existence queers female gender roles and expectations for what it means to be a woman within the confines of the cisheteropatriarchy.

It was Adler who documented the birth and growth of Neo-Paganism in her 1979 book, *Drawing Down the Moon*. In a section on Witchcraft and feminism, Adler notes how Wicca, witchcraft and the Triple Goddess intertwined with second wave feminism to empower women and motivate them to political action. She describes how many of the literature and poetry magazines in feminist bookstores bore titles such as '*Hecate, 13th Moon, Dykes and Gorgons, Hera, Wicce,* and *Sinister Wisdom*', illustrating 'the connection between Witchcraft and goddess worship and the women's movement'.[11] Thus, 'the step from [the second wave conscious-raising] group to the coven was not long'.[12] Some of these covens, known as Dianic Covens after the Roman goddess of women, the moon and the hunt, took efforts to completely isolate themselves from the influence of men in order to better engender their own unique sense of power and identity. According to Dianic Priestess Morgan McFarland, the Triple Goddess's iconography was especially powerful for such women, most of whom were lesbians. She notes that 'while most of the members of the [initial] Neo-Pagan movement [were] heterosexual or bisexual, ... the feminist Craft and the movement toward feminist spirituality [seemed] to have a larger percentage of lesbians than either'.[13] Lesbians frequently formed their own feminist covens, creating a space to actively resist patriarchal cultural norms and celebrate their queer sexuality.[14]

Other groups took more direct measures. Started in New York City on Halloween 1968, W.I.T.C.H. (Women's International Terrorist Conspiracy from Hell) was – and is – part protest group, part coven. As their first manifesto states, W.I.T.C.H. is 'an awareness that witches ... were the original guerrillas and resistance fighters against oppression – particularly the oppression of women – down through the ages'.[15] Protests frequently take the form of guerrilla theatre, whereby participants employ props, costuming and other theatrical elements to bring attention to particular social issues. Although the group had disbanded in 1970, W.I.T.C.H. resurfaced in 2016 to participate in the protests against the recently elected Republican president, Donald Trump. When the Women's March on Washington (January 2017) and the March for Science (April 2017) flooded Washington, DC, members of W.I.T.C.H. appeared in the throng, dressed in black smocks and veils to keep their identity anonymous.[16] Like its previous incarnation, the W.I.T.C.H. of today is intensely feminist with an unrelenting focus on intersectionality, especially LGBTQIA+ rights. In their guidelines for establishing new chapters, W.I.T.C.H. PDX (Portland, Oregon) states, 'WE WOULD LOVE IT IF PRIORITY IN STARTING AND ORGANIZING CHAPTERS WERE GIVEN TO PEOPLE OF COLOR AND QUEER & TRANS PEOPLE [sic]'.[17] These guidelines indicate a mission to not only prioritize queer voices in the coven's activism, but a determination to use queer witch power to create a future that 'has no gender'.[18]

While W.I.T.C.H.'s queer craft emphasizes political theatre, activism and intersectional empowerment, other witches employ more traditionally occult techniques as a means of political resistance, that is, casting spells and performing rituals to resist the cissexist, homophobic, transphobic patriarchy in which they live. Catland Books, a metaphysical/occult space in Bushwick, Brooklyn, made international news when it hosted a ritual to hex Donald Trump's Supreme Court nominee (now sitting judge) Brett Kavanaugh. According to co-owner Dakota Hendrix, who organized the event, witchcraft 'has always been practiced by the most downtrodden, disenfranchised and oppressed peoples who have used it as a tool for survival ... to be the arbiter of their own justice since it would be denied by the powers that be'.[19] Such political resistance is woven throughout Hendrix's own practice, creating 'a supernatural form of self-defense that ... includes amulets that fight off miss-gendering [sic], rituals that provide protection when walking down the street, and paying honor to queer and trans ancestors who don't have descendants of their own'.[20] Given the enthusiastic support for Catland's hexing event – 1,800 people marked themselves as 'going' on the event's Facebook page – it is reasonable to assume that Hendrix is not alone in their philosophy.[21]

Emerging power: Coraline as the Maiden

While not all witches worship and invoke the Triple Goddess in their practice, She is nevertheless a powerful figure within the Craft, especially among feminist and queer traditions such as Dianic Wicca. The Triple Goddess manifests as the Maiden, Mother, Crone, or an entity that combines all three. Because 'each aspect reflects different ways in which women can realize their potentials in the world', witches can develop and strengthen their magical abilities by invoking various aspects of the Triple Goddess in their own practice.[22] Of all the Goddess's aspects, Coraline is most closely aligned with the Maiden, who 'represents women's right to own themselves, to be self-directed, and to have a wide variety of skills, talents, and competencies upon which to draw'.[23] As a woman delves into her relationship with the Maiden and her own Maiden self, 'she becomes aware of her strengths, potentials, and abilities to know and understand herself'.[24] Equally, Coraline's narrative focuses on her potential magical abilities and the realization of that potential – the same latent power that the Maiden represents. Thus, like the queer witches who call on the Maiden to help them discover their own magical power, Coraline's arc turns on her potential to be, and her first steps toward becoming, a queer witch.

When the audience first meets Coraline, it is clear she is often dismissed and ignored by the people around her. Her family has just moved into an old Victorian home known as "The Pink Palace', forcing Coraline to leave behind her friends in Michigan. Her parents, caught up in unpacking and working on a gardening catalogue, are too busy to give her any attention. In fact, when Coraline tells her mother she 'almost died', her mother offers a non-committal 'uh-huh' before finally sighing, 'Coraline, I don't have time for you right now'. Coraline's father similarly dismisses her, sending her away to explore the house on her own. Her invisibility and voicelessness extend into her community. Her neighbours, Mr Bobinsky, Wybie Lovat, Miss Forcible and Miss Spink, all consistently call her 'Caroline' and ignore Coraline's efforts to correct them. However, Coraline is not completely powerless: details hinting at her potential strength as a witch are threaded throughout the film. At her first appearance onscreen, she is dowsing for water, a magical practice used to help locate groundwater, and looking for an old, abandoned well. Standing in a fairy ring, wind whipping around her, Coraline chants a spell: 'Magic dowser, magic dowser, show me the well!' (Figure 9.1).[25] Although Coraline does not realize she is standing on the well, that she still finds

Figure 9.1 Coraline, dowsing for water.

it speaks to the potential within her. Wybie seems to subconsciously recognize this potential as well, even if he ignores *her*. He describes her dowsing as 'water-witching' and then calls her a 'Michigan water witch'. Coraline's father also has some intuition of her latent abilities, however obliquely. As he serves dinner, he sings, 'oh my twitchy witchy girl, I think you are so nice'. Later, as Coraline goes to finish off the Other Mother once and for all, she takes up the song for herself. That she does so illustrates the progress she makes over the course of the film: Coraline has reached within herself and started to claim her own 'twitchy witchy' magic.

As with many witches, Coraline has a familiar: the black cat that prowls the grounds of the Pink Palace. Traditionally a witch and her familiar form a pact: the witch promises to care for their familiar while the familiar promises to aid the witch in all her magical dealings. Familiars in early modern Britain would first appear before the witch when she was powerless and 'in some kind of need', wherein the familiar 'would offer help'.[26] This 'help' took multiple forms, including 'making its magical powers available to [the witch]', healing powers, divination and speaking to the dead.[27] In discussing her experiences with her four familiars, witch and writer Marietta Williams elaborates further, noting familiars will 'pass on their vast metaphysical experience and wisdom' and act as a 'wonderful educator in the metaphysical and the craft'.[28] While Coraline and the black cat do not make the traditional pact that Williams describes, Coraline does care for them while the cat guides her through the Other Mother's world.[29] Like the familiars of early modern Britain, the cat first appears to Coraline in a time of need and, like the familiars Williams describes, they offer protection and guidance. When Coraline first tries to leave the Other Mother, one of the Other Mr Bobinsky's circus mice starts to sound an alarm. The cat kills it, removing its glamour and revealing that it is, in fact, one of the Other Mother's spies. The cat also helps Coraline find her missing parents by leading her to a mirror that reflects an image of the Joneses, shivering and covered in snow. These last two details are key in that they help Coraline realize that her parents are locked inside a snow globe on the Other Mother's mantle. Once Coraline decides to rescue her parents, the cat warns, 'You know, you're walking right into her trap.' Coraline insists, to which the cat responds, 'Challenge her, then. She may not play fair, but she won't refuse. She's got a thing for games.' On the cat's council, Coraline then devises a game that plays to her strengths, enabling Coraline to save her parents and the Other Mother's previous victims.

The film further hints at Coraline's potential witch power when she acts as a medium and a healer for the Other Mother's victims. When the Other Mother throws Coraline through a mirror and into a small, abandoned room, she meets three ghost children with buttons for eyes. The ghost children tell her that they gave up their true eyes – and thus their souls – and cannot pass on into the next life. They ask Coraline to help them escape and Coraline agrees. She challenges the Other Mother to a 'finding things game': if she can find the ghost children's lost eyes and her missing parents, the Other Mother has to let all of them go. If Coraline loses, however, then she must stay with the Other Mother forever. Coraline ultimately wins the game and escapes the Other Mother. In her true home at last, she dreams of the ghost children, envisioning them as golden angels free to move on into the afterlife. As Emma Wilby notes, 'cunning folk [i.e. witches] were … valued for their roles as mediators between the living and the dead', and 'it was commonly believed that a ghost who wished to complete unfinished business would be able to communicate it' to a witch.[30] Thus, the witch was summoned to help the ghost resolve their issues and release them to the next life. In restoring the ghost children's eyes, and thus their souls, Coraline acts as a spirit worker as per Wilby's description, thereby releasing the ghost children into the peace of the next life.

Raising power: Coraline meets the (Other) Mother[31]

In the examples above, Coraline's queer witch power remains untapped. Throughout the film, she is unaware of her potential to be a witch, nor does she deliberately use magic, that is, she does not cast a spell to communicate with the ghost children or to defeat the Other Mother. Instead, it is through her trials with the Other Mother that Coraline's latent queer power finally comes to fruition. If Coraline is the Maiden in the film's queer Triple Goddess formulation, then the Other Mother is the Mother, albeit inverted. Traditionally the Mother helps women embrace and develop their own motherly qualities, including those involved in 'birthing, healing, nurturance, sexuality, organization and love'.[32] By working with the Mother, women 'can focus on empowering themselves through reclaiming the positive aspects of such powers ... [and] finding in them sources of strength, pride and direction'.[33] Where the Mother is sensual, however, the Other Mother is frigid and castrating. Where the Mother is nurturing, the Other Mother is devouring and negligent. What is more, the Other Mother is not a mother at all, but the Beldam: a powerful crone who steals children's souls in order to preserve herself. It is only by vanquishing the Other Mother that Coraline finally unlocks her own queer power.

The Other Mother is an inversion of the sensual and sometimes erotic Mother aspect of the Triple Goddess in that she evokes fears of the castrating feminist/ lesbian who haunts modern-day discourse about powerful women. Those who wish to undermine strong-minded, independent women – or delegitimize feminism in general – often refer to such women as 'lesbian' and 'witch' – epithets that allude to men's fears of the castrating woman. Conservative blogger and 'Feminist Fixer' Suzanne Venker illustrates this fear when she warns readers that all feminists want 'is to neuter the American male'.[34] In Venker's estimation, a lesbian and/or queer woman is more threatening because their world is one where 'men, regardless of their social status, are repeatedly told that ... [they] are no longer needed – that women can manage just fine on their own'.[35] Wiccan and Pagan communities are historically more liberal than Venker and her cohorts and thus more accepting of feminist, lesbian and queer women. Yet even within these circles there is a reluctance in letting women become *too* powerful, lest they emasculate male witches. As Alison Harlow notes, 'until several years ago most Craft people had bought the media image of the feminists. For these people, the popular stereotype of the radical feminist and lesbian is more frightening than the traditional stereotype of the Witch is to people outside the Craft.'[36]

The castration anxieties the Other Mother evokes play out in the way she treats the Other Father and the Other Wybie. The Other Father is essentially her puppet, denied any semblance of independence. When Coraline first meets him, the Other Father sings to her from a piano that is an agent of the Other Mother. The piano, outfitted with mechanical arms and gloves that slide over the Other Father's hands, 'plays [him]' like a marionette. Later, when Coraline finds him absently plinking on the keys, he tries to talk to her, but the piano silences him: 'Mustn't talk when Mother's not here', he tells her. What little agency he does possess is further diminished at the climax of the film. When Coraline returns to the Other Mother's world in the hope of rescuing her parents and the ghost children, she discovers that the Other Father has been reduced to a babbling, bumbling pumpkin creature. As he attacks Coraline, he tells her, 'Sorry, so sorry, Mother making me. Don't wanna hurt you.' The Other Father does not demonstrate any sense of autonomy until the end, when he rebels against the Other Mother and gives Coraline the first set of ghost eyes. The Other Mother treats the Other Wybie in much the same way, creating him to be Coraline's personal companion. When Coraline first meets the Other Wybie, she rolls her eyes, brightening only when the Other Mother says, 'I thought you'd like him more if he spoke a little less, so I fixed him' – 'fixed' both in that she did not give the Other Wybie a voice and as a euphemism for 'castrated'. Like the Other Father, the Other Wybie must remain happy and compliant, lest he faces the Other Mother's wrath. The moment the Other Wybie frowns, the Other Mother 'fixes' him further by sewing his mouth into a permanent, close-lipped smile. Much like the Other Father, the Other Wybie's only act of independence is helping Coraline escape the Other Mother's realm.

The Other Mother's inverted nature also emerges in the way she antagonizes, clings to and devours her 'children' instead of loving and caring for them. Aside from her first encounter with Coraline when she showers her with presents and affection, the Other Mother only nurtures Coraline through provocation and resistance, which forces Coraline to become strong enough to overcome the challenges the Other Mother presents. The Other Mother's love is selfish: when Coraline demands to be set free and returned to her real parents, the Other Mother locks her in a shadowy room, telling her, 'You may come out when you learn to be a loving daughter.' As Coraline makes her escape with her parents and the ghost children's souls, the Other Mother screams, 'Don't leave me, don't leave me, I'll die without you!' Indeed, if she cannot feed on Coraline's life, the Other Mother will literally starve. The ghost children tell Coraline that the Other Mother 'locked us here and ate up our lives'. In fact, the Other Mother is no mother at all, but an old crone. The ghost children call her 'the Beldam', a creature who feasts on her young victims' lives and keeps the spectral remains. Neil Gaiman notes that 'a Beldam was originally a Middle English way of saying "grandmother", which then came to be used for "crone" (a more metaphorical grandmother) and then, sometimes, off at the edges of that, "witch"'.[37] Thus, the Other Mother is no true M/mother, but a darker, inverted version: a powerful crone who lures children to her web and devours their love and life.

Sharing power: Coraline and the Crone(s)

While Coraline's reluctant cat familiar and the Other Mother are key figures in her journey to becoming a powerful queer witch, her elderly lesbian neighbours, Miss Miriam Forcible and Miss April Spink, are arguably the most crucial. Like goddesses foretelling the heroine's future and arming her to meet her fate, Forcible and Spink foresee the Other Mother in Coraline's tea leaves and give her the green, perforated stone – a hag stone – that helps her win her contest with the Other Mother (Figure 9.2).[38] Multiple cues throughout *Coraline* point to both Miss Forcible and Miss Spink's lesbian relationship and their ties to the Triple Goddess's Crone aspect, thus making them the queer Crones to Coraline's Maiden.

Director Henry Selick's focus on Forcible's and Spink's former careers in burlesque visually signals the couple's queerness.[39] North American burlesque began in the nineteenth century, where performances consisted of 'a chaotic and nebulous combination of dancing, singing, minstrelsy, witty repartee, political commentary, parodies of plays and scant clothing'.[40] It is in burlesque that those with queer, non-normative bodies, that is, 'the circus freak, the tattooed lady, the diminutive woman, the Amazon', make their home, revelling in the sensuality and sexuality of the bodies patriarchal society rejects.[41] Forcible and Spink fit into this framework, as their much older and more corpulent bodies are no longer seen as conventionally attractive. That they still retain the sensuality of their burlesque days – Miss Forcible with her ample bosom and revealing dressing

Figure 9.2 Miss Spink gives Coraline the hag stone.

gown and Miss Spink with her flirtatious wink – emphasizes the queerness of their sexuality as compared to the young, lithe female bodies that are so often displayed for masculine consumption. Contemporary burlesque's inclusion of drag and parody of heteronormative gender roles further queers Forcible and Spink's relationship by association, even if they do not engage in more modern iterations of the art form. According to David Owen, the burlesque community itself is incredibly queer. He notes that burlesque is a safe environment where both performers and audiences can test their boundaries, creating 'a cultural space where gender is open for interpretation and expression of sexuality by diverse bodies is explored and encouraged'.[42] Thus, by aligning Forcible and Spink with the burlesque scene, rather than theatre, Selick further signals their queerness.

Not only are Miss Forcible and Miss Spink lesbians, they are the queer Crones of the film. The Crone is 'an old woman, past child-bearing age, who is wise, independent, capable of meeting her own needs or of sharing with others, and who is often associated with choice, change, death, transformation, and challenge'.[43] The Crone is also a teacher, a woman who has experienced the fullness of life and passes on her wisdom to younger witches, thus continuing the cycle of life, death and rebirth. Forcible and Spink do the same for Coraline, passing on their knowledge and tools to help her face the Other Mother. Some of that wisdom is irrelevant, such as Miss Spink's warning to 'never wear green in your dressing room' or Miss Forcible's advice to 'acquire a very tall stepladder'. Nevertheless, it is Miss Spink who reads Coraline's tea leaves and admonishes her to 'be very, very careful': a warning to stay away from the Other Mother and her realm. Coraline, too enchanted with the Other Mother to notice the danger she is in, initially dismisses Miss Spink's advice. Still, the tea leaf reading and the warning become extremely useful when Coraline finally rejects the Other Mother and chooses to challenge her instead.

Frequently, the Crone passes on more than wisdom to her students, bequeathing magical objects that can aid them on their journey. For Miss Forcible and Miss Spink that object is the hag stone: the small green stone with a natural hole in the middle that they give to Coraline. Hag stones, also known as mare-stanes, mare-stones or lucky stones, have been part of British superstitious practices since at least the nineteenth century. They are still used among witches today, even if their usage has changed over the centuries. A document from 1888 notes that a hag stone was used to 'ward off bad dreams' or stave off nightmares.[44] A. W. Buckland, writing for *The Antiquary: A Magazine Devoted to the Study of the Past*, notes that hag stones 'are used for driving away hags or witches, especially the nightmare'.[45] Today, hag stones are used among witches of various paths for a number of reasons, including seeing into other realms or finding invisible spirits and creatures. Witch Grim Rowntree, owner of the occult shop Stone Tree, notes on their blog that hag stones 'are also used as windows or doorways to see "otherworlds", invisible spirits, or how a being "really" looks beyond their glamoury'.[46]

Coraline's hag stone draws on both its traditional and current usages. The Other Mother's realm is a kind of nightmare, a place that Coraline initially only visits after she has gone to bed. Her true mother even refers to Coraline's first visit as 'a dream'. By using the hag stone in her challenge, Coraline dispels the nightmare and defeats the witch that would do her harm. Moreover, when Coraline peers through the stone, the Other Mother's world appears flat and colourless, making the ghost children's eyes glow against the grey background. Thus, it is thanks to Miss Forcible and Miss Spink that Coraline wins the game and defeats the Other Mother.

The queer witch power that Coraline unearths with the help of these two Crones becomes evident in the final few moments of the film. When Coraline returns home, she emerges more confident and self-assured, more powerful, than when she left. This newfound power ripples outward, starting with Wybie. After her victory, Wybie calls her 'Coraline' for the first time, as if he is *seeing* her for the first time. Coraline also acts as a positive force in her community, uniting all of the residents of the Pink Palace under a common cause: reviving their long-dead garden. Coraline's first act as an emergent queer witch, then, is to bring her disparate neighbours – a semi-reclusive Eastern European circus mouse trainer (Mr Bobinsky), two lesbian ex-burlesque stars (Miss Forcible and Miss Spink), her lone friend at the Pink Palace (Wybie), her own parents and a semi-feral black cat – out into the openness of the garden for an entirely queer goal, that is, creating new life for a non-procreative, community-building purpose.

Conclusion

LAIKA's *Coraline* is a film about resistance and courage, about drawing power from within yourself to stand up to those who mean you harm. In the context of today's political climate, *Coraline* can also be read as a narrative of magical queer resistance. In a Western culture where members of the LGBTQIA+ community feel more and more powerless to fight back against queerphobic, homophobic and transphobic policies and leaders, many turn to witchcraft as a source of power when more traditional avenues have failed. Part of that Craft is the veneration of the Triple Goddess, the female deity who presides over the cyclical nature of life through her aspects as the Maiden, the Mother and the Crone. The Triple Goddess is more than the Craft's main deity; she appears again and again in literature, through authors such as *Coraline*'s own Neil Gaiman and British fantasy writer Sir Terry Pratchett, among others.[47] Thus, it is useful to model Coraline, the Other Mother and Miss Forcible and Miss Spink on the three aspects of the Triple Goddess to trace a narrative of queer empowerment: Coraline as the young Maiden, only just coming to grips with her magical power and her queer identity; the Other Mother as the corrupted Mother who seeks to prevent Coraline from realising her power; and Miss Forcible and Miss Spink as the Crone(s) who, like LGBTQIA+ community elders, encourage Coraline's magical ability and give her the tools necessary to awaken her latent power. Coraline thus becomes an inspiration, a character the queer community can look to when their own strength begins to wane. Such a witchcraft-based, queer reading of *Coraline* disrupts the assumed 'straight' reading to allow radical new understandings from non-normative viewpoints to join the discourses on and around the film. This framework can be further expanded to other films, including mainstream animated features and children's films overall, to the same effect: disassembling assumed heteronormative readings to make space for the queer, thereby giving queer people more opportunities to thrive.

Acknowledgements

I would like to extend my deepest thanks to Misha Mihailova and Janine Hatter for their patience and guidance, Ellen Ricketts and Jonathon O'Donnell for conversations on lesbianism and queer witchcraft, Jed Edwards, Simon Walker, Bee Bentall, and Barbara Grabher for being excellent cheerleaders and Annie Maier and Charlie Ward for their unflagging love and support.

Notes

1   Neil Gaiman, 'Fairy Tales Are More Than True: Not Because They Tell Us That Dragons Exist, but Because They Tell Us That Dragons Can Be Beaten', *Tumblr*, 18 November 2014. https://neil-gaiman.tumblr.com/post/102947175291/fairy-tales-are-more-than-true-not-because-they (accessed 13 November 2019).

2   Neil Gaiman, '@notdoingmywork Asked: What Was the Point of the Story Coraline?', *Tumblr*, 21 April 2017. https://neil-gaiman.tumblr.com/post/159843218331/what-was-the-point-of-the-story-coraline-because (accessed 13 November 2019).

3   'Witchcraft' can refer to both the secular practice of channelling one's personal power with the help of personally or traditionally significant props (e.g. candles, crystals, chants) to supernaturally effect one's will and the religious system that employs this practice as part of its praxis. Here the former will be referred to with a lowercase 'w' ('witchcraft') and the latter with a capitalized 'W' ('Witchcraft', sometimes shortened to 'the Craft').

4   A note on terminology: while there are numerous ways to refer to the lesbian, gay, bisexual and transgender community, this chapter will use LGBTQIA+ (lesbian, gay, bisexual, transgender, queer, intersex, asexual and others) for inclusivity.

5   Critical theorist and queer scholar J. Halberstam criticizes *Coraline* as being 'a deeply conservative narrative where Coraline goes from 'a protofeminist critic of the family, boys, and normativity into a submissive girl and dutiful daughter, committed not to production but reproduction'. See J. Halberstam, *The Queer Art of Failure* (Durham, NC: Duke University Press, 2011), pp. 180–1. This chapter serves

as a rebuttal to Halberstam's discussion, elaborating on ways in which Coraline develops her queer/feminist power.

6   Moira Smith, 'The Flying Phallus and the Laughing Inquisitor: Penis Theft in the "Malleus Maleficarum"', *Journal of Folklore Research*, vol. 39, no. 1 (2002), p. 87.

7   Ibid.

8   Ibid., p. 88.

9   Madeline Miller, 'From Circe to Clinton: Why Powerful Women Are Cast as Witches', *The Guardian*, 7 April 2018. https://www.theguardian.com/books/2018/apr/07/cursed-from-circe-to-clinton-why-women-are-cast-as-witches (accessed 13 November 2019).

10 Margot Adler, *Drawing Down the Moon: Witches, Druids, Goddess-Worshippers and Other Pagans in America* (New York: Penguin Group, 2006), p. 185.

11 Ibid.

12 Ibid., p. 184.

13 Ibid., p. 186.

14 Lynda Warwick, 'Feminist Wicca: Paths to Empowerment', *Women & Therapy*, vol. 16, no. 2–3 (1995), p. 127.

15 Adler, *Drawing Down the Moon*, p. 181.

16 Liz Posner, 'You May Be a Witch and Not Even Know It: The Resurgence of W.I.T.C.H. Activism Under the Trump Administration', *AlterNet*, 30 October 2017. https://www.alternet.org/2017/10/resurgence-witch-activism-and-witches-under-trump-administration/ (accessed 13 November 2019).

17 W.I.T.C.H. PDX, 'W.I.T.C.H.: STARTING NEW CHAPTERS', PDF File, No date. https://static1.squarespace.com/static/58bc4014db29d66bb3b20966/t/59c6e45fd7bdce9acafab603/1506206816220/NEW-W.I.T.C.H.-CHAPTERS.pdf (accessed 13 November 2019). Capitalization included in text.

18 W.I.T.C.H. Boston (@witchboston), 'ANONYMOUS | INTERSECTIONAL | INCLUSIVE | UNIFIED', Instagram photo, 27 January 2017. https://www.instagram.com/p/BPx5jAFh5kj/ (accessed 13 November 2019).

19 Unnamed, 'New York Witches Place Hex on Brett Kavanaugh', *BBC News*, 21 October 2018. https://www.bbc.co.uk/news/world-us-canada-45928212 (accessed 13 November 2019).

20 Moira Donovan, 'How Witchcraft is Empowering Queer and Trans Young People', *Vice*, 14 August 2015. https://www.vice.com/en_us/article/zngyv9/queer-trans-people-take-aim-at-the-patriarchy-through-witchcraft (accessed 13 November 2019).

21 Catland Books, 'Ritual to Hex Brett Kavanaugh', Facebook event, 20 October 2018. https://www.facebook.com/events/179836286297165/ (accessed 13 November 2019).

22   Warwick, 'Feminist Wicca', p. 124.

23   Ibid.

24   Ibid.

25   'Coraline (2009)'. Animation screencaps. https://animationscreencaps.com/
     coraline-2009/3/#box-1/152/coraline-disneyscreencaps.com-512.jpg?strip=all
     (accessed 31 January 2020).

26   Emma Wilby, *Cunning Folk and Familiar Spirits: Shamanistic Visionary Traditions
     in Early Modern British Witchcraft* (Brighton: Sussex Academic Press, 2010), p. 66.

27   Wilby, *Cunning Folk*, pp. 67–9.

28   Marietta Williams, '[Familiars 2017: Part 4] How a Familiar Serves the Witch', 17
     November 2017. http://www.witchywords.com/2017/11/familiars-2017-part-4-
     how-familiar.html (accessed 13 November 2019).

29   While the cat in *Coraline* is voiced by male actor Keith David, they are not given a
     name, nor are they explicitly given pronouns. In Gaiman's novel, the cat is referred
     to as 'it' but 'with a man's voice'. See Neil Gaiman, *Coraline* (New York: Bloomsbury,
     2002), p. 35. Because of this ambiguity, I will be referring to the cat by neutral
     'they/them' pronouns to emphasize their queerness and potential queer identity.

30   Wilby, *Cunning Folk*, p. 40.

31   In witchcraft, building the energy one needs for a spell is called 'raising power'.
     The Other Mother also essentially 'raises' Coraline to be a queer witch. Thus, the
     section's title.

32   Warwick, 'Feminist Wicca', p. 125.

33   Ibid.

34   Suzanne Venker, 'The Neutering of the American Male', 9 March 2018. https://
     www.suzannevenker.com/feminism/the-neutering-of-the-american-male/
     (accessed 13 November 2019).

35   Suzanne Venker, 'Men Called. They Want Their Balls Back', 30 April 2018. https://
     www.suzannevenker.com/relationships/men-called-they-want-their-balls-back/
     (accessed 13 November 2019).

36   Adler, *Drawing Down the Moon*, p. 213.

37   Neil Gaiman, '@lesbiantrevorbelmont Asked: I Was Wondering, in The Kindly
     Ones, One of the Things Cluracan Calls Nuala is "La Belle Dame Sans Merci" ',
     Tumblr, 3 April 2018. https://neil-gaiman.tumblr.com/post/172565660631/i-was-
     wondering-in-the-kindly-ones-one-of-the (accessed 13 November 2019).

38   'Coraline (2009)'. Animation screencaps. https://animationscreencaps.com/
     coraline-2009/44/#box-1/16/coraline-disneyscreencaps.com-7756.jpg?strip=all
     (accessed 31 January 2020).

39   Gaiman has confirmed their lesbian relationship multiple times on his blog. Neil
     Gaiman, '@reivaxm Asked: Hello. I Was Reading Coraline Again',

'@aweirdvegan-blog Asked: Are Ms. Spink and Forcible Together?' and '@uwudroj Asked: Hello I Was Just Wondering, are Miss Spink and Miss Forcible a Couple?', *Tumblr* posts, 31 August 2014, 24 October 2016, 6 July 2018. https://neil-gaiman. tumblr.com/post/96248654066/hello-i-was-reading-coraline-again-and-something, https://neil-gaiman.tumblr.com/post/152237746756/are-ms-spink-and-forcible-together, and https://neil-gaiman.tumblr.com/post/175615960441/hello-i-was-just-wondering-are-miss-spink-and (accessed 13 November 2019).

40   Claire Nally, 'Grrly Hurly Burly: Neo-Burlesque and the Performance of Gender', *Textual Practice*, vol. 23, no. 4 (2009), p. 622.

41   Ibid., p. 631.

42   David Owen, 'Neo-Burlesque and the Resurgence of Roller Derby: Empowerment, Play, and Community', *Canadian Theatre Review*, vol. 158 (2014), p. 36.

43   Warwick, 'Feminist Wicca', p. 125.

44   Earl of Ducie, 'Exhibition of Three "Mare-Stanes," or "Hag Stone"', *Journal of the Anthropological Institute of Great Britain and Ireland*, vol. 17 (1888), p. 135.

45   A. W. Buckland, 'The Significance of Holes in Archaeology', *The Antiquary: A Magazine Devoted to the Study of the Past*, vol. 32 (1896), p. 336.

46   Grim Rowntree, 'Hag Stone Lore', 30 October 2012. http://cauldroncraftoddities. blogspot.com/2012/10/hag-stone-lore.html (accessed 13 November 2019).

47   The Triple Goddess is particularly prominent in Neil Gaiman's *The Sandman* series, and She frequently appears in the comics. See Neil Gaiman, *The Sandman* (New York: Vertigo Comics, 1989–96). In addition, Rose Walker, a key character, is part of a Triple Goddess formulation with her mother and her grandmother. A second Triple Goddess formulation appears in the fifth trade paperback, *A Game of You*: recently pregnant Hazel is the Mother, Foxglove, Hazel's partner, is the Maiden and the ancient witch Thessaly is the Crone. See Neil Gaiman, *The Sandman: A Game of You* (New York: Vertigo Comics, 1993). In Sir Terry Pratchett's famed *Discworld* series, the main Triple Goddess formulation consists of Granny Weatherwax (Crone), Nanny Ogg (Mother) and Magrat Garlick (Maiden). See Terry Pratchett, *Discworld* (New York: Penguin Random House, 1983–2015). Elsewhere, lesbian playwright Carolyn Gage's *The Triple Goddess: Three Plays* is modelled on the Triple Goddess, with each play focused on one of Her aspects. See Carolyn Gage, *The Triple Goddess: Three Plays* (lulu.com, 2009). Academics and critics have also used the Triple Goddess in their analyses, from Roz Keveney's examination of the *Alien* movie franchise to Jeanne Addison Roberts' discussion on Shakespeare's plays. See Roz Keveney, *From Alien to the Matrix: Reading Science Fiction Film* (London: Bloomsbury Academic, 2005) and Jeanne Addison Roberts, *The Shakespearean Wild: Geography, Genus, and Gender* (Lincoln: University of Nebraska Press, 1991).

10

Becoming-puppet: Failed interpellation and the uncanny subjection in *Coraline*

Eric Herhuth

When Neil Gaiman completed his manuscript for *Coraline*, he asked his agent to send it to Henry Selick. Gaiman appreciated Selick's stop-motion work and believed he was the most suitable director for animating the story. Its dark imagery suited Selick's style, as did the narrative's investment in a child's bravery and independence.[1] Released in 2009, the movie occupies a significant position within the transitional era of digital cinema or what some scholars call post-cinema.[2] It also established LAIKA animation studio as a popular brand known for stop-motion feature films. The movie offers a fantasy pleasing to parents and children in its emphasis on a child's heroism and the restoration of family, which also makes it conducive to psychoanalytic readings. And, as Gaiman's choice of director indicates, the focus on uncanny aesthetics, animation and puppets invites reading the movie as a commentary on developments in technology, especially those that affect creativity and ideas about what is alive, intelligent and autonomous. In an attempt to think about how these events, themes and aesthetics interweave, this essay examines the movie through one of its overarching technological themes: namely, the fear-inducing possibility that losing one's identity is comparable to becoming a puppet.

This idea is central to the story of *Coraline*, which follows a girl who has recently moved with her family across the United States to a new home. Coping with isolation, the young Coraline meets a series of strange neighbours and finds a small door in her house that leads to another world created and controlled by her 'Other Mother'. The Other Mother looks like Coraline's real mother except for a pair of button eyes. In this Other World Coraline meets alternative versions of her father and neighbours, all of whom have button eyes and, to Coraline, seem preferable to their normal-world counterparts. After Coraline ventures to the Other World multiple times, the Other Mother invites her to stay but only if Coraline allows the Other Mother to sew buttons in the place of her eyes. Coraline rejects the offer, and the Other Mother tries to trap her. Coraline escapes but is, ultimately, lured back to rescue her parents and the souls of three children whom the Other Mother abducted long ago.

For Coraline, acquiring button eyes in the Other World would mean surrendering to the Other Mother's control and appetite. This amounts to losing her identity and life in the normal world while becoming a puppet of sorts in the Other World. The three ghost children tell Coraline that the Other Mother is a Beldam or witch who 'ate up [their] lives'. And in the book they say, 'She stole our hearts, she stole our souls.'[3] In addition to consuming souls, the Other Mother, as Coraline learns, controls the characters in the Other World, and their button eyes are markers of the Other Mother's puppeteer-like control. Coraline's fear of losing her eyes is thus linked to a fear of losing her autonomy and soul. This threat in the Other World correlates with her identity crisis in the normal world following her family's move to a new home and region. In other words, Coraline's coherent formation as a subject – that is, her identity constituted by social categories such as daughter, neighbour, friend, student, etcetera – maintains her non-puppet status. As her identity destabilizes in the normal world, Coraline faces the threat of becoming a puppet in the Other World. Defeating her Other Mother, rescuing her parents and the ghost children and avoiding becoming a puppet in the Other World enables Coraline to re-establish her sense of self and reconstitute her family and community. This structure resembles the mirror worlds found in other stories – for example, *Alice in Wonderland* or *Wizard of Oz* – but it raises the question of what it means to become a puppet, to acquire button eyes and be controlled and consumed by the Other Mother. How does the process, which I will call becoming-puppet, express the loss of identity or self? What does the threat of this process in the fiction suggest about human-technology relations in real life? And what does it say about puppets?

The philosophical relevance of puppets

Puppets remain culturally significant in large part because of everyday experiences with avatars, robots and animation that resemble or remediate forms of puppetry or perhaps simply evoke the concept through aspects of manipulation and control. These include operating an avatar in a videogame, remotely programming and controlling a toy or animating a character using your own movements recorded in real time (e.g. through Adobe Character Animator). Beyond manipulation and control however, philosophical and literary accounts tend to discuss how puppets expose a repressed belief in the supernatural or express a thingness and alienness that resonates with human experience.[4] Whether wooden marionette or sock, a puppet presents vitality and activity but also a dead, inanimate materiality. In *Coraline*, there are many types of puppets and puppet-like figures – from the dolls and characters controlled by the Other Mother to the stop-motion puppets themselves – that offer a range of expressions derived from their materiality and functionality.

My approach to these types follows that of Chiara Cappelletto, who distinguishes marionettes and hand puppets from dolls and automata but proposes that they are all part of a spectrum. For Cappelletto, dolls are passive, doing nothing on their own, and automata by definition act independently. The puppet, however, lies between these two poles. This in-between state resonates with the duality of human experience in which a person finds her body, emotions and thoughts at once under her control and beyond her control.[5] We might think of this as the human capacity to *experience* experience – for example, to not just be angry but to feel one's anger as it builds and unfolds. Cappelletto's doll-puppet-automata spectrum does not distinguish precisely when a doll becomes a puppet or vice versa, but it does clarify how puppets serve analyses of the divided human subject who experiences their self as under and beyond their control. In this sense, the puppet is defined as a medium that expresses agency as a problem, as existing in a conflicted space between autonomy and passivity, between controlling oneself and being controlled by other forces. In addition to inner conflict and psychical divisions (e.g. Freud's ego, id, superego), Cappelletto acknowledges a romantic understanding of puppets as expressions of a grace and unity unavailable to humans. This idea remains influential today and is often traced back to Heinrich von Kleist's 1810 essay 'On the Marionette Theatre', and a brief discussion of this tradition will illuminate a couple of ways to think about becoming-puppet that contextualize *Coraline* within contemporary arguments about technology and politics.

For Kleist marionette puppets have a grace and innocence that humans cannot match because these puppets are not self-conscious and are without affectation. They have no knowledge of gravity and their bodies do not need rest in the manner of human bodies. The marionette does not present disharmony when it is pulled by strings because the marionette is also an extension of the puppeteer, akin to a prosthetic limb.[6] In this sense, the marionette presents harmony between diverse (organic and inorganic) elements working in coordination as part of an apparatus or network. This harmony contrasts with the disharmony of the individual whose self-consciousness or self-knowledge creates discord amongst the parts of their being – conflicts between reason and emotion, instinct and culture, desire and restraint, etc. Among Kleist's examples is that of a young man who discovers his own attractiveness, becomes increasingly vain and therein loses his natural charm, innocence and bodily grace.[7] For Kleist, grace can appear either 'in that human bodily structure that has no consciousness at all – or has infinite consciousness – that is, in the mechanical puppet, or in the God'.[8]

Writing about post-cinematic media, Deborah Levitt suggests that Kleist's view of puppets offers a valuable model for critiquing anthropocentric hierarchies in that it shows how a 'media-technical object' (Levitt extends Kleist's ideas beyond the marionette) overcomes or alters the constraining human experience of self-consciousness.[9] In other words, the media-technical object – whether a wooden puppet, doll, robot or animated character – can have a representational function and may even simulate human behaviour, but it also exceeds these and introduces new ways of being to the human interacting with it.[10] A puppet, for example, is more than a representation or an avatar; it has its own materiality and mode of existence. This is hyperbolically expressed in *Coraline* by the doll that resembles the protagonist but spies on behalf of the Other Mother. This portrayal underscores the otherness that lurks behind the doll's resemblance. Levitt's premier example is Mamoru Oshii's *Ghost in the Shell 2: Innocence* (2004), which features artificially intelligent humanoid characters, but these characters and the movie itself tend to value doll-like puppet consciousness as a critical alternative to human consciousness.[11] In short, the otherness of the puppet or technical media is valued over its resemblance to the human because it offers new ways of relating to and being in the world – that is, a return to innocence. This line of reasoning recurs in Levitt's analysis of culturally significant puppets, dolls and simulacra and supports her contention that a transition has occurred during the computer age in which animation has become central to cultural production. This culture-producing formation or *animatic apparatus* releases images from their representational ties to the world and decouples bodies from biological destiny.[12] Like Kleist's graceful marionette, puppets in this context are not appreciated for their resemblance to or representation of the human but for offering a generative, technical otherness associated with possibility and radical reconfigurations of self and community.

In *The Soul of the Marionette* political philosopher John Gray also returns to Kleist's ideas in order to critique anthropocentric humanism, specifically the harms caused by myths of progress. He argues that many modern societies have tended to adopt ideologies that seek transcendence and freedom through knowledge. The basic idea is that greater awareness of self and environment will make humans less like puppets and more like gods, to use Kleist's terms. Gray finds revised versions of this belief common among 'contemporary evangelists for evolution, trans-humanists and techno-futurists'.[13] But he also finds that this pursuit for transcendent knowledge has not removed violence and suffering from the world and that it leads to paranoid attempts to explain everything, including the irrational, conflicted experience of human self-awareness. In opposition to this idea, Gray argues that humans should accept their condition between puppets and gods in a fashion comparable to Kleist's appreciation of the grace of an unknowing marionette.[14] Instead of trying to transcend the human condition, the recommendation is to acknowledge the freedom in not knowing who or what is pulling all of the strings and that the mystery and conflict of consciousness is a defining attribute of human experience. This sentiment runs counter to digital utopianism and notions of technological progress that seek to eradicate mystery and inner conflict from human experience.

Levitt and Gray share an appreciation for processes of becoming-puppet even though each has a different political valence. Levitt's analysis features an optimism about the worldmaking and self-experimentation facilitated by the contemporary, animatic media environment. Gray's analysis is more pessimistic and contrarian because he is convinced that overconfidence in technological innovation and human knowledge production results in less freedom and fails to diminish violence and suffering. In both accounts, however, puppetry is not valued as a Pinocchio-type expression of the non-human becoming human or wanting to become human, nor is it valued for evoking the human ambition for transcendent knowledge – to leave behind the condition of feeling like a puppet and become a god. Instead, it functions as a critical counterpoint to notions of becoming-human and becoming-god. In this critical usage, the idea of becoming-puppet challenges facets of anthropocentrism, but, following Kleist, it does so through a kind of prelapsarian fantasy. Puppetry examples in these arguments recall an idealized state of innocence, possibility and contentment. The puppet's lack of autonomy and awareness and its otherness are admired in a romantic fashion comparable to idealized fantasies about childhood.

This raises questions for *Coraline*, which is a fantasy about childhood, and addresses many of the themes that appear in the arguments of Levitt and Gray. First, the movie depicts becoming-puppet as an unpleasant fate that the protagonist must avoid. Even though the film's production utilized animation and digital practices paradigmatic of Levitt's animatic apparatus, it differs from her examples in that it is more akin to a Pinocchio story than an anti-Pinocchio story. It does not affirm the non-human aspects of technology and representation – that is, the potential represented by dolls, puppets and artificial intelligence (AI) that in no way aspire to be human or to save humans. Second, *Coraline*'s popularity as an innovative movie adaptation of a book directly engages the discourse of technological progress, the subject of Gray's critique. This is apparent in LAIKA's promotion of its brands which package together the business of studio filmmaking and the craft of stop-motion animation. The remainder of this essay will elaborate these points and consider how the movie's treatment of becoming-puppet responds to the techno-political context that concerns Levitt and Gray but offers a contrasting puppet fantasy. The depiction of becoming-puppet in *Coraline* is not that of an idealized, childlike innocence but rather the unsettling and uncanny experience of misrecognition and the trauma of becoming a subject.

Stop-motion puppets and LAIKA's progressive image

Coraline marks a significant technological and aesthetic development in stop-motion animation. It was the first movie to combine stop motion and digital 3D production, and it helped establish conventions for 3D aesthetics in the era of digital cinema – namely, the use of depth over protrusion.[15] *Coraline* launched the LAIKA animation studio's brand and marketing strategy, which involves promoting stop motion's meticulous hand labour and the latest digital technologies. This includes using computers to create storyboards, 3D models and replacement parts for the stop-motion puppets printed with a 3D printer. It also includes using a digital motion picture camera for shooting in stereoscopic 3D, checking each frame on a monitor during the animation process and, finally, editing in software to clean up lines, seams and wires visible on the puppets.[16] These techniques gave the puppets and the diegesis an enhanced precision that was not available to earlier stop-motion processes. In the movie, the puppets look clean, and their movements are relatively smooth and lively. The material reality of their silicone bodies is apparent, but it is subdued rather than flaunted. The uncanniness of this puppet world stems not from jittery movement or visible wires/seams/thumbprints (as in older stop motion), but from an uncertainty about the nature of the materiality and tangibility of the puppets.

Stop-motion puppets are distinct from marionettes and hand puppets that perform in real time. Stop motion can include any kind of material, but its frame-by-frame animation technique adds a significant layer of mediation. The puppet is at rest when photographed and moved or modified between frames. In terms of the spectrum ranging from dolls to automata invoked by Cappelletto, the stop-motion puppet is basically a doll when photographed, but the film or digital recording approaches the category of automata when it is projected or played for an audience. In a sense, the stop-motion puppet retains the in-betweenness of puppetry by combining doll and automata, inorganic and organic elements (puppets and puppeteers). The cut between frames, however, creates a discontinuous performance. In contrast to the marionettes that inspired Kleist, the movement of the stop-motion puppet is not graceful to the extent that grace refers to uninterrupted, coordinated movement of puppet and puppeteer. The grace of the puppet for Kleist does not rely on movement alone, however. The puppet also possesses grace and innocence through its non-conscious, non-human ontology; it does not suffer the burden of human self-consciousness. The stop-motion puppet retains this non-human, non-conscious quality, but its agency is distributed through a network that differs from that of the live-performance marionette. Frame-by-frame animation techniques can be appreciated for offering a god-like control that resonates with notions of human transcendence and Pinocchio narratives. But they can also cultivate an appreciation of the otherness of the materials, the technical media, with which one works. As Donald Crafton notes in his study of performance in frame-by-frame animation, both animators and puppeteers vary on this point. They may relish the sense of god-like control or the otherness of the puppets/characters that exceeds that control.[17]

LAIKA's branding and marketing certainly tend towards valuing a combination of human control and craft, technological innovation and the vitality of the non-human puppets. The stop-motion processes used in *Coraline* may not be discernible to some viewers, but many are likely to intuit a complex production process behind the scenes. They can learn about the replacement animation and 3D photography through interviews, LAIKA's promotional materials and DVD extras. These paratexts complement the uncanny aesthetic of the movie and LAIKA's brand in that they present the production process as utilizing high-tech tools and low-tech methods to produce something that seems intimate, familiar, part of an earlier cinematic moment, but also novel and innovative.[18] In addition to the digital tools and techniques already mentioned, the studio's more traditional methods include drawing character and set designs, storyboarding, building puppets by hand (which includes engineering a moveable skeleton, painting, sculpting and fabricating clothes and wigs), replacement animation and frame-by-frame stop-motion photography.

Promotional commentary for *Coraline* often exaggerates this mix of old and new: 'Although the techniques of stop-motion animation have essentially remained unchanged since the early days of cinema, for *Coraline* the animators at LAIKA reinvented the process to bring it into the digital age.'[19] This complimentary line betrays a techno-capitalist ethos that believes the real cure for stop motion's supposed stagnation is an innovative, well-funded company. Indeed, the studio's commitment to innovation has been driven by corporate investment and leadership starting with Philip Knight's takeover of Vinton Studios.[20] The studio's self-representation may downplay its corporate culture, but there is a clear effort to associate the brand with technological innovation, occasionally treating past (or less expensive, independent) stop-motion practices as obsolete.

The movie's production and aesthetic style address the transition between cinema and the animatic apparatus, to use Levitt's terms, in their mix of old and new techniques, tools and stop-motion aesthetics at a moment when moving-image media and creative industries more broadly are adopting new digital technologies and animation aesthetics that are less reliant on cinema's indexical reality effect. The ambiguity generated by this mix enhances the movie's focus on domestic, familiar (*heimlich*) spaces and characters that become other-worldly and strange (*unheimlich*). The pro-filmic process of taking small versions of familiar objects and magnifying them through photographic perspective entails multiple layers of defamiliarization. The small models of furniture and domestic space are a strange version of familiar things to begin with. Rendering them life-size through photography and manipulating those images through software creates multiple mediated versions. The diegesis of the movie echoes the duplication and transformation within the production through its uncanny doubling of characters and settings in its two worlds.

These uncanny and transformative aesthetics and practices support Levitt's account of animation's capacity for worldbuilding, reconfiguring the self and what she calls animation's an-ontology or its lack of a stable essence or referent. The opening sequence, after all, begins with the Other Mother's needle hands disassembling a doll, presumably designed after Wybie's grandmother's missing twin sister, and then creating Coraline's doll. This opening scene resembles that of many movies and series about androids, robots and artificial life such as the *Ghost in the Shell* films and the HBO series *Westworld*. Often in these creation scenes human hands are noticeably absent and there is an emphasis on the technology that mediates and facilitates creation. In *Coraline* the dolls do not have a human origin at all. They are simulacra in that they resemble human figures but are not part of the same ontological order. The dolls originate from the Other Mother and serve as spies in Coraline's ordinary world. They do not seek to become or serve humans; instead, they belong to another life force bent on capturing, collecting and possibly consuming Coraline. By presenting these anti-Pinocchio types in the service of a villain, however, the movie's narrative takes on a distinct Pinocchio structure in contrast to the examples appreciated by Levitt. Even though the protagonist character is performed through a stop-motion puppet, the narrative characterizes puppets as different from and a threat to Coraline.

The title sequence also evokes the trope of self-figuration common to cartoon animation.[21] As in the case of Chuck Jones's cartoon *Duck Amuck* (1953) which reveals Bugs Bunny to be the animator behind a highly reflexive Daffy Duck sequence, here, the Other Mother is the creative, animating force. Behind the animation, there is only more animation. Despite LAIKA's promotional display of their own stop-motion production processes, which includes time-lapse video of the animators at work, the opening sequence of *Coraline* aligns itself with a technological fantasy of alien creativity. The Other Mother's needle hands demonstrate a graceful precision unavailable to fleshy fingers. But this Kleistian moment aligns with the Other Mother's deception. The opening presents spectators with a vision of non-human (puppet) creativity, but again framed by the Other Mother's villainy. Analogous to Coraline's encounter with her Other Mother in the narrative, the fantasy of non-human creativity represented in the opening sequence can be read as a tempting but creepy illusion that should not be trusted. In short, the movie's anti-Pinocchio elements serve a generic Pinocchio narrative produced by a company deliberately associating its brand with technological progress. Instead of deploying becoming-puppet as a critical framework, the movie presents it as a threat and compares the appeal of a puppet's alterity to a deceptive fantasy. We might say that through *Coraline*,

LAIKA champions technological innovation on one hand while vilifying the radical otherness of technical media on the other.

Much of this treatment derives from Gaiman's book, but the movie elaborates it through several formal devices that speak to an unpleasant and unsettling feeling of returning to a state of ignorance and uncertainty. When placed in dialogue with Kleistian themes, the movie illuminates the philosophical and psychological nature of the divide between understanding becoming-puppet as a return to a childlike state of freedom and innocence and understanding it as a return to a childlike state of uncertainty, fear and misrecognition.

Failed interpellation and uncanny subjection

Coraline's first on-screen encounter is with a black cat who startles and stalks her as she looks for an old well. Shortly after this, Coraline meets Wybie, who deliberately tries to scare her before introducing himself. During their introduction, Wybie asks, 'Caroline what?' and Coraline must correct him. This encounter begins a pattern of misrecognition that continues through Coraline's encounters with her other neighbours: Mr Bobinsky, Miss Forcible and Miss Spink. In addition to the trepidation caused by the strangeness of each encounter, Coraline appears frustrated by her new neighbours' lack of sincere attention. In addition to not knowing her, they have little interest in listening to her (let alone getting her name correct), and they would rather tell her about themselves and what they assume to be true about her.

The movie refines this pattern through several audiovisual cues and stylistic elements. There is an important shot-reverse-shot that characterizes the initial encounter between Coraline and Wybie. Even before the two begin their banter about names, Wybie targets Coraline through his night-vision mask and Coraline appears in persecutory fashion through an iris frame (Figures 10.1a and 10.1b). The mask conceals Wybie's face and enhances his vision, which creates a menacing gaze that startles Coraline and presumably some viewers. Coraline does not know who he is, she cannot see him, and she does not know what he sees through the mask. Accompanying the mispronunciation of Coraline's name, then, is the visual trope of the mask, which we might say represents the opacity of the other and the capacity to conceal. The movie's early sequences utilize similar point-of-view shots to generate a sense that others are targeting and stalking Coraline, and this pattern continues in the

Figure 10.1 (a) Wybie, concealed by a night-vision mask, peers down at Coraline and (b) Coraline in an iris frame appears persecuted by Wybie's masked gaze.

meetings between Coraline and Mr Bobinsky, and then Miss Spink and Miss Forcible. In these scenes, Coraline is viewed suspiciously and surveilled, and this contributes to characterizing her suffering under conditions of mistrust and misrecognition.

Such encounters exacerbate Coraline's isolation and her frustration towards her parents, who are preoccupied with their work. On multiple occasions Coraline calls out to her parents who, being busy, are slow to respond. This quotidian parental negligence supplies a conventional set up for a child-adventure story and the parent-child scenes foreshadow precise reversals with the Other parents. Another crucial shot-reverse-shot is deployed with a zoom effect when Coraline meets her Other Mother. The Other Mother responds immediately to Coraline's call, turns around and offers direct eye contact to Coraline, save for the fact that she has buttons in the place of eyes. This face-to-face encounter is a key variation on the earlier repetition of uncanny encounters. Coraline knows this is not her mother, but the scene presents a successful hailing or interpellation in contrast to what occurs earlier when Coraline struggles to win the attention of her parents.

These scenes of misrecognition and recognition establish a link between Coraline's loss of identity and her journey into the Other World. The misrecognition theme itself has roots in Neil Gaiman's naming of the titular character: 'I had typed the name Caroline, and it came out wrong. I looked at the word "Coraline" and knew it was someone's name. I wanted to know what happened to her.'[22] In this remark, Gaiman reveals how his error as author created a name that called to him as a reader. This calling, which includes a form of concealment, masking or mystery ('what happened to her'), seems to have had a large influence on the story and the subsequent movie.[23] After all, the story begins by establishing Coraline's feelings of isolation in her new home where no one knows her or her name and her parents are preoccupied with their work. The Other World calls to Coraline and promises fulfilment and meaningful recognition, but she must learn to see that call as deceptive. Coraline learns that those who really care for her well-being may not show it, and those who appear to care may not really mean it.

Coraline's story of overcoming fear, misrecognition and deception is a fantasy about a child's successful development, whether understood as her entering the Symbolic Order or realizing authenticity and autonomy.[24] But the stop-motion aesthetics and narrative moments of hailing, the verbal and visual recognition and misrecognition, link this fantasy to a fundamental uncanny aspect of subject formation – namely, as Louis Althusser argued, that it does not take place in our heads but in the world.[25] Althusser described interpellation as the process of hailing that transforms an individual into a subject of and within ideology. The classic example is that of a police officer calling out to a pedestrian, 'Hey, you there,' in response to which the pedestrian immediately turns around. *Coraline*, meanwhile, focuses on familial practices but, comparable to Althusser's idea, envisions interpellation as a two-way process. If child or parent never responds to the other's hailing, then their status as parent or child is not constituted. Their subject position in the family is in question. Successful interpellations give continuity to individual identities and the institutions sustaining them. Indeed, children in many contexts interpellate their parents (whether in word or gesture) and parents respond because it is obviously (i.e. ideologically) the correct thing to do, not unlike turning around in response to the police. Gaiman, who dedicated the book to his two daughters and wrote it while they were growing up, demonstrates an understanding of the kinds of calls children place on parents. Interpellation has an uncanny puppet aspect to it in that it describes not only how institutions and discourses control one's identity but also how that identity can give a person a feeling of control (i.e. agency and self-knowledge). Coraline's encounters with her parents and neighbours present moments of failed interpellation, which leave Coraline feeling uncertain, powerless and alone.

The encounters that trouble Coraline are divided between those with actual, normal-world parents and neighbours and those of the Other World, and the narrative sides with the former despite the extravagance of the Other World. This is in part indicated by the button eyes. Even though they know how to please Coraline and make her comfortable, the Other characters cannot reciprocate visual recognition. Their button eyes prevent Coraline from seeing them see her. This is significant because the movie emphasizes point of view through its use of shot-reverse-shot scenes and depictions of surveillance, and, generally speaking, reciprocal recognition produces a kind of common ground. Without the capacity for mutual recognition, the Other characters are even more untrustworthy than the normal-world characters. Furthermore, they are the puppet creations of the Other Mother. Unlike the real Wybie who removes his mask after meeting Coraline for the first time, the Other characters in the Other World remain masked and deceptive. The Other Mother functions as a puppet master controlling the Other characters behind the scenes, and it is not entirely clear what she is or wants.

This depiction of otherness through not only puppets but also failed interpellation in both visual and verbal encounters all within the purview of family dynamics facilitates a range of psychoanalytic readings. This includes the idea that *Coraline*'s failed interpellations can be understood as evoking earlier misrecognitions that haunt subject formation. This is a critical point because it elaborates even further how the movie presents a counter fantasy to Kleistian theorizations of puppetry. There are numerous reasons for misrecognition to be unpleasant – it can be disrespectful or indicate disregard – but its uncanny aspect urges retrospection – for example, if they don't know who I am, then who am I? This prompt can accompany uncanny feelings to the extent that moments of misrecognition that occur later in life recall earlier moments, perhaps even unconscious memories from early childhood.[26] Even Althusser's idea of interpellation, which was influenced by Lacanian psychoanalytic theory, features a strange relation to the past. This is evident in the critical questions scholars use to challenge it: why does the subject turn around in response to the call and how could a subject respond to such a call if it is the call that constitutes the subject?[27] Indeed, Althusser refers to interpellation as a 'theoretical theatre' given for convenience because in actuality 'the existence of ideology and the hailing or interpellation of individuals as subjects are one and the same thing'.[28] We usually cannot recall our earliest encounters with the values and ideas that form us, but these familiar ideas and values must have once been new and strange. Interpellation is a fiction, a story we tell about early subject formation that remains largely unavailable and, following the movie *Coraline*, seems capable of haunting the subject.

This line of reasoning accords with Freud's comments about uncanny experience causing a subject to doubt their own epistemological foundations when repressed, frightening feelings or primitive beliefs return to the subject.[29] Many of Coraline's interactions can be interpreted this way, especially the scenes in which she encounters her new neighbours and eventually becomes suspicious of her Other Mother. Uncanny experience in general is a kind of misrecognition that triggers a sense of an unavailable but formative past. Examples often include confusing something mechanical for something biological because such experiences evoke a sense of childlike perception that does not consistently differentiate between the two categories. The person who experiences an uncanny misrecognition regresses to an extent and becomes unstable and potentially afraid without solid epistemological grounding. The character Coraline performs this kind of uncanny subject through failed interpellation and, also, the figure of the puppet. Coraline's fear of becoming-puppet amounts to a loss of self-knowledge that can be understood as a fear of regression for a sovereign subject who is supposed to be self-possessed and self-knowing.

Furthermore, the movie's use of depth metaphorically represents the threat of returning to an earlier form of consciousness and identity. *Coraline* primarily explores depth through its 'shoebox diorama aesthetic', and enhances the depth of the Other World through its use of 3D.[30] Commentators writing on the book and movie debate the extent to which the tunnels, rooms and well lend themselves to vaginal and womb-like symbolism.[31] The sequence in which Coraline first crosses the tunnel and meets her Other Mother in the kitchen does suggest a return-to-the-womb fantasy in that Coraline is retreating to a warm, motherly, comforting space. But it is a deceptive and uncanny fantasy, since Coraline very quickly becomes suspicious of the Other World and learns that the Other Mother does not offer authentic recognition and is a force that she must overcome.

This is not the appreciative reading of the puppet proposed by Kleist. Coraline's loss of self-knowledge and identity threatens to return her to an earlier, more enigmatic and helpless state of being. The movie's valuation of the human gaze over the puppet gaze (i.e. the button-eyed, Other World characters prove to be more treacherous) corresponds to this conflict. But I hope the foregoing analysis reveals an interesting complexity within the movie.

Namely, that becoming-puppet is compared to the loss of identity through the two-world structure of the story, but then the loss of identity understood as failed interpellation seems capable of relieving a subject from the pull of a given identity over which they have little control, so long as they don't suffer violence from the cop/parent/child who hails them. The latter aggression takes a different form when it is the child who calls upon the parent. In this case, the child's inability to receive recognition diminishes their agency, making it more difficult to do or get what they want, as when Coraline is ignored by her parents and misunderstood by her neighbours. Having a name and identity that is recognized equips a subject with agency as well as self-esteem and security but that recognition comes with strings attached, so to speak.

This dilemma is represented in the scene in which Coraline turns down the Other Mother's offer to stay in the Other World. Presented with the buttons that would be sown in place of her eyes, she decides this is not a good deal, despite the recognition, pleasure and security of the Other World. This bad offer makes Coraline's situation in her normal world more tolerable. But does not the button offer refer precisely to the early, unrecallable, interpellative moment when in order to gain agency in the world the subject is forced to choose the identity and worldview offered by those around them? The subject does not really have the opportunity to say no, hence the power of the fantasy in *Coraline*, in which the protagonist says no and thereby avoids becoming an (ideological) puppet. Rejecting the Other Mother's offer actually enables Coraline to be a better subject in the normal world because she feels she has chosen the better deal. Perhaps this narrative even helps viewers sustain the fantasy of choice affirming their own identity and ideological commitments.

Coraline is located in the transition to an increasingly animated media environment in which animation concepts and technologies intersect across diverse areas of science and cultural production. The Kleistian approach represented by Gray and Levitt finds puppetry particularly relevant in this context. The puppet does not feature self-consciousness or autonomy, but its own graceful, innocent mode of being. Technical media can evoke this innocent condition for humans, but this seems to rely inevitably on a romantic fantasy akin to the idealization of childhood. The fantasy posits a childlike state in which the subject has very little control over their conditions but also very little ambition or fear in terms of self-knowledge and self-preservation. They are vulnerable but unafraid because they do not know any better, and therein are open to different forms of becoming.

Coraline presents a different fantasy. In this uncanny return to a kind of prelapsarian moment, the protagonist becomes frightened and disoriented as they lose self-knowledge and recognition and discover potential threats and deceptive, masked characters. This is an unpleasant return to a vulnerable state, not a return to innocence and possibility. Lurking in this uncanny experience is the repressed memory of a forced choice in which one gains identity and agency by agreeing to terms not of their choosing. The puppet remains a useful figure for expressing this idea not only through its location between autonomy and passivity but also through its uncanny otherness which resonates with the opacity of our own early development. *Coraline* does not present a fantasy that values becoming-puppet because, in this film, fantasy functions to help the human subject cope with the state of having already become a puppet.

Notes

1 Stephen Jones, *Coraline: A Visual Companion* (New York: HarperCollins, 2009), p. 29.

2 Shane Denson and Julie Leyda, eds, *Post-Cinema: Theorizing 21st-Century Film* (Falmer: REFRAME Books, 2016). http://reframe.sussex.ac.uk/post-cinema/.

3 Neil Gaiman, *Coraline* (New York: HarperCollins, 2012), p. 95.

4 For discussions of puppets expressing human duality and thingness, see Chiara Cappelletto, 'The Puppet's Paradox: An Organic Prosthesis', *RES: Anthropology and Aesthetics*, no. 59/60 (2011), pp. 325–36 and Tzachi Zamir, 'Puppets', *Critical Inquiry*, vol. 36, no. 3 (2010), pp. 386–409. For a discussion of puppets' expression of repressed spirituality, see Victoria Nelson, *The Secret Life of Puppets* (Cambridge: Harvard University Press, 2003).

5 Cappelletto, 'Puppet's Paradox', p. 331.

6 Heinrich Von Kleist, 'On the Marionette Theatre', trans. Thomas G. Neumiller, *The Drama Review*, vol. 16, no. 3 (1972), p. 23.

7 Ibid., p. 25.

8 Ibid., p. 26.

9 Deborah Levitt, *The Animatic Apparatus: Animation, Vitality, and the Futures of the Image* (Washington: Zero Books, 2018), p. 39.

10 Ibid., p. 46.

11 Ibid., p. 44.

12 Ibid., p. 2.

13 John Gray, *The Soul of the Marionette: A Short Inquiry into Human Freedom* (New York: Farrar, Straus and Giroux, 2015), p. 164.

14 Ibid., p. 165.

15 Scott Higgins, '3D in Depth: *Coraline, Hugo*, and a Sustainable Aesthetic', *Film History: An International Journal*, vol, 24, no. 2 (2012), p. 198.

16 For an overview of the production process see Jones's *Coraline: A Visual Companion*, especially chapter 2.

17 Donald Crafton, *Shadow of a Mouse: Performance, Belief, and World-Making in Animation* (Berkeley: University of California Press, 2013), p. 17.

18 For additional commentary about the new technology and the hand-crafted feel of stop motion, see Ellen Wolff, 'Digital Puppeteers: Pete Kozachick and Brian Van't Hul on *Coraline*', *Millimeter* (January/February 2009), pp. 18–21.

19 Jones, *Coraline: A Visual Companion*, p. 102.

20 See Zachary Crockett, 'How the Father of Claymation Lost His Company', *Priceonomics*, 9 May 2014. priceonomics.com/how-the-father-of-claymation-lost-his-company/ (accessed 3 March 2020).

21 Donald Crafton, *Before Mickey: The Animated Film 1898–1928* (Cambridge, MA: MIT Press, 1987), p. 11.

22 Neil Gaiman, 'Introduction', *Coraline* (New York: HarperCollins, 2012), p. xxi.

23 The emphasis on hailing Coraline's name influenced Caetlin Benson-Allott's essay which also considers the movie as a transitional object in a post-cinematic context but utilizes an incidental homonymic correspondence between *khōra* and Coraline. See Caetlin Benson-Allott, 'The CHORA Line: RealD Incorporated', in Shane Denson and Julia Leyda (eds), *Post-Cinema: Theorizing 21st-Century Film* (Falmer: REFRAME Books, 2016). http://reframe.sussex.ac.uk/post-cinema/3-3-benson-allott/.

24 There are several articles that analyse Gaiman's novel in psychoanalytic terms and contest how Coraline's character should be understood as developing agency within the Symbolic Order – Jacques Lacan's term for the domain of culture, language and social authority. See Kara K. Keeling and Scott Pollard 'The Key Is in the Mouth: Food and Orality in *Coraline*', *Children's Literature*, vol. 40 (2012), pp. 1–27. See also Richard Gooding, ' "Something Very Old and Very Slow": *Coraline*, Uncanniness, and Narrative Form', *Children's Literature Association Quarterly*, vol. 33, no. 4 (2008), pp. 390–407; David Rudd, 'An Eye for an I: Neil Gaiman's *Coraline* and Questions of Identity', *Children's Literature in Education*, vol. 39, no. 3 (2008), pp. 159–68.

25 Louis Althusser, 'Ideology and Ideological State Apparatuses', trans. Ben Brewster [1970], Marxists.org. https://www.marxists.org/reference/archive/althusser/1970/ideology.htm (accessed 3 March 2020).

26 As Judith Butler notes, a subject's 'proper name and gender must surely arrive as enigmatic noise that requires an interpretative response'. Later misrecognitions recall earlier enigmatic noise. Butler considers such statements as 'I cannot believe you are my mother!' and 'Is this my child?' Judith Butler, *Senses of the Subject* (New York: Fordham University Press, 2015), p. 14.

27 Won Choi, 'Inception or Interpellation? The Slovenian School, Butler, and Althusser', *Rethinking Marxism*, vol. 25, no. 1 (2013), pp. 23–37.

28 Althusser, 'Ideology and Ideological State Apparatuses'.

29 Sigmund Freud, *The Uncanny*, trans. David McLintock (New York: Penguin, 2003), p. 154.

30 Higgins, '3D in Depth', p. 201.

31 See Benson-Allott, 'The CHORA Line'; Keeling and Pollard, 'The Key Is in the Mouth'; and Elizabeth Parsons, Naarah Sawers and Kate McInally, 'The Other Mother: Neil Gaiman's Postfeminist Fairytales', *Children's Literature Association Quarterly*, vol. 33, no. 4 (2008), pp. 371–89.

11

The wandering child and the family in crisis in Henry Selick's *Coraline*

Jane Batkin

'We are told: the only safe place is home.'¹ – Stephanie Coontz

Henry Selick's *Coraline* (2009) charts the exploits of an 11-year-old girl as she discovers the secrets of her family's new home. At its core, the film explores what family means, through issues of identity, belonging and the 'othering' of characters. Within Selick's morose, colourless real world, Coraline struggles to establish herself as an individual and is subsequently drawn to the witchy, shadowy side of home where her doppelgänger parents take more notice of her and encourage her feelings of self-fulfilment. Underpinning this story is the physical act of wandering that Coraline undertakes as she explores these vastly different representations of home and family. The portal/tunnel she crawls through is a corridor between the real and unreal, the mundane and fantastic, the invisible and vibrant. It links two distinctive worlds and simultaneously highlights their differences, asking where home actually lies. At the heart of this is the wandering child who searches for her own identity and the answer to a question: where exactly does she fit in, and is 'home' something to be sought after or something to dread?

The crisis of childhood identity and the family unit leads explicitly to roaming in Selick's film (see Figure 11.1). Coraline's invisibility, depicted through how others perceive her, is significant to the film's theme of crisis, as is the representation of the contemporary family. Identities are in flux, inasmuch as they shift and change shape within the film, and the family unit as a whole remains under constant threat. Isabel Heinemann suggests that 'in the United States the family has always been perceived as the most important social unit next to the individual'; family and childhood are at the core of American

Figure 11.1 Coraline wanders the area around her new home.

society and have always been viewed traditionally as a foundation for individual and collective identities.[2] They have evolved, however, morphing into other versions of themselves in the late twentieth and early twenty-first centuries: the traditional family 'with a homemaking mother and a bread-winning father' is no more, and childhood has become a site of contention, both in terms of its identity and in terms of the way in which children play, inside and outside of the home, and why they wander across neighbourhoods and landscapes (and, in Coraline's case, worlds) in search of wholeness.[3] Marilyn Coleman and Lawrence Ganong argue that the American family today is more diverse than it was in the past and that it is viewed as being, conversely, both in decay and as having adapted to broader social and economic changes.[4] Because family and the child have been transformed thus, belonging is contested and wandering, in a physical sense as well as an emotional one, may occur. Wandering is central to many cultures, but Samuel P. Huntingdon writes about the wandering nature of Americans, citing their pioneer past as the foundation for this.[5] Mike Savage et al. argue that individual identities have become more transient today; because of changes in the workplace and in the family dynamic, identities have shifted on a national as well as global scale and are formed, more increasingly, on the move.[6]

Animation – in this case stop motion – is an effective medium for the depiction of shifting representations of childhood and society because of its physical malleability, as well as its ability to broach the dark themes of childhoods in crisis within an acceptable, 'safer' form than live action suggests. This chapter will explore the wandering child and the disintegrating, reimagined family in Selick's adaptation of Neil Gaiman's British novel *Coraline*, reading the film itself as an American text, and one that is reflective of American society.

Contextualizing *Coraline*

The film's central themes and issues are certainly prevalent within both American culture and the American family unit itself. Dennis Wiseman suggests that the traditional family is no more,[7] and Stephanie Coontz supports this notion, calling the traditional family 'mythical'.[8] Film, as a mirror to society, often addresses cultural concerns, and American cinema in the 2000s questioned family and belonging at the turn of the century, as well as, crucially, the difficulty in deciphering truth and meaning within interior and exterior objective realities.[9] Live-action films such as *Memento* (Christopher Nolan, 2000) and *Donnie Darko* (Richard Kelly, 2001) played with perceptions of fiction versus the real, of memory versus dark fantasy. In the latter film, in particular, Donnie does not fit in with his family or society and wanders, mentally, to an alternate space, where belonging is more attainable. Animation also significantly addressed alternate worlds and ideas of the real versus non-real during this era; in *Monsters, Inc.* (Pete Docter, 2001), the idea of traversing between worlds through a portal (and becoming trapped within one or the other) is a central theme, and Richard Linklater's *Waking Life* (2001) explores the idea of wandering into and out of dreams and consciousness, taking a philosophical approach to question what is real. The witchy, fantasy elements of Neil Gaiman's book *Coraline* are heightened in Selick's adaptation, leading us into alternate realities where eerie doppelgängers inhabit the space. Children in animated cinema of the 2000s wander far away from the parental home, and the act of wandering itself becomes entangled with a crisis of identity (of self and of fitting into one's environment).

Coraline can be read as a study of shifting identities and worlds, one that considers the impact of these shifts on the child. Parenthood and its responsibilities are questioned, and the nuclear family is dissected and criticized, just as notions of childhood and the child's place in society are contested. Within the film, child voices and adult identities are silenced in unsettling acts of erasure and othering, and it is a story that, even as it offers a happy resolution, depicts a haunting representation of the traditional family and of home.

Home and family

If, as Henry Giroux claims, animated film belongs to popular culture and 'is the primary way in which youth learn about themselves', their relationships and how they see themselves fitting into the world, the lessons learned from *Coraline* are dark and disturbingly real.[10] Gaiman's original story is told in an adult's voice that reveals the child's thoughts and feelings, and the story, rather than evoking the supernatural, hints at subtle meanings in a mature way. The novella itself has been discussed widely in terms of its uncanny qualities; David Rudd, applying Freud's theory of the '*heimlich*' and '*unheimlich*', explores the relationship between 'the symbolic and the Real' through home and the familiar and the mirroring of the fantasy realm.[11] Richard Gooding, similarly, positions the house in Gaiman's story as unheimlich.[12] This supports the idea that the home in *Coraline* is something that is fractured, then broken and missing – and also that it might actually be something to fear. Two homes exist in the film, and, whilst on a surface level they both appear to represent safety, the Real home is damaged through the parents' neglect of their child's needs and desires, whilst the Other home represents a dangerous site of abduction and abuse. Indeed, Saeed Hosseinpour and Nahid Maghadam stress that the fictional world in the original story is a 'double-sided reality with a two-lane highway', alluding to the easy traversing of worlds by Coraline herself, but this traversing becomes difficult and fraught with fear and then horror, as she crawls away from the clutches of the child-stealing Beldam.[13]

What is clear, from these discussions, is that home and 'Other' home, as well as the border between the real and the fantastic, are core, disturbing themes of the story, as are the representation of the family unit and the child's place within it.

Home, in the 'real' world, is a barren, uninviting place in Selick's film. The Pink Palace apartments suggest nostalgia for home, rather than home itself. Gaiman states that the house was too big to be owned by Coraline's parents, but there is a sense, in the film, of a grand old house that may once have been a single home; it has a turret and a gabled roof that pitches in different directions and the rambling house nestles in the hillside.[14] The house's appearance also hints of mystery; it is often shrouded in mist or rain, and towers over muddy, uninviting grounds. The resident cat moves with a jerky liveness, resembling the stuffed, rigid dogs in Miss Spink and Miss Forcible's basement, who have angel wings sewn into their sweaters when they pass away. Coraline and her parents occupy two floors of the residence, a vacuous space with high ceilings and ample areas of solitude. It is dreary, unloved and devoid of colour or cosiness, and the space in which the family reside can be viewed as a mirror to the neglect and apparent dysfunctionality of their own family unit.

Coraline's family are still unpacking from their recent move, and her parents are engaged in freelance work together, an increasingly widespread occupation in the late twentieth and early twenty-first centuries. The family's well-being depends on the success of the catalogue they are creating; thus, they are living and working in a pressurized environment with little time to give to their daughter. Coraline's sense of invisibility in this world leads to her wandering, firstly through the grounds and house and then into the fantasy realm. The wandering child is not a new phenomenon, but childhood itself has naturally evolved alongside the nuclear family, resulting in a different sort of relationship between child and parent and, subsequently, in a different sort of child – changes that are reflected in *Coraline*.

There is a sense of upheaval in the film that points to current anxieties about a lack of fixedness in American society, specifically relating to family and its identity, and the problem of how to view the family is fundamental to this argument. As mentioned above, Coleman and Ganong suggest that there are two opposing views of the American family in the twenty-first century: that it has grown more diverse and has adapted, and that it is currently in decline.[15] Coontz also challenges ideas of the family, suggesting that the traditional family is an illusion and arguing instead that the family has always been in flux, and it has often been in crisis.[16] In the 1990s, the abbreviation SNAF was coined by Dorothy Smith to represent the Standard North American Family (this being the working father, homemaker mother and two children). Tasha Howe argues that this standardization of the family unit led to an 'ideological code' by which other types of family, who didn't fit into this thought process, were judged (and, one imagines, 'othered').[17] The idea that families could be standardized in this way seems highly problematic, given that this type of family is observed today as being largely defunct. In *Coraline*, both parents are working as freelancers on the same project, a gardening magazine, and their home-caring duties are equally blurred: mother can't cook and father doesn't tend the garden. The traditional family is absent in the real world here. It is only when Coraline wanders into the magical realm that she witnesses the traditional family adhering to their stereotypical roles and appearing to enjoy them.

Identity and fracture lines

David Rudd argues that the story of Coraline is 'centrally concerned with how one negotiates one's place in the world'.[18] The appeal of the fantasy Other World is understandable for a child who is as invisible as Coraline. Her position is compromised because of her parents' lifestyle, and she experiences feelings of displacement within their new home. Her mother remarks, 'I don't have *time* for you' and her father demands, 'Let me work!' When the spirited Coraline challenges her mother, she is told, as a matter of fact, 'Your dad cooks, I clean and *you* stay out of the way.' The parent, under pressure, does not have time to spare or to share. The alternative for Coraline becomes a dangerous adventure in the realm of the fantastic. Coraline's identity is constantly under threat; she is vocal and vociferous, but she is perpetually ignored and her own identity is challenged by adults who constantly forget her name. After protesting on a number of occasions, she decides to accept that those around her really cannot remember it. Coraline's invisibility is also mirrored in the doppelgänger doll of herself, who also represents a physical mirror. When Coraline loses the doll, she asks it, 'Alright little me, where are you hiding?'[19] This can be interpreted literally and metaphorically; the doll is a little Coraline and simultaneously Coraline may be questioning her own identity and invisibility, through the doll. Unaware of the doll's secret (that it is sewn and altered to resemble each victim that the Beldam wants to acquire), Coraline adopts a maternal attitude towards it, conscious that others lack empathy towards her as she tries to be seen and heard, whilst also addressing the doll as one who hides and is invisible.

Wybie suffers from similar issues. He hovers in the background, intent on befriending Coraline, but is constantly aware of his grandmother's voice calling him home. He is Coraline's shadow in a sense; he is often invisible to her, but he (unlike Coraline) is visible and needed by his family. His grandmother has already lost her own child sister, whose kidnapping (he tells Coraline that she was 'stolen') hints at the danger about the world that these children inhabit. Other Wybie becomes trapped in the Other World and his mouth is stitched up, rendering him silent, and Coraline initially expresses her grim delight at this, until she discovers that Wybie wants to help her escape. When she asks him to leave with her, however, his hand dissolves into dust and he shakes his head. Other Wybie understands his imprisonment and dark fate in this fantasy realm; after all, like the other inhabitants, he is a doll here. These scenes of children put in peril through their silencing and loss of control function as disquieting reminders of abduction and abuse. The notion of childhood as something precious and valuable, and as a time of life that is necessarily safeguarded, is challenged within the film. Children disappear, their eyes are removed and replaced with buttons, their mouths sewn shut and their souls captured. Childhood identity is addressed in an unnerving way, evoking horror, and it appears as a mirror (through the ghost children whose lives were eaten up, the missing girl who was 'stolen' and Wybie's silencing) to serious real-life concerns.

Lindsay Myers argues that the 'family film' has come to address 'real life traumas, broken homes and troubled child heroes'.[20] *Coraline* certainly reveals a disconcerting representation of modern parenthood and the family unit. Whilst Coraline's mother sits in the kitchen, working, her father is hunched over his computer in another room. The family is fractured, distanced and preoccupied. This bland and lonely existence leads Coraline to exaggerate stories to get her parents' attention: 'I almost fell down a well … I could have died,' to which her mother merely replies, 'Mmm hmm'. Coraline's parents find interacting with her frustrating, and here the narrative reflects real-world issues. Coraline's mother and father, immersed in their own work and deadlines, struggle to connect with their daughter and the stories of her excursions. Samuel Huntingdon, writing in 2004, stresses Americans' work ethic and the guilt felt when they are not engaged in work activities, while Cindy Aron comments that Americans have become prisoners of the workplace, suspending the time they spend away from it.[21] Coraline's parents reflect these views through their actions; when not working, they appear fractious, such as when Coraline's mother takes her shopping for clothes or when dinner is being prepared. Interacting with their child becomes the thing that they struggle with the most, as they try, and fail, to balance workloads with family life. We see the errors that the titular heroine's parents make in their inattentiveness towards their child who, literally, is on the periphery of their vision. Her real mother seems aware of her own shortcomings as a parent; she frowns in doorways and hovers uncertainly in rooms, announcing her daughter's name like a question when she has nothing else to say. When she eventually buys Coraline the gloves she wanted, she simply slides them under the bed covers in silence and leaves the room.

Coraline's parents fail to hold the family securely together, and this leads to a crisis of belonging for Coraline herself. Savage et al. suggest that there lurks a fear in American society that 'the stability of belonging and the sanctity of belonging are forever past', in relation to the concept of belonging as well as attitudes towards it.[22] Belonging is something that is in crisis because of the rise of the mobile, transient population; how does one belong to society and to the family unit itself, if movement is what defines us?

Samuel Huntington explores identity and the migratory nature of the United States, charted through its history of settlers, claiming that Americans 'acquire no attachment to Place: But Wandering about Seems engrafted in their Nature [*sic*]'.[23] Stephen Vincent Benet states that 'Americans are always moving on', referring to their pioneer status in US history, but this can also relate to the migratory nature of those who move to seek work across state lines, thus suggesting problems in achieving a sense of belonging anywhere in particular.[24] What is clear is that place and belonging are being increasingly challenged in late-twentieth- and early-twenty-first-century society and the theme of wandering, itself, ties back in with concerns about the family unit. Savage et al. argue that the home, as a place, 'is a crucial, possibly *the* crucial, identifier of who you are'.[25] Home, in *Coraline*, however, is an unfamiliar and unsettled place. It is contested and becomes uncanny and Coraline's own identity crisis can be seen to link directly with her lack of belonging within the family unit. She must search for her sense of herself through wandering between worlds because 'home' does not give her the answer. Wandering, itself, occurs once the move from place to place has already happened. We can see a kind of transience, as well as crisis, of the family unit and the frustration of a child wanting to belong; she is willing to journey to find her own wholeness, despite the dangers that may be lurking in the elsewhere, because her family is fractured. The solution, for Coraline, is to wander into a world where her name matters and her identity *appears* to be solidified.

The wandering child

Wandering across neighbourhoods and cyberworlds is what children naturally do in search of personal fulfilment and a sense of belonging. Today, migrant children physically wander across landscapes and seascapes to belong somewhere, often without parents, their haunted faces etched into social and political history and memory. To wander is to travel aimlessly, evoking different meanings than to 'move', which stipulates that something definitive changes (job, house, location/position, place, progress). Coraline's parents *move*, whilst Coraline *wanders*.

I have mentioned child identity as a key theme, above, and studies into childhood are imperative in order to underpin Coraline's actions and motives in the film. Various theories of childhood exist; Dominic Lennard discusses images of childhood and children in his book *Bad Seeds and Holy Terrors – The Child Villains of Horror Film* and argues that there is still an assumption in today's society that the child remains fragile and in need of adult protection.[26] Michael Wyness explores the notion of a childhood in crisis at the dawn of the new century, finding that this 'crisis' exists in the idea that children are now 'out of place'.[27] What he means by this is that the idea of childhood has been contested to such an extent by culture and society that the child no longer understands what its role is within society, how it will be governed or by whom. As parents step away from the home, busy with their own working lives, state laws continue to attempt to govern minors. Paula Fass's book *Childhood in America* claims that 'children are convenient symbols for our better selves, and we use them to make points, make laws and win elections'.[28]

Another important factor to consider, as we explore the wandering child, is that of the concept of 'play'. Children throughout history have always played outside of home and its confines; conversely, twenty-first-century play has become increasingly streamlined into new media, meaning that children are now far less likely to wander from their own bedrooms. The pre-internet child, however, was adept at physical play. Anne Scott MacLeod's essay 'American Girlhood in the Nineteenth Century' contains anecdotes of energetic, active girls who enjoyed and took full advantage of their freedom, climbing trees, falling into rain barrels and fishing in horse troughs. One child set her sights on climbing everything in her neighbourhood, often badly injuring herself in the process, and her mother's only comment was, 'You must learn to climb better'.[29] Gaiman's depiction of childhood and its freedom seems to reflect this early American period, and Coraline can be seen as a mirror to these girls; the only computer in the house is the one that her father uses – the same one she inadvertently switches off. Coraline behaves as a child of the pre-internet age; she wanders and plays outside of the home and creates her own amusement in all weathers. Gaiman and Selick have placed the wandering child into a contemporary family unit, wherein the child is forgotten as the adults are preoccupied with making a living and pondering their options. Coraline is a little deflated by her parents' inattentiveness, but she is not overtly damaged by it. She is very capable of wandering off on her own to have playful adventures, she is curious about the possibilities of the Other World and its inhabitants and she is able to replace her own parents at different points of her journey (although this alludes more to her missing them than her independence). For example, Coraline uses Other Mother and Other Father to replace her parents and subsequently recreates her family using pillows. This show of bravado, that she is the wandering, adventurous child, falters here as she realizes that she needs them and that she is alone and afraid in the empty, uncanny home. Like the climbing child in the anecdote above, Coraline needs affirmation from a parent that she is ok, and safe.

The tunnel through which Coraline uses to wander is easily traversable, both to and from the Other World, at least to begin with. This renders the fantasy realm accessible and, to some extent, normalizes this Other World for the viewer and for Coraline. The passage between these worlds is organic and womb-like, as if Coraline is seeking a way back to the maternal in its purest form in response to her real family's dysfunctionality. Selick leads the viewer through a portal into a contrasting world of colour and magic, and this wandering is perceived, initially, as a positive journey for Coraline. Her identity flourishes in a place where she is at last the focus of her Other parents' attention.

American cinema in the 2000s commonly performed these intersections between the real and fictional, as I have discussed earlier. The fantasy genre commonly introduces alternate worlds, shown as conflicting with, or offering escape from, the real. As Paul Wells puts it, 'to be "down the rabbit hole" or "through the looking glass" is an acknowledgement of a transition into a fantasy state; a shift of perception into an altered world'.[30] In many fantasy films the child can be seen venturing into the unknown to overcome whatever obstacles arise, and characters are able to thwart evil in this magical world because of the absolute absence of the real. In Henry Selick's 1996 feature *James and the Giant Peach* (another adaptation of a British story), the titular character encounters and outsmarts external forces and foes on his wandering journey, just as Coraline is able to outwit the Beldam and save her real mother and father. Animation is a natural facilitator of fantasy, but also mirrors the real, and the animated child is able to wander and play just as the real child is, into these fantasy realms. James and Coraline represent real child concerns: fear of monsters, being erased and losing one's family. Because *Coraline*, in particular, is nightmarish and frequently questions the real, it is important for us to believe wholly in Coraline's ability to thwart evil.

Michael Wyness explains that children today have begun to take more responsibility for their own affairs, rather than relying on adults for protection, and claims that they often police themselves and each other.[31] Today's children are occasionally forgotten or overlooked by their parents/caretakers. Coraline must solve the mystery of the Other realm and of what happened to the missing children; she must save their souls and defeat the demon mother without assistance from her real parents (whom she has to free from the snow globe). By completing these tasks, Coraline proves that she knows exactly who she is and what she can achieve. She is an inter-world wanderer who can thwart the monsters and find home again. In doing so, however, she performs a dissection and, to some extent, a destruction of her own childhood.

The Other family

Wandering opens up thoughts and fears of the unknown, of the wasteland of what is not understood, mentally, as well as the physical wasteland that creates the barrier between two worlds. Philosopher Richard Kearney writes about a no-man's land of difference and that it is in this no-man's land that otherness flourishes. He writes that it is in the space between worlds that 'the Other passed from the horizon of reflective understanding into the invisible, unspeakable, unthinkable dark'.[32] Kearney is talking about strangers and monsters moving between our consciousness of what we know or assume to know and the void of the unknown that opens up and introduces horror. This theory of a no-man's land allowing the Other to flourish can be applied to Coraline, whose wandering

Figure 11.2 Coraline's Other parents treat her to a sumptuous meal.

leads her between worlds, through the womb-like tunnel. When Coraline tries to escape the fantasy realm, it fractures into a white expanse of space, a no-man's land that the cat calls 'the empty part of this world'. It is the unmade part that the Beldam didn't bother making, a realm of the unknown.

The otherness of the alternative parents inhabiting this magical realm becomes immediately apparent and is important in establishing the danger of their fantasy world. Coraline's Other Father is controlled by the piano, whilst Other Mother gestures with her hands and taps her long, spindly fingers as she waits for Coraline's stunned responses when they sit at the dinner table, particularly when the Beldam asks if she can sew buttons into Coraline's eyes and announces, 'Other Mother knows you best, like the back of her hand', alluding to the real mother's failure to understand her daughter. Other Mother manipulates Coraline on an emotional level through her dialogue and apparent kindness, creating a juxtaposition between the two mothers. The contrast between the worlds is also significant. In the fantasy realm, mist seeps out from beneath the house and the plants and flowers in the grounds intertwine in autumnal colours, creating Halloweeny tapestries that symbolize witchcraft. There is constant movement in the Other World, in contrast to the stillness of the real one; it is a constantly animated alter-dimension, one which Coraline views, initially, as being more attractive than 'home', even though she understands that it isn't home. When she calls her father the 'Other Father', her Other Mother insists, 'Your better father, dear', but Coraline remains unconvinced. She is adept at wandering, and is curious about the Other World, yet retains a level of cynicism about its magical properties.

For her, belonging to the family in the Other World is tempered by an acutely heightened awareness of what is real and what is not. Coraline, familiar with unhappiness and abandonment issues, does not believe that this magical world is real or true. She experiences doubt at the strange familiarity of the fantasy home and its inhabitants because this world is colourful, musical and homely, a stark contrast to her real home life, and when Other Father comments that 'everything's right in this world, kiddo', she instinctively knows that it is not.

Coraline begins to understand what makes her Other parents uncanny, just as she understands that Wybie's silencing and the silencing of her Other Father is unnatural. When Other Mother presents her with a gift of button eyes and a needle for sewing them onto her face, announcing, 'Soon you'll see things our way', Coraline embraces the fear that has been curdling beneath the surface and hurries off to bed so that she can wake up in the 'real' world. It is at this point that her wandering becomes a threat rather than a promise of adventure, and she understands the danger that she is in, just as the children before her must have realized, too late. Home as a safe place is certainly contested at this point, and it becomes something far more nightmarish. The answer to the question of which world is better is finally revealed through Other Mother's unveiling of her murderous self.

The realm of the fantastic evokes very real concerns about child safety and the horror of child abduction in Selick's film adaptation. Wybie refers to his grandmother's sister, the child who was 'stolen' or who may have simply run off, as no one at the time knew what happened to her. The ghost children tell Coraline how the Beldam ate up their lives, keeping them prisoners in her Other World and, when Coraline escapes through the tunnel, the Beldam screams, 'Don't leave me, don't leave me, I'll die.' She needs the children; she feeds off them and keeps them as wispy pale trophies. The magic elements of the Other parents' world offer delight and distraction, whilst the sinister underlying themes drag it back into the real. Ideas of parenthood and parental responsibility are called into question, just as the fantastic and grotesque lead us further into the dark uncanny.

'Belonging'

From other mothers to silenced, tortured children, *Coraline* is a film about identity and displacement, and its themes, as we have seen, extend into the fabric of modern life. The question of how one belongs in the family and the negotiation that occurs, through wandering, in order to find one's place, is at the core of *Coraline*. This happens against a backdrop of magic and socially important, relevant issues that are particularly salient for a children's film, such as the dissolving family and child identity. The film broaches the question of identity as it traverses the difficult void between the real and the fantastic; characters are placed in precarious situations and must overcome real fears of abduction, abandonment and displacement. We see how Coraline loses and eventually finds herself in her quest to establish firmer ideas of home and family and also in her and Wybie's attempt to survive the imminent danger that threatens them and their loved ones.

Childhood is clearly displaced in the film. Coraline is neglected and left to wander (into danger), whilst Wybie is a character who appears, hovers and disappears regularly, unable to function within either setting of the real or fantastic world. Belonging is only achieved at the denouement of Selick's film; childhood and its safety is in peril throughout. This is accentuated particularly by the appearance of the child ghosts, who, in Gaiman's original story, warn Coraline of her impending fate:

> She will take your life and all you are and all you care'st for, and she will leave you with nothing but mist and fog … A husk you'll be, a wisp you'll be, and a thing no more than a dream on waking, or a memory of something forgotten.[33]

In Selick's adaptation the ghosts are visual reminders of the dangers that befall children in the Beldam's world, telling Coraline, 'We don't remember our names … she lured us away … she said that she loved us but she locked us up here and ate up our lives.'

Displacement of childhood and family has become part of modern life. Globalization renders identities 'diasporic, mobile and transient'.[34] Identity is malleable and it adapts to situations, to places and to others around us. Identity within contemporary culture is very much connected to the idea of wandering, Rapport and Dawson suggest,[35] which ties in with the notion of belonging being 'unstable'.[36] It seems reasonable to propose, therefore, that the wandering in Selick's *Coraline* may be viewed as normal by its audience. Home is created, somewhat haphazardly, as the Joneses move into a strange residence and surround themselves with boxes. The house remains largely unlived in until Coraline's mother tasks her with the unpacking. The family is not settled or safe, and the setting itself represents mystery and, later, danger.

As the notion of identities as fixed things becomes contested, and the family unit breaks down, otherness creeps between Coraline's worlds and begins to tear at the fabric of life. Coraline's sense of her own belonging becomes displaced, as magic and horror intersect and pull together, like the rough stitches sewn across the child dolls' mouths and bellies. The allusion to child abuse is subtle but present, and home and family become both something sought after and something to dread. Coraline begins her adventure with gutsy excitement and an eagerness to become visible, but, as her adventure progresses and her fear begins to build, she longs for the stability of her real family.

Empowered by her adventures, Coraline rejects her own position as a child in need of protection and becomes the hero of her family and neighbourhood. As Coontz posits, we should abandon the myth of the traditional family; it never existed and even if it did, it certainly does not anymore.[37] Coraline learns to adapt to the worlds she inhabits and recognizes that home and family are more important than adventure and that her parents' work commitments and their celebration of their milestone achieved is part of this family life. Coraline's awareness of the world and its monsters has been enhanced by her adventures; she has wandered, played and survived very much on her own terms. If Gaiman's story is a lesson learned, it is as much one of child empowerment through wandering as it is of valuing family.

Wandering is part of the nature of twenty-first-century life; it happens both mentally and physically, as we distance ourselves from place and social interaction. In the climate of the nuclear family, parents find themselves questioning their own decisions and values, and wandering occurs. Coraline wanders in search of her identity and her own place in the world – whichever world is the best fit – and this reflects the unsettled family unit and its values today. Wandering eventually leads back to family, but family doesn't always mean belonging and home isn't always safe; the child must adapt in order to survive.

Notes

1   Stephanie Coontz, *The Way We Never Were: American Families and the Nostalgia Trap* (New York: Basic Books, 1992), p. 207.

2   Isabel Heinemann, *Inventing the Modern American Family: Family Values and Social Change in 20th Century United States* (Frankfurt: Campus Verlag, 2012), p. 7.

3   Ibid., p. 8.

4   Marilyn J. Coleman and Lawrence H. Ganong, *The Social History of the American Family: An Encyclopedia*, vol. 1 (London: SAGE, 2014), p. xxxi.

5   Samuel P. Huntingdon, *Who Are We? The Challenges to America's National Identity* (New York: Simon and Schuster, 2004).

6   Mike Savage, Gaynor Bagnall and Brian Longhurst, *Globalization and Belonging* (London: Sage, 2005).

7   Dennis Wiseman, *The American Family: Understanding Its Changing Dynamics and Place in Society* (Springfield: Charles C. Thomas, 2008), p. 17.

8   Coontz, *The Way We Never Were*, p. 278.

9   Timothy Corrigan, ed., *American Cinema of the 2000s: Themes and Variations* (New Jersey: Rutgers, 2012), p. 140.

10   Henry Giroux, *The Mouse That Roared: Disney and the End of Innocence* (Lanham, MD: Rowman & Littlefield, 1999), p. 2.

11 David Rudd, 'An Eye for an I: Neil Gaiman's Coraline and Questions of Identity', *Children's Literature in Education*, vol. 39, no. 3 (2008), p. 164.

12 Richard Gooding, 'Something Very Old and Very Slow: Coraline, Uncanniness and Narrative Form', *Children's Literature Association Quarterly*, vol. 33, no. 4 (2008), p. 394.

13 Saeede Hosseinpour and Nahid Shahbazi, 'Magical Realism in Neil Gaiman's Coraline', *Prague Journal of English Studies*, vol. 5, no. 1 (2016), p. 87.

14 Neil Gaiman, *Coraline* (London: Bloomsbury, 2009), p. 11.

15 Coleman and Ganong, *The Social History of the American Family*, p. xxxi.

16 Coontz, *The Way We Never Were*, p. x.

17 Tasha R. Howe, *Marriages and Families in the 21st Century: A Bioecological Approach* (Chichester: Wiley-Blackwell, 2012), p. 4.

18 Rudd, 'An Eye for an I', p. 160.

19 Ibid.

20 Lindsay Myers, 'Whose Fear is It Anyway? Moral Panics and Stranger Danger in Coraline', *Lion and the Unicorn*, vol. 36, no. 3 (2012), p. 246.

21 Cindy Aaron quoted in Samuel P. Huntingdon, *Who Are We? The Challenges to America's National Identity*, p. 72.

22 Savage, Bagnall and Longhurst, *Globalization and Belonging*, pp. 1, 11.

23 Lord Dunmore quoted in Huntingdon, *Who Are We? The Challenges to America's National Identity*, p. 50.

24 Stephen Vincent Benet quoted in Huntingdon, *Who Are We? The Challenges to America's National Identity*, p. 50.

25 Savage, Bagnall and Longhurst, *Globalization and Belonging*, p. 207.

26 Dominic Lennard, *Bad Seeds and Holy Terrors – the Child Villains of Horror Film* (New York: SUNY Press, 2014), p. 8.

27 Michael Wyness, *Contesting Childhood* (New York: Falmer Press, 2000), p. 8.

28 Paula S. Fass and May Ann Mason, eds, *Childhood in America* (New York: New York University Press, 2000), p. 1.

29 Anne Scott MacLeod, 'American Girlhood in the Nineteenth Century', in Paula S. Fass and May Ann Mason (eds), *Childhood in America*, p. 88.

30 Paul Wells, 'Wonderlands, Slumberlands and Plunderlands: Considering the Animated Fantasy', in Christopher Holliday and Alexander Sergeant (eds), *Fantasy/Animation: Connections between Media, Mediums and Genres* (London: Routledge, 2018), p. 24.

31 Wyness, *Contesting Childhood*, p. 1.

32 Richard Kearney, *Strangers, Gods and Monsters: Interpreting Otherness* (London: Routledge, 2005), p. 7.

33 Gaiman, *Coraline*, pp. 101–2.

34 Savage, Bagnall and Longhurst, *Globalization and Belonging*, p. 1.

35 Nigel Rapport and Andrew Dawson, *Migrants of Identity: Perceptions of Home in a World of Movement* (Oxford: Berg, 1998), p. 24.

36 Savage, Bagnall and Longhurst, *Globalization and Belonging*, p. 11.

37 Coontz, *The Way We Never Were*, p. 278.

12

Fa(r)ther figures: Locating the Author Father in *Coraline*

Nicholas Andrew Miller

For Georgia

Devotees of Henry Selick's 2009 stop-motion film, *Coraline*, might be excused for dismissing the notion that the tale has anything of importance to say about fathers.[1] It is an 'Other Mother', after all, who stands at the centre of the narrative's vortex of terror. In this tale of a brave daughter, the alien presence residing at the heart of domestic life is the maternal itself, cast as a rapacious force of desire that threatens, in the tradition of fairy-tale witches, evil queens, and predatory stepmothers, to consume the child it purports to love.[2] By contrast, the power of the paternal seems vague and amorphous, barely registering as a factor in Coraline's quest to deliver her family from the malevolence that lives on the Other side of her house. Her father, Charlie Jones, is a schlubby, unobtrusive, at times wholly ignorable figure in the narrative. Dutifully subservient to his overtaxed and querulous wife, he epitomizes the father as deputy parent, surfacing here and there to deliver the odd dad-joke or to cook another inedible concoction for his family's dinner.[3] His doppelgänger, the Other Father, meanwhile, carries this paternal diminution to its logical extreme: a tool, quite literally, of the Other Mother's will, he is little more than a spineless sack of doughy existence that, shaped to her specifications, can appear to play an enchanted piano or drive a robot praying mantis garden tractor, but assessed on his own merits is decidedly more dud than dad.

It is striking, then, to note that the film's own 'parent' text, Neil Gaiman's 2002 novella of the same name, locates *Coraline*'s origins in a daughter's encounter not with her Other Mother but with her Author Father. Traversing the volume's front matter, we come upon two unpunctuated sister sentences marching in paired rhythm across an otherwise empty page:

I started this for Holly

I finished it for Maddy

Holly Gaiman, as the author explains in a brief afterword titled 'Why I Wrote Coraline', was five years old when her father began composing a 'refreshingly creepy' story for children; Maddy, her younger sister, was roughly that age when he completed it a decade later.[4] That *Coraline* came into being as a tale addressed by a father to his daughters might seem a dismissible bit of context, but this point of origin reverberates intriguingly in a narrative as centrally focused as this one is on the force – particularly the potentially threatening force – of the maternal. What could Gaiman, or any father for that matter, have wanted with such material? Gaiman's ready answer is as compelling as it is personal: 'I'd wanted to write a story for my daughters', he explains, 'that told them something I wished I'd known when I was a boy: that being brave didn't mean you weren't scared. Being brave meant you were scared, really scared, badly scared, and you did the right thing anyway.'[5]

The private character of Gaiman's expressed motivation here suggests a certain reframing of *Coraline* itself. This tale about maternal horror is in a primary sense a fable of paternal pedagogy, a literary bequeathing to daughters of their father's acquired emotional wisdom. From this vantage, Gaiman's textual dedication of the work to Holly and Maddy raises a number of questions not only about his aims in concocting a story about the threat of maternal evil but also about the role fathers may play, as Coraline's does to some degree, in passively abetting and even perhaps encouraging that evil. Charlie Jones's relatively flaccid presence in the story belies the forceful, protective masculinity that is frequently presumed to animate paternal devotion as such; Gaiman's writerly intervention remaps that devotion onto the figure of a guardian storyteller and pedagogue. Between these two fathers, the fictional character and the real author, the tale of Coraline's encounter with a monstrous mother unspools as a curious and complex communication between dads and daughters.

It seems clear that Gaiman fashioned his protagonist rather precisely with his story's didactic aims in view. A young, self-assured heroine with whom little girls might readily identify, Coraline credibly deflates bravery's traditional associations with knights, soldiers, explorers and other figures frequently gendered as exclusively male. But beyond this, Gaiman's ambition to tell his daughters 'something I wished I'd known when I was a boy' suggests a desire to address a failure of the adult world in general, and of fathers in particular, to give children the tools necessary to knowing how to act in spite of fear. The creator of *Coraline* is not in this sense merely a spinner of yarns but also his heroine's Author Father; her capacity to manage fear as bravery's companion and not its adversary is the measure of his own emotional intelligence and mentorship. Coraline's role in demonstrating that courage can be powerfully represented in the actions of a small girl thus points towards a more expansive reading of her story, one that has the potential to reconfigure the landscape of paternal masculinity as a force that can shape, for good or ill, a daughter's experience of her own bravery.

This chapter seeks to explore the paternal in *Coraline*, and in doing so to investigate three points in particular: first, as I have already suggested, that the extraordinary power of the tale is rooted to a significant extent in its invention by a father for his daughters; second, that the story may have something to teach us about the structural role father figures play within representations of maternal evil, a richly developed tradition of which can be found in the narrative legacies of fairy and folk tales across many cultures and contexts;[6] and third, that Selick's stop-motion refashioning of Gaiman's material offers a constructive critique of this tradition, particularly concerning the parameters within which fatherhood itself is too often defined in terms of power and discipline, values frequently presumed to be synonymous with masculinity in general. Simply put, the force of maternal wickedness that pulses at the core of *Coraline* is activated by a paternal dyad – fictional father and Author Father – that grounds and structures the tale itself. Gaiman's assertion that he 'started this for Holly' and 'finished it for Maddy' is an invitation to consider the story's portrait of daughterly grit and fearlessness as one drawn specifically by and for fathers. Selick's film takes this invitation seriously, redirecting the paternal forces at work both in the novella and in its creation in order to investigate the possibility of a frequently discounted but extremely powerful father–daughter dynamic that relies on the child's perspective of her parent not as masculine, distant and wise, but as vulnerable and human.[7]

A gifted child

There are plenty of children for whom moving to a remote, draughty, hundred-and-fifty-year-old mansion like the Pink Palace might prove traumatic. Not so Coraline Jones. An explorer at heart, she takes it upon herself to investigate her new surroundings, wandering alone through the overgrown garden and up into the hills above the house, an improvised dowsing rod in hand to aid in locating a hidden well. Curious and sociable, Coraline makes the rounds to meet her neighbours, including April Spink and Miriam Forcible, the aging burlesque actresses who keep Scottie dogs (both alive and stuffed) in their basement flat, and Sergei Alexander Bobinsky, the loopy Russian gymnast who trains circus mice in the rooms upstairs. She befriends the local nameless feral black cat, apologizing for at first calling him a 'wuss-puss', and deals assertively with the banana-slug-hunting, homemade-steampunk-electric-bike-riding Wybie, whom she immediately dislikes as a creepy 'stalker' and know-it-all, and by whom she is not intimidated in the slightest. Initially spooked by a strange cry she hears while searching for the well (it turns out it's only the cat), she proceeds in short order to establish her bona fides as a confident, self-possessed 11-year-old, getting her clothes dirty, contracting a poison oak rash and squashing bugs in the bathroom with her bare hands. Selick places a light but conspicuous emphasis on these and other details missing from Gaiman's book, as if to suggest that Coraline is the sort of daughter who already knows what it means to be brave.

The bold and self-governing child adventurer is a distinctly parental fantasy, one that Coraline's own busy father and mother cannot help but indulge. Mel and Charlie Jones are writers whose work producing gardening catalogues seems to occupy most of their waking hours. They type away at their keyboards, frantically churning out copy to meet a looming deadline. Such are the professional pressures they face that they barely have time to grocery shop or unpack boxes from the move, much less entertain an energetic young daughter. To such parents, a child content to amuse herself is a dream come true. Of course, it is impossible for the daughter the Joneses might *prefer* to accord at all times with the daughter they *have*, and when a downpour curtails her outdoor explorations, Coraline's efforts to comply with her guardians' go-away-we're-working parenting style are upended. By driving her inside, the rain forces her to intrude directly upon her parents' work-blinkered awareness. Confined to the house, she becomes exactly what they wish they could ignore, a noisy presence to accommodate and a responsibility – *their* responsibility. In short, she becomes a regular kid.

In Gaiman's novella, the Joneses' occupation is only vaguely delineated.[8] The film is, on the contrary, explicit both about what their work entails and about the fact that they are, essentially, defined by it. They write. They edit. They stress over deadlines. Activities of a non-professional sort, such as eating, sleeping, running errands and raising daughters, are essentially side engagements, shoehorned into the interstices of a life devoted to work. As married working professionals who happen also to be parents, Mel and Charlie Jones offer a compelling vision of filial abandonment as a normal and acceptable practice, perhaps even one to be celebrated. 'Coraline, I don't have time for you right now' is their go-to mode of address, a mantra that masks as necessity what is actually a personal, parental choice. Compelled by stress rather than malice, the Joneses' policy of benign neglect is nonetheless what occasions their daughter's initial encounter with the Other Mother. Exiled to her room for declaring that her father's cooking 'looks like slime', Coraline awakens in the night, alone and hungry, and descends the stairs to discover the tunnel behind the secret door. In a narrative sense, it is thus the breach opened within the family space by Mel and Charlie's averted gazes that precipitates her entry to the Other World, a surreal elsewhere defined as much by the familiar absence of her real mother and father as by the extravagant presence of their uncanny familiars.

The fact that the Other Mother and Other Father mirror Coraline's own parents seems initially to suggest that they merely represent a correction to her actual home life. Precisely responsive to Coraline's individual needs, the Other side of the house offers an avalanche of wish fulfilment. Welcomed 'home' by her Other parents, Coraline finds herself in a space that is brightly lit, warm and reassuring, in which she eats food that is delicious and abundant, goes to sleep in a snug room populated by magical stuffed animal friends and wears uniquely expressive clothing made especially for her.[9] The Other Mother in particular stands at the centre of this golden-hued dream vision as the obverse of Coraline's actual experience, a mother whose otherness consists in providing the maternal attention her real mother does not. The Other Mother is thus easily located within *Coraline*'s narrative landscape as a sort of symptomatic expression of parental abandonment. In her overwhelming responsiveness to Coraline, she represents the 'everything' that is the material antithesis of the emotional and psychological 'nothing' that the girl confronts at home.

However, this clean distinction between Coraline's mothers may prove too neat. In a curious sense, the Other Mother's defining maternal feature can be glimpsed most clearly in the strange confluence of material superabundance and emotional insufficiency that she embodies. What is perversely maternal in the Other Mother is that her idealized beneficence, rather than compensating Coraline for her real parents' deficiencies, threatens to engulf and consume her. A sort of enchanted and enchanting supermom, she is in precisely this sense not a mother at all – a *smother* rather, her preternatural capacity to anticipate and fulfil Coraline's every wish expressing maternal solicitude in inverted form as a veiled threat. For Coraline, the effect is a bewildering fusion of maternal affection and desire; the Other Mother's material profligacy becomes indistinguishable from her voracious emotional need. In fact, it is this blurring of motives that makes her terrifying, the embodiment of an *amor matris* that will eventually suffocate Coraline's own will and gobble up her very existence. 'Why does she want me?' Coraline asks the cat. 'She wants something to love, I think,' he replies, 'something that isn't her. Or maybe she'd just love something to eat.'

This inscription of maternal desire as ravenous and consumptive, of 'mothering' as 'smothering', complicates rather significantly the Other Mother's appearance in *Coraline* as a symptom of mere material neglect. Coraline's encounter with the Other Mother is an expression not of her own desires as a daughter, satisfied in the form of imaginary roast chicken dinners and stylishly expressive clothing, but of the collapsing of maternal love and emotional need. This collapse is in fact the defining feature of Coraline's home life where, in her interactions with her mother and father, acceptance is provisional and temporary, recognition is accompanied by avoidance and expressions of concern are synonymous with demands that she go away. 'Family' as such is familiar to Coraline only as a concept defined and grounded in the merging of conflicting parental desires. The Other side of the house materializes as the imaginative articulation of Coraline's response to this merging of love and need, a liminal elsewhere in which she can quite literally 'get lost'. The Other Mother is thus not an unconscious projection of a preferred fantasy parent, but the embodied expression of Coraline's own creative response to emotional conflicts that are all too familiar.

In her sensitivity and responsiveness to her parents, Coraline establishes herself as an example of what pioneering Polish-Swiss psychologist Alice Miller called the 'gifted child'.[10] The term 'gifted' here refers not to cognitive intelligence but to a capacity for emotional awareness that is universally visible in children's interactions with their caregivers.[11] In Miller's account, children are highly sensitive barometers of the emotional environment in which they find themselves. Attuned to those upon whom they depend for their happiness, safety and very existence, they respond from infancy to the cues their behaviour elicits in the adults around them. 'The child', Miller writes, 'has a primary need from the very beginning of her life to be regarded and respected as the person she really is at any given time'.[12] The parent who because of his own unaddressed anxieties and insufficiencies cannot acknowledge his child in this way inexorably exhibits his own dependence for emotional equilibrium 'on the child's behaving in a particular way'.[13] In response, the child stifles her own need to be seen in order to gratify her parents' desire to feel competent.

Understood as the attributes of a gifted child, Coraline's most salient and recognizable qualities – her independence, adventurousness and curiosity – acquire a certain compensatory sheen. Charlie and Mel's devotion to their work communicates a parental need that, to a daughter navigating a new environment and relationships and dependent entirely on her parents' capacity to provide or withhold what is necessary for stability and security, is at an emotional level indistinguishable from the parental expression of love. It is by becoming the child her parents need her to be – absent, undemanding, 'out of the way' – that Coraline can experience herself as the child they love. The enactment of parental attachment as consumption, of 'mothering' as 'smothering', here comes fully into focus: the Other Mother's love can only achieve expression as a famished greed for the extinction of the child's own authentic emotional experience. For the gifted child, being loved fundamentally entails the destructive absorption – the 'swallowing up' – of the child she *is*. In Coraline's familiar world, what mothers want is 'something to love' that is also 'something to eat'.

The father in the mirror

It is against this particular vision of maternal love, *amor matris* figured as an annihilating force of affection, that daughters, it seems, must learn to be brave. In writing *Coraline*, Gaiman explicitly mobilized his own resources as an Author Father on his daughters' behalf, implying that teaching them what it means to act courageously in the face of such maternal love is an expressly paternal undertaking. While Charlie Jones is a mostly passive figure within Gaiman's fiction, the author's dedication of the volume gestures towards his endorsement of a traditional role for the paternal in this tale, the real father operating behind the scenes as the indispensable instrument of protection. It is striking, therefore, that it should be precisely in his visual depiction of Coraline's dad that Selick effectively subverts Gaiman's authorization of the daughter's deliverance by a wise and courageous father. In doing so, he points as well to a solution to the gifted child's fundamental dilemma, her capacity to find parental love only by allowing herself to be consumed by her caregivers' emotional needs.

Our first glimpse of Charlie Jones arrives a scant ten minutes into Selick's film, as Coraline pushes open a heavy wooden door to reveal her father's study. His back to the viewer, Charlie bends over an old monitor, two long index fingers poking methodically at the keyboard as he composes an article for the garden catalogue. The scene is dimly illuminated, its visual palette ranging from drab to sombre, Charlie's stooped body dwarfed by the precarious towers of unpacked moving boxes that surround him. In this initial exchange, Mr Jones comes off as a somewhat robotic, if essentially harmless, fellow. Wholly absorbed in his screen and keyboard, he avoids his daughter's requests for attention first by ignoring them, then by abdicating responsibility and finally by sending Coraline off on a pointless window-counting expedition designed to keep her occupied. He is the epitome of the inaccessible grown-up, and as viewers encountering him for the first time, we share fully in Coraline's disappointment.

In many respects, the film's visualization of Charlie fills out the contours of the preoccupied, generic dad that appears early in Gaiman's text. But Selick's attention to mise-en-scène underscores particular dimensions of paternal vulnerability and confinement that Gaiman de-emphasizes. In the film, Charlie's study resembles the den of some pale, reclusive, light-averse creature. Cramped and poorly lit, the room seems less a workspace than an extension of his introverted personality, a shell in which he privately dwells. Indeed, Charlie himself appears tortoise-like, hunched and physically compact, hemmed in by the dishevelled stacks of boxes, his bespectacled head and neck extending horizontally from a green Michigan State sweater. He pursues his writing with dutiful, passionless verve, marshalling the energy and attention the task requires and no more. His hunt-and-peck typing technique evokes at once childish ineptitude and mindless automatism while his sleepy, heavy-lidded eyes, flitting from keyboard to screen and back, betray a very adult state of surrender to work-inspired ennui. This is writing visualized both figuratively and literally as 'copy' – not, that is, as creative expression but as repetitive, mechanistic chore.

Figure 12.1 Father and daughter: a study in confinement.

In a remarkable bit of visual framing, Selick subtly but powerfully suggests Charlie's vulnerability, not only as a writer chasing a deadline but also as a father beset by greater, unspoken pressures. A cut-in to an over-the-shoulder shot reveals his face dimly reflected in the computer screen, traversed by the lines of copy he is required rather than inspired to write. Enclosed within the flat confines of the monitor, the elongated oval of his visage suggests a disembodied puppet head floating in a dark void. Beside it we glimpse the full-length figure of Coraline waiting restlessly behind him (Figure 12.1). The impression is overwhelmingly one of confinement, father and daughter mutually constricted by boredom, technology and the banality of their respective family roles. In this regard the image exposes the root cause of the Joneses' family crisis, at the same time foreshadowing Coraline's crucial encounter with a second mirrored portrait late in the film, that of her parents imprisoned by the Other Mother behind the hallway mirror. Despite the displacement of her own form in the earlier reflection by her mother's in the later one, the visual rhyme is explicit and unmistakable. Now, as then, textual figures – letters and words – cover and enclose human ones, Charlie's anxious typing on the reflective computer monitor presaging his wife's plea for help as she traces with her finger a desperate message on the obverse surface of the mirror: 'HELP US' (Figure 12.2).

Revisiting Gaiman's literary description of the mirror scene reveals the care Selick exercised in replicating the sequence. As in the novella, Coraline watches in horror as the mirror goes dark, and then gathers herself for the decisive act

Figure 12.2 A parental plea: 'HELP US'.

of bravery that will compel her return to confront the Other Mother. 'I have to go back,' she tells the cat. 'They are my parents.' However, this fidelity to his source material has the paradoxical effect of underscoring what is most striking about Selick's treatment as a whole, namely the enormity of what it leaves out. In the original, Gaiman brings the plot to a grinding halt as Coraline, about to turn the key that will unlock the secret door, pivots instead to face the cat and, improbably, tell a story. Neither excessively brief nor particularly cogent, the anecdote she relates seems a strikingly odd insertion at this moment in the narrative. It tells of a long-ago expedition with her father to explore an urban 'wasteland' in which they were attacked by angry wasps. As the insects swarm, Coraline's father tells her to run away, himself remaining behind to ensure her escape. After returning home, they assess the damage: she has been stung only once, while he has 'thirty-nine stings, all over him'. In the tale's coda, Coraline's father returns to the wasteland, knowing that he will be stung again, to retrieve his glasses which he dropped as he ran. Here Coraline imparts to the cat the story's moral in a voice ventriloquizing Gaiman's own: 'When you're scared but you still do it anyway ... *That's* brave.'[14]

While the wasp episode suspends narrative momentum at a critical juncture, it is difficult to ignore the fact that, given Gaiman's acknowledged paternal aims in writing *Coraline*, it constitutes what is arguably *the* crucial passage in the entire tale. It is here, after all, that the father character teaches his daughter what it means to be brave. In his spoken commentary on the DVD edition of the film,

Selick reflects ruefully on this point, calling the wasp story, which he ultimately had to cut, 'a beautiful tale … setting up what bravery is and what are necessary things you just have to do'. That the suspension of narrative drive could not be made to work cinematically is hardly surprising, but the excision of the episode also raises an important question about the role of the paternal in Selick's film. In Gaiman's original tale the father's function in demonstrating bravery is the indispensable mechanism by which Coraline accesses her own courage; his is the pedagogical act without which she, standing at the threshold of the secret door, would not herself prove capable of turning the key. By cutting the story of the wasps, Selick effectively removed the very heart of *Coraline* as an instructive tale. The force of the father's teaching, and in a crucial sense the value of the paternal as such, recedes as Selick's Coraline is left profoundly alone to turn the key of bravery herself.

In Gaiman's telling, the daughter's defeat of the Other Mother depends on her father's ability to enact a model bravery for her to imitate; his paternal effectiveness lies in his capacity to act as her mirror, to cause her to see her own potential, her own *self*, reflected in his actions. It is precisely through the elimination of this particular father figure, the moral didact, the heroic, wasp-stung dad, that Selick's film preserves the possibility of Coraline's rescue of her parents as her own action, the authentically brave deed of a gifted child. To understand this paradox, we have to return to the space of the paternal as Selick visually represents it. We have to look again at that hard-working figure Coraline finds hunched over his computer. We have to reconsider the terms of that father's actual relationship to the daughter who swings impatiently on the door behind him, eager for him to notice her. And we have especially to ask what these two figures of confinement and vulnerability, father and daughter, owe to the Author Father who dreamed them up in the first place.

Fa(r)ther figures

Gaiman recounted the story of *Coraline*'s compositional gestation twice, once in his 2002 afterword and again in his introduction to the novella's 2012 tenth-anniversary edition. Between these two accounts, it is possible to calculate that the two lines of Gaiman's textual dedication, 'I started this for Holly' and 'I finished it for Maddy', mark a temporal ellipsis of roughly a decade.[15] After initiating the project, Gaiman composed several dozen pages and then abruptly stopped. 'We moved to America', he explains. 'The story, which I had been writing in my own time, between things that people were waiting for, ground to a halt. Years passed. One day I looked up and noticed that Holly was now in her teens, and her younger sister, Maddy, was the same age Holly had been when I had started it for her.'[16] What compelled Gaiman's return to the project was a father's worry that the teaching he had intended for his children might in the end only be received by them as adults: 'I started it again', he writes, 'because I realized that if I didn't, my youngest daughter, Maddy, would be too old for it by the time I was done.'[17] It is striking in this context that the immediate compositional task to which Gaiman turned following this hiatus was none other than the wasp episode, the crucial articulation of what he would later acknowledge as the tale's central motivation and meaning. With the urgency not merely of a writer but of an Author Father, he marked his return to *Coraline* precisely by promoting the paternal to a place of major significance in the tale itself.

The story of the wasps is not, ultimately, about Gaiman's young female protagonist at all; its purpose is to transform a determinedly passive father figure, Charlie Jones, into the heroic author of Coraline's emotional formation as a young girl capable of bravery. In this sense, Gaiman's insertion of the wasp story upon returning to *Coraline* suggests a certain authorial solipsism, a self-regard that in fact serves neither the fictional Coraline nor his own daughters, but primarily Gaiman himself. I do not mean to suggest that Gaiman's motivations were in a trivial sense selfish, but simply that the wasp story reveals his own presence, particularly in the guise of the paternal nurturer and pedagogue, as an important element of the father–daughter dynamic in *Coraline*. In putting off work on the project, Gaiman had in effect delayed, both figuratively and literally, his dedication to Holly and Maddy. Locating a valiant father and his thirty-nine wasp stings at precisely the place in the narrative at which that figure could most effectively exonerate him offered an effective, if only symbolic, fictional bulwark against the spectre of paternal neglect. At the same time, by inscribing Coraline's recollection of the wasp episode at the decisive, critical juncture of her own story, Gaiman appropriates to the father an act of bravery that in a fundamental sense can no longer belong to his daughter-heroine; passing through the door to confront the Other Mother can only ever be for Coraline an act of filial mimicry. Acting bravely to rescue her parents confines her within a learned practice of imitation in which she can only be the author of her own actions to the extent that she is 'just like her dad'.

Coraline, in these terms, is in its original literary form essentially a paternal fantasy. Gaiman's strategy, while it succeeds in mapping the origins of Coraline's courageous action for the reader, essentially subverts her power and autonomy as a heroine. Paradoxically, if less apparently, it also effects a certain distancing of the father himself from the scene of his daughter's development. Through the story of the wasps, Charlie Jones (and by implication Gaiman as well) is inscribed in the tale not as an actual father but as a type, a stock figure whose supposedly masculine qualities of strength, self-sacrifice, wisdom, persistence and of course bravery are meant to articulate the paternal as such. The father Coraline knows, boxed-in, harried, inadequate, burdened, *human*, is replaced by a gallant ideal, a model father who is transcendent, refined and distant, a fa(r)ther figure who performs bravery as a quality intrinsic to the paternal pattern his daughter is invited to emulate but that can never be authentically her own.

Like the mother as 'smother', the father as 'fa(r)ther figure' reveals a compensatory structure at work in Gaiman's fiction, the symptom of an emotional gap spanned by a father's expedient fantasy of daughterly heroism. Ironically, the wasp story robs Coraline not only of the assertion of her own emotional experience as valid and true but also of her father as *a* father. It locates him instead at an elevated remove, an exemplary model and 'father in the mirror' to replace the actual, human father whose attention she seeks. The key feature of the daughter's emotional development in such an instance is not the meeting and overcoming of her own fear, but the submersion of that emotion: to be brave, she must become so in her father's image. By eliding the wasp story, Selick removed its structural role in defining bravery for the tale's heroine. In effect, he proscribed the possibility of Charlie Jones's serving as a paternal ideal, a fa(r)ther figure, for Coraline in the film. Instead, Charlie remains a father, his emotional proximity to his daughter measurable in terms that are imperfect and variable, subject to the vagaries of work distractions, poorly developed cooking skills, playful impulses, deadline stress and weather. Absent the heroic wasp story, Charlie is confirmed in his work-induced absence as a paternal presence, a non-archetypal father figure who remains for all his flaws and inadequacies nevertheless resolutely human in his interactions with his daughter.

Recognizing Charlie in Selick's portrayal not as an exemplary fa(r)ther figure but as an actual father, vulnerable to fear as well as capable of being rescued, it becomes possible to discern that his filial neglect masks a hunger of his own.

What is obscured by Gaiman's focus on Coraline's paternal education in bravery is given focused visual attention in the film: the Charlie Jones that viewers encounter is a parent who experiences the stresses and emotional confinement of adulthood without needing to swallow up his daughter's vitality. A study in lethargy and depletion, he presents the image of a man curiously sheltered from his own natural exuberance and indeed, in a certain profound sense, from his own life. His surroundings, material and familial, constrict rather than sustain him; his world, reflected in the limited field and sombre colours of the computer screen, is literally and figuratively too small for him. His physical presence eloquently expresses this state of affairs: twisted and hunched, his body resembles nothing so much as an inverted question mark, a shape that suggests at once his inability to stretch and extend himself and the fact that his existence has itself become essentially a form of bewilderment and alienation.

Selick represents the challenge to Coraline in encountering this all-too-human dad as scaled to the interests and longings of a bright, curious, bored 11-year-old. Coraline's interaction with her father in his study clearly displays her disappointed desire for paternal attention; as she swings on his office door complaining that there is nothing to do, her impatience is manifest, her frustration palpable and the attractions of finding a means to replace her dud of a dad with an idealized father-hero obvious. What is most striking, however, is the way Selick's visual presentation underscores Coraline's observation of her father as a moment of self-discovery. In the image reflected in Charlie's computer screen, Coraline glimpses the lively, brightly hued, full-length figure of a child hovering beside a male adult's tired, pinched and disembodied countenance. The visual contradiction is unmistakable and leaves an impression of stark emotional contrast, the bright yellow of her slicker and Wellington boots erupting like the energy of childhood itself inside the dull, constrained space of adulthood.

The visual juxtaposition here is especially powerful because it makes palpable not only her father's plight as an adult but also the maturity that awaits Coraline herself. The spectacle of beleaguered adult confinement she observes directly and explicitly presages the image of parental captivity she later confronts in the hallway mirror. In that instance, as her parents fade from view, their figures are replaced by her own, a visual confirmation of the truth Coraline will presently acknowledge verbally, that they are not coming back and that it is she who will have to act with a bravery all her own. In Selick's film, Coraline's decision to save her parents is not an emulation of an idealized paternal model but the straightforward act of a little girl who has stumbled upon the world in which her parents live, a barren, colourless wasteland defined by obligation and professional burdens, in which it is the adults who are in urgent need of rescue.

Coraline's act of bravery, decisive, forthright and unequivocal, prompts a reassessment of her appeals for parental attention early in the film and of the Other World as her creative response to the emotional dilemma of the gifted child. Her attempts to breach the state of stressed concentration that consumes her parents' lives are essentially reminders that the child's basic emotional right is to express herself and in doing so to be heard, seen and appropriately acknowledged.[18] This need for self-expression and recognition is fundamental to the development of every child; it begins with the infant's cry and continues throughout the changing circumstances of every life, extending into and through adulthood. As Alice Miller points out, to be recognized as the person one is and no other, possessed of particular emotions, thoughts and ideas at any given time, is a human requirement as irreducible and fundamental as oxygen, food and shelter. Confronted with the avoidance or outright refusal of her appeals, the gifted child reacts by fashioning herself as the precise and direct response to her parents' expressed need.[19] In Coraline's case, this means 'getting lost', subjecting herself to the temptation/threat of donning button eyes and becoming an Other Daughter.

Coraline's 'discovery' of the Other Mother is the clearest indication that she has registered at an emotional level her parents' need for her to get lost. The Other side of the house is the place that she disappears in, obliterating the child her parents reject and becoming the child they need and therefore love. The Other Mother's existence expresses Coraline's plight as a function not simply of her parents' neglect but of her responsiveness to that neglect, her creative awareness that it is her parents' emotional imprisonment that her bravery must address. By giving visual emphasis to Coraline's parents' distressed emotional lives, Selick makes available to his stop-motion heroine a form of action that is effectively closed off to her literary counterpart. His decision to suppress the need for a traditional father-hero's intervention opens a space in which Coraline's action is authentically and unequivocally her own, and in which she manages not only to save her parents but also to transform her family.[20] Understanding Coraline as a 'gifted' child in Miller's sense clarifies her confrontation with the Other Mother as a quest not to restore her family and her home to some idyllic and imaginary vision of wished-for abundance, but to obviate the emotional confinement on which her parents rely for their own sense of purpose, stability and security. While Coraline's responsiveness to her parents' need is expressed in the form of a powerful malicious maternal figure, her path to understanding that need and her potential independence from it lies through an encounter with a human, and humanly vulnerable, father.

Notes

1 I am grateful to Victoria Bartolomeo and Jillian Fury for conversations that both spurred and sustained my curiosity about the role of paternal 'mirroring' in *Coraline*, as well as for their generous and perceptive readings of this chapter in draft.

2 The tradition of the devouring mother trope in western fairy and folktales is rich and varied. See especially Maria Tatar, *The Hard Facts of the Grimms' Fairy Tales* (Princeton: Princeton University Press, 1987) and Bruno Bettelheim, *The Uses of Enchantment: The Importance and Meaning of Fairy Tales* (New York: Random House, 1976).

3 Insofar as it implies a certain miscarriage of parental nurturing, Charlie's bad cooking suggests an interesting framing of the father's role within the devouring mother tradition.

4 Neil Gaiman, *Coraline* (New York: HarperCollins, 2002).

5 Neil Gaiman, *Coraline* (New York: HarperCollins, 2012), p. xvii.

6 In the original *Cinderella* tale, for example, variations of which appear in virtually every world cultural tradition, it is a widowed father's illicit desire to marry his own daughter that ultimately leaves her vulnerable to the wicked stepmother. See Jack Zipes (trans., ed.), *The Great Fairy Tale Tradition: From Straparola and Basile to the Brothers Grimm* (New York: W.W. Norton, 2001), pp. 26–50.

7 With respect to Selick's rewriting of the paternal role in particular, it is worth considering *Coraline* in relation to other prominent explorations of the father–daughter relationship in animation. See especially Hayao Miyazaki's *My Neighbor Totoro* (Japan, 1988), Michaël Dudok de Wit's *Father and Daughter* (Netherlands, 2000), Keiichi Hara's *Miss Hokusai* (Japan, 2015), Han Yang and Basil Malek's *The Tree* (France, 2018) and Daria Kashcheeva's *Daughter* (Czech Republic, 2019).

8 Gaiman, *Coraline* (2002), p. 5.

9 Selick employed a number of visual tools to distinguish the Other World as vibrant and alive, including expansive 3D effects, a brighter colour palette, and sets built with greater allowance for spatial depth in contrast to the 'raked', or flattened, sets used to shoot the 'real world' of Coraline's home environment. See Henry Selick, *Coraline*, 'Feature Commentary' (Laika, Inc., 2009), DVD.

10 Throughout her career, Alice Miller argued that society's deep commitment to excusing and protecting parents creates a strong incentive in adults to recall their childhood origins as idyllic. Miller's clinical studies frequently revealed the grounding of such personal histories in memories that are selective or even largely imagined. See especially *The Drama of the Gifted Child*, 3rd edn (New York: Basic Books, 1997) and *Thou Shalt Not Be Aware: Society's Betrayal of the Child*, 1st edn (New York: Farrar, Straus and Giroux, 1998).

11 See Edward Tronick et al., 'The Infant's Response to Entrapment between Contradictory Messages in Face-to-Face Interaction', *Journal of the American Academy of Child Psychiatry*, vol. 17, no. 1 (1978), pp. 1–13; See also Lauren B. Adamson and Janet E. Frick, 'The Still Face: A History of a Shared Experimental Paradigm', *Infancy*, vol. 4, no. 4 (2003), pp. 451–73.

12 Miller, *The Drama of the Gifted Child*, p. 6.

13 Miller suggests that unconscious insecurities in adults are frequently rooted in their own childhood experiences of emotional neglect which can now be met through the vulnerable person of their own child. See *The Drama of the Gifted Child*, pp. 8–13.

14 Gaiman, *Coraline* (2012), pp. 54–7.

15 Gaiman, *Coraline* (2002); Gaiman, *Coraline* (2012).

16 Gaiman, *Coraline* (2002).

17 Gaiman, *Coraline* (2012), p. xv.

18 Miller, *The Drama of the Gifted Child*, p. 6.

19 Ibid., pp. 4–19.

20 In the film's final sequence, the entire cast of Coraline's neighbours and allies assembles in the garden. We are left with a portrait of togetherness, collaboration, and mutual enjoyment that makes plain that the measure of Coraline's bravery was, all along, a transformed family.

A guide to further research

This non-comprehensive guide offers a representative mixture of popular press and academic sources on *Coraline* and studio LAIKA (which remains active as of this book's publication date), as well as broader topics directly relevant to the film, such as stop-motion animation, 3D filmmaking and animated children's horror. It is intended as a starting point for future research, rather than an exhaustive round-up of available material on these subjects.

Coraline

Fordham, Joe. '*Coraline*: A Handmade World', *Cinefex*, no. 117 (2009), pp. 40–61.

Cinefex is a visual effects journal aimed at industry professionals and layperson afficionados alike. This non-academic article offers a wealth of behind-the-scenes production information (along with photographs), including highly specific and detailed descriptions of the camera equipment and puppet crafting materials used by LAIKA's team.

Jones, Stephen. *Coraline: A Visual Companion* (New York: HarperCollins, 2009).

This is a detailed, lavishly illustrated guide to the production of *Coraline*, designed for general audiences. It includes a foreword by Neil Gaiman, and sections on the book, film, key characters and various other *Coraline* adaptations (graphic novel, audiobook, theatrical productions).

Studio LAIKA

Alger, Jed. *The Art and Making of ParaNorman* (San Francisco: Chronicle Books, 2012).
Brotherton, Philip. *The Art of The Boxtrolls* (San Francisco: Chronicle Books, 2014).

Haynes, Emily. *The Art of Kubo and the Two Strings* (San Francisco: Chronicle Books, 2016).
Zahed, Ramin. *The Art of Missing Link* (San Rafael, CA: Insight Editions, 2019).

These four coffee-table artbooks dedicated to LAIKA's other feature films contain material that would fascinate animation fans and may prove particularly useful for researchers. They feature quotes by various production crew members, behind-the-scenes photos, concept art, storyboards, character design sheets, etc.

Hury, David. 'The Little Factory of the Great Thrill: Studio LAIKA', *Marimo* no. 2 (2018), pp. 38–48.

This issue of animation journal *Marimo*, titled 'Phantasmagoria', dedicates a number of pages to LAIKA, focusing on the studio's blend of stop motion and visual effects, especially in its most recent films. This overview article is followed by one-page interviews with art director Alice Bird and director Chris Butler, as well as a short analysis of LAIKA's approach to storytelling.

Stop-motion animation

Comiskey, Andrea. '(Stop)Motion Control: Special Effects in Contemporary Puppet Animation', in Dan North, Bob Rehak and Michael S. Duffy (eds), *Special Effects: New Histories/Theories/Contexts* (London: Palgrave, 2015), pp. 45–61.

Comiskey's excellent chapter on the recent evolution of stop-motion practices in the digital age examines the role of digital technologies and aesthetics in eight Anglo-American stop-motion features produced since 1993, including *Coraline*. The author's discussion of the incorporation of computer-generated imagery (CGI) work in the film and the importance of the 'handmade imperative' to its promotion is an especially valuable approach to understanding not only *Coraline* itself, but its place in the broader context of contemporary puppet filmmaking.

Giesen, Rolf. *Puppetry, Puppet Animation and the Digital Age* (Boca Raton, FL: CRC Press, 2019).

Giesen's book (which includes a discussion of some of LAIKA's films) focuses on the role of puppet animation in digital-age filmmaking, arguing for a reconsideration of the view of stop motion as a niche practice. This study features interviews with practitioners, as well as historical context and comparative studies of CGI and puppet aesthetics.

Harryhausen, Ray, and Tony Dalton. *A Century of Stop-Motion Animation: From Méliès to Aardman* (New York: Watson-Guptill, 2008).

In this book, stop-motion legend Ray Harryhausen and his co-author Tony Dalton offer a detailed history of the craft, from its earliest days to the present moment. Richly illustrated, this essential volume contains rare archival photographs and sketches, explanatory diagrams and industry trivia.

Pallant, Chris. 'The Stop-Motion Landscape', in Chris Pallant (ed.), *Animated Landscapes: History, Form and Function* (London: Bloomsbury, 2015).

Introducing a new critical angle to the study of stop-motion animation aesthetics, this chapter analyses the distinguishing formal characteristics of the stop-motion landscape, defining three distinct categories: instrumental landscapes, symbolic landscapes and narrative landscapes.

Priebe, Ken A. *The Advanced Art of Stop-Motion Animation* (Boston, MA: Cengage Learning, 2010).

Aimed mainly at practitioners, this excellent, updated in-depth guide includes sections on puppet building, digital cinematography and visual effects (among others). The book will also be of interest to scholars, as it includes a section on the history of the form, as well as interviews with key figures in contemporary stop-motion filmmaking (both commercial and independent) and a useful 'further reading' section.

Ruddell, Caroline, and Paul Ward, eds. *The Crafty Animator: Handmade, Craft-Based Animation and Cultural Value* (Cham, Switzerland: Palgrave Macmillan, 2019).

While this excellent edited collection is focused on the notion of craft and its many meanings and applications within the study and process of animation (with an emphasis on issues of labour and gendered practices), many of the chapters directly engage with or touch upon stop motion in particular. As craft and craftsmanship have been central to LAIKA's production and marketing ethos since *Coraline*, this volume offers productive new ways of engaging with this film and the studio's larger oeuvre.

3D filmmaking

Benson-Allott, Caetlin. 'The *Chora* Line: RealD Incorporated', *South Atlantic Quarterly*, vol. 110, no. 3 (2011), pp. 621–44.

In this close reading of *Coraline*'s 3D aesthetics, the author argues that the film mobilizes the inherent uncanniness of stereoscopic animation in order to offer a new experience of visual verisimilitude that moves away from indexical realism. Benson-Allott reads the film as a key moment not only in the history of digital projection but also in the development of a greater understanding of post-indexical spectatorship.

Higgins, Scott. '3D in Depth: *Coraline, Hugo,* and a Sustainable Aesthetic', *Film History*, vol. 24, no. 2 (2012), pp. 196–209.

This essay places *Coraline* in the context of 3D aesthetics, singling the film out as a historically significant moment in the development of the technology's formal qualities. It argues that Selick's film, together with Martin Scorsese's *Hugo* (2011), articulates a depth-oriented aesthetic that directly ties stereoscopic effects to character-driven storytelling.

Prince, Stephen. *Digital Visual Effects in Cinema: The Seduction of Reality* (New Brunswick, NJ: Rutgers University Press, 2012) [specifically chapter 5, 'Immersive Aesthetics, pp. 183–220].

In this seminal work on contemporary visual effects, Prince counters the tired claim that the so-called 'digital revolution' has brought about a radical departure from traditional Hollywood filmmaking. Instead, he demonstrates that effects-driven films can be seen as a continuation of well-established aesthetic and narrative norms. The fifth chapter, devoted to 3D aesthetics, contains a brief discussion of *Coraline*'s stereoscopic design.

Zone, Ray. *3-D Revolution: The History of Modern Stereoscopic Cinema* (Lexington: University Press of Kentucky, 2012) [specifically chapter 28, 'Immersed in *Coraline*', pp. 317–24].

This comprehensive book chronicles the history of modern 3D cinema from the 1950s through James Cameron's *Avatar* (2009). Neatly divided into key time periods and their relevant technological and aesthetic developments, Zone's work is a valuable resource on the industry, culture and art of 3D cinema. In a short chapter devoted to *Coraline*, Zone briefly touches upon the reception of *Coraline*'s 3D visuals and includes an interview with Brian Gardner, who worked as a stereoscopic advisor on the film.

Animated children's horror

Lester, Catherine. 'The Children's Horror Film: Characterizing an "Impossible" Subgenre', *Velvet Light Trap*, no. 78 (2016), pp. 22–37.

As Lester argues, the relationship between horror and the child demographic (a topic central to *Coraline*'s reception, as Rayna Denison points out in this volume) has historically remained complex and burdened by tensions and misconceptions. This article focuses on animated horror films in order to trace the development of children's horror as a Hollywood subgenre and tease out the ways in which such films mediate their content in order to cater to their intended audience while still honouring genre conventions.

Troutman, Megan. 'It's Alive ... AGAIN: Redefining Children's Film Through Animated Horror', in Casie Hermansson and Janet Zepernick (eds), *The Palgrave Handbook of Children's Film and Television* (Cham, Switzerland: Palgrave Macmillan, 2019), pp. 149–65.

This volume analyses contemporary global film and television developed for children and youth. Troutman's chapter focuses on American animated children's horror (including *Coraline*), arguing that these features challenge dominant notions of childhood currently entrenched in mainstream children's film genres in the United States.

Notes on contributors

Jane Batkin is a Senior Lecturer and Enterprise Lead at the University of Lincoln, UK. She is the author of *Identity in Animation: A Journey into Self, Difference, Culture and the Body* (2017) and recently completed her PhD on identity in animated film. She has published book chapters on duality, othering and family in *Toy Story: How Pixar Reinvented the Animated Feature* (2018) and in *Aardman Animations: Beyond Stop Motion* (2020). Her chapter on framing Snow White within 1930s America appears in *Snow White and the Seven Dwarfs: New Perspectives on Production, Reception, Legacy* (2021).

Malcolm Cook is Associate Professor of Film at the University of Southampton. His book *Early British Animation: From Page and Stage to Cinema Screens* was published by Palgrave Macmillan in 2018 and was runner-up in the Norman McLaren/Evelyn Lambart Award for Best Scholarly Book in Animation. He is currently researching the role of advertising in the history of animation and has written several chapters on this topic, which appear in *The Animation Studies Reader* (2018) and *Aardman Animations: Beyond Stop-Motion* (2020). Dr Cook has also co-edited (with Dr Kirsten Moana Thompson) the collection *Animation and Advertising* (2019).

Rayna Denison is Head of Department and a Senior Lecturer for the Film, Television and Media Studies at the University of East Anglia. Her research and teaching interests centre on Japanese film and animation. She is the author of *Anime: A Critical Introduction* (2015), the editor of *Princess Mononoke: Understanding Studio Ghibli's Monster Princess* (2018) and the co-editor of the Eisner Award-nominated *Superheroes on World Screens* (with Rachel Mizsei-Ward, 2015). She has also edited several special issues on animation and adaptation including for the *Journal of Japanese and Korean Cinema*, the *Journal of East Asian Popular Culture* and *Animation Studies*. Her scholarly articles can be found in many leading journals, including the *Journal of Cinema and Media Studies*, *The Velvet Light Trap*, *Japan Forum* and the *International Journal of Cultural Studies*.

Miriam Harris is a Senior Lecturer in Digital Design at the Auckland University of Technology, New Zealand. She studied Fine Arts and Literature at the University of Auckland, and Digital Animation and VFX at Sheridan College, Canada, and is both an animation practitioner and theorist. Her output includes award-winning short animated films, as well as a number of essays on experimental, digital and Eastern European animation. Together with Lilly Husbands and Paul Taberham, she co-edited the book *Experimental Animation: From Analogue to Digital* (2019). In 2020 she was appointed co-editor – alongside Samantha Moore – of the international animation academic journal *Animation Practice, Process & Production*.

Eric Herhuth is Assistant Professor of Communication and Director of Film Studies at Tulane University. His research areas include animation and film studies, aesthetics and politics, and media and film theory. He has published in the *Quarterly Review of Film and Video, Cinema Journal, animation: an interdisciplinary journal, Theory & Event*, and he is the author of *Pixar and the Aesthetic Imagination: Animation, Storytelling, and Digital Culture* (2017).

Norman M. Klein is a cultural historian and a novelist. His books include *Seven Minutes: The Life and Death of the American Animated Cartoon, The History of Forgetting: Los Angeles and the Erasure of Memory, Vatican to Vegas: The History of Special Effects, Freud in Coney Island*, the award-winning database novel *Bleeding Through: Layers of Los Angeles, 1920–85, The Imaginary 20th Century* (co-authored with Margo Bistis) and *Tales of the Floating Class: Essays and Fictions, 1982–2017*. The expanded second edition of *Bleeding Through* will appear in early 2021 (co-edited by Jens Martin Gurr). Later that year, *Archaeologies of the Present: The Dismantling of the American Psyche* is due out. Klein is a professor at California Institute of the Arts.

Kodi Maier is currently working on their thesis on the Disney Princess franchise at the University of Hull. Their most recent article, 'Kids at Heart?: Exploring the Material Cultures of Adult Fans of All-Ages Animated Shows', was published in June 2019 in the *Journal of Popular Television*. Other publications include 'Princess Brides and Dream Weddings: Investigating the Gendered Narrative of Disney's Fairy Tale Weddings' in the book *Discussing Disney* (2019) and 'Camping Outside the Magic Kingdom's Gates: The Power of Femslash in the Disney Fandom' (2017) in *Networking Knowledge: Journal of the MeCCSA Postgraduate Network*.

Mihaela Mihailova is Assistant Professor in the School of Cinema at San Francisco State University. She has published in *Feminist Media Studies, animation: an interdisciplinary journal, Studies in Russian and Soviet Cinema,*

Flow, and *Kino Kultura*. She has also contributed chapters to *Animating Film Theory* (with John MacKay), *Animated Landscapes: History, Form, and Function, The Animation Studies Reader*, and *Drawn from Life: Issues and Themes in Animated Documentary Cinema*. Dr. Mihailova is the co-editor of *Animation Studies* (https://journal.animationstudies.org/) and currently serves as Secretary of the Society for Animation Studies.

Nicholas Andrew Miller is Associate Professor of English and Director of Film Studies at Loyola University Maryland. His areas of interest include film animation, early cinema, and the intersections between modernist print and visual cultures. He has published in *James Joyce Quarterly, Eire-Ireland: An Interdisciplinary Journal of Irish Studies*, and *Clues: A Journal of Detection*, and has contributed chapters to *Animation and Memory* (2020), *Aardman Animations: Beyond Stop Motion* (2020), as well as a recent blog post on the origins of the phenakistiscope to *Animation Studies 2.0*. His current project is an interdisciplinary study of metamorphosis and metaphor in modernist visual culture. He is the author of *Modernism, Ireland, and the Erotics of Memory* (2002).

Ann Owen lectures in animation and visual effects, teaching the history and theory of animation, and stop-motion animation and puppet making. She studied animation at the University for the Creative Arts in Surrey and after graduating in 1998 went on to work as a production animator in Manchester for Hot Animation, working on the award-winning children's show *Bob the Builder*. After leaving the studio, she took up an appointment teaching stop-motion animation in Surrey and progressed to become a lecturer in the history and theory of animation. Her research interests lie in the growing area of neuroaesthetics, a discipline that involves researchers from both science and the arts. Her own focus is on the relationships between the mechanisms of visual perception (in the human brain) and animation spectatorship and production. She has led panels and presented her research at international conferences in Athens, Los Angeles, Toronto, Canterbury and Singapore.

Jane Shadbolt is a senior lecturer in Visual Communication Design at the University of Newcastle, Australia. She is a stop-motion animator and academic with research interests in stop-motion production, particularly cameras, visual effects and virtual production.

Dan Torre is a senior lecturer in the School of Design at RMIT University in Melbourne, Australia. He is the author of a number of books, including *Animation – Process, Cognition and Actuality* (2017), *Cactus* (2017), *Carnivorous Plants* (2019) and co-author of *Australian Animation – An International History* (2018) and *Grendel Grendel Grendel – Animating Beowulf* (2021).

Bibliography

Adamson, Lauren B., and Janet E. Frick. 'The Still Face: A History of a Shared Experimental Paradigm'. *Infancy*, vol. 4, no. 4 (2003): 451–73.

Adler, Margot. *Drawing Down the Moon: Witches, Druids, Goddess-Worshippers and Other Pagans in America* (New York: Penguin Group, 2006).

Aguilar, Carlos. 'Take a Look at the Painstaking Craft behind Laika's "Missing Link"'. *Cartoon Brew*, 10 April 2019. https://www.cartoonbrew.com/stop-motion/take-a-look-at-the-painstaking-craft-behind-laikas-missing-link-172509.html (accessed 10 May 2020).

Althusser, Louis. 'Ideology and Ideological State Apparatuses'. Trans. Ben Brewster, Marxists.org. https://www.marxists.org/reference/archive/althusser/1970/ideology.htm (accessed 3 March 2020).

Altick, Richard D. *The Shows of London* (Cambridge, MA: Harvard University Press, 1978).

Amidi, Amid. *Cartoon Modern: Style and Design in Fifties Animation* (San Francisco: Chronicle Books, 2006).

Amidi, Amid. 'A Peek into the Art of "Coraline" Book That Never Was'. *Cartoon Brew*, 2 July 2015. https://www.cartoonbrew.com/auctions/a-peek-into-the-art-of-coraline-book-that-never-was-gallery-108716.html (accessed 11 October 2019).

Amidi, Amid. '"Missing Link" Bombs at the Box Office'. *Cartoon Brew*, 14 April 2019. https://www.cartoonbrew.com/box-office-report/missing-link-bombs-at-the-box-office-172729.html (accessed 10 June 2019).

Anon. 'Abrams Boldly Goes to Trekkie Heights'. *Sunday Business Post*, 10 May 2009.

Anon. 'Movies: New This Week'. *Atlanta Journal-Constitution*, 6 February 2009, p. 8E.

Anon. 'Opening This Weekend'. *New York Observer*, 6 February 2009.

Antunes, Filipa. 'Rethinking PG-13: Ratings and the Boundaries of Childhood and Horror'. *Journal of Film and Video*, vol. 69, no. 1 (2017): 27–43.

Ashley, Tim. '*Coraline* Review – Creepy Adaptation of Neil Gaiman's Tale Will Turn Kids on to Opera'. *The Guardian*, 30 March 2018. https://www.theguardian.com/music/2018/mar/30/coraline-review-neil-gaiman-barbican (accessed 5 November 2020).

Atkinson, Michael. 'The Night Countries of the Brothers Quay'. *Film Comment*, vol. 30, no. 5 (1994): 36–44.

Bailey, Jason. 'The Stop-Motion Animation Studio That Created *Coraline* Is Still Toiling Away'. *Vulture*, 9 April 2019. https://www.vulture.com/2019/04/inside-laika-stop-motion-studio-that-made-missing-link.html (accessed 10 June 2019).

Barker, Martin, and Julian Petley. 'Introduction'. In Martin Barker and Julian Petley (eds), *Ill-Effects: The Media/Violence Debate* (London: Routledge, 1997), pp. 1–11.

Bazin, André. 'The Myth of Total Cinema'. Trans. Hugh Gray, in *What Is Cinema? Vol. 1* (Berkeley: University of California Press, 2005), pp. 17–23.

BBFC. 'Case Studies: Coraline'. *British Board of Film Classification.* http://www.bbfc.co.uk/case-studies/coraline (accessed 1 September 2018).

Bear, Mark F., Barry W. Connors and Michael A. Paradiso. *Neuroscience: Exploring the Brain* (Philadelphia: Lippincott Williams & Wilkins, 2007).

Beck, Jerry. 'The Ranft Bros. in *Coraline*'. *Cartoon Brew*, 10 February 2009. https://www.cartoonbrew.com/feature-film/the-ranft-bros-in-coraline-11228.html (accessed 23 September 2020).

Benson-Allott, Caetlin. 'The *Chora* Line: RealD Incorporated'. *South Atlantic Quarterly*, vol. 110, no. 3 (2011): 621–44.

Berlina, Alexandra, ed. *Viktor Schklovsky: A Reader* (London: Bloomsbury, 2016).

Bettelheim, Bruno. *The Uses of Enchantment: The Importance and Meaning of Fairy Tales* (New York: Random House, 1976).

Bigelow, Joe. 'King Kong'. *Variety*, 6 March 1933. http://www.variety.com/review/VE1117792322/ (accessed 9 December 2019).

Briggs, Caroline. 'Gromit Film 'a Force for Britishness''. *BBC News*, 9 October 2005. http://news.bbc.co.uk/1/hi/entertainment/4309544.stm (accessed 17 March 2020).

British Board of Film Classification (BBFC). 'Same Difference? – A Comparison of the British and American Film and DVD Rating Systems'. *British Board of Film.* https://forum.blu-ray.com/showthread.php?t=309139 (accessed 8 September 2018).

Brotherton, Philip. *The Art of The Boxtrolls* (San Francisco: Chronicle Books, 2014).

Brown, Noel, and Bruce Babington. 'Introduction: Children's Films and Family Films'. In Noel Brown and Bruce Babington (eds), *Family Film in Global Cinema: The World Beyond Disney* (London: I.B. Tauris, 2015), pp. 1–18.

Braund, Simon. 'Through the Looking Glass'. *Empire*, no. 239 (May, 2009).

Buccino, Giovanni, Lui Fausta, Nicola Canessa, Ilaria Patteri, Giovanna Lagravinese, Francesca Benuzzi, Carlo A. Porro and Giacomo Rizzolatti. 'Neural Circuits Involved in the Recognition of Actions Performed by Nonconspecifics: An fMRI Study'. *Journal of Cognitive Neuroscience*, vol. 16, no.1 (2004): 114–26.

Buchan, Suzanne, ed. *Pervasive Animation* (London: AFI Reader/Routledge, 2013).

Buchan, Suzanne. 'The Animated Spectator: Watching the Quay Brothers' "Worlds"'. In Suzanne Buchan (ed.), *Animated 'Worlds'* (Eastleigh: John Libbey, 2006), pp. 15–38.

Buchan, Suzanne. *The Quay Brothers: Into a Metaphysical Playroom* (Minneapolis: University of Minnesota Press, 2011).

Buckland, A. W. 'The Significance of Holes in Archaeology'. *The Antiquary: A Magazine Devoted to the Study of the Past*, vol. 32 (1896): 335–41.

Buckley, Chloé Germaine. 'Psychoanalysis, "Gothic" Children's Literature, and the Canonization of *Coraline*'. *Children's Literature Association Quarterly*, vol. 40, no. 1 (2015): 58–79.

Bukatman, Scott. *Matters of Gravity* (Durham, NC: Duke University Press, 2003).

Bukatman, Scott. *Poetics of Slumberland* (Berkeley: University of California Press, 2012).

Bukatman, Scott. *Terminal Identity* (Durham, NC: Duke University Press, 1993).

Burr, Ty. '*Coraline*: Alice in Freudland'. *Boston Globe*, 6 February 2009. http://archive.boston.com/ae/movies/articles/2009/02/06/alice_in_freudland/ (accessed 1 September 2018).

Butler, Judith. *Senses of the Subject* (New York: Fordham University Press, 2015).

Campanario, Gabi. 'A Weird, Whimsical – and Somewhat Eerie – "Coraline"'. *Seattle Times*, 5 February 2009. https://www.seattletimes.com/entertainment/movies/a-weird-whimsical-8212-and-somewhat-eerie-8212-coraline/ (accessed 10 September 2020).

Cappelletto, Chiara. 'The Puppet's Paradox: An Organic Prosthesis'. *RES: Anthropology and Aesthetics*, no. 59/60 (2011): 325–36.

Carroll, Lewis. *Alice's Adventures in Wonderland* (Chicago, IL: VolumeOne, 1998).

Carroll, Noël. 'Medium Specificity Arguments and Self-Consciously Invented Arts: Film, Video and Photography'. *Millennium Film Journal*, no. 14/15 (1984–5): 127–53.

Carroll, Noël. 'The Specificity of Media in the Arts'. *Journal of Aesthetic Education*, vol. 19, no. 4 (1985): 5–20.

Catland Books. 'Ritual to Hex Brett Kavanaugh'. Facebook Event, 20 October 2018. https://www.facebook.com/events/179836286297165/ (accessed 13 November 2019).

Character Design References. 21 July 2017. https://characterdesignreferences.com/art-of-animation-3/coraline (accessed 5 July 2019).

Choi, Won. 'Inception or Interpellation? The Slovenian School, Butler, and Althusser'. *Rethinking Marxism*, vol. 25, no. 1 (2013): 23–37.

Cianciolo, Patricia J. *Picture Books for Children*. 4th edn (Chicago, IL: American Library Association, 1997).

Clark, John. 'Adding Dimension to the Storytelling'. *New York Times*, 1 February 2009, p. 16.

Coleman, Marilyn J. and Lawrence H. Ganong. *The Social History of the American Family: An Encyclopedia*, vol. 1 (London: SAGE, 2014).

Comiskey, Andrea. 'Special Effects in Contemporary Puppet Animation'. In Dan North, Bob Rehak and Michael S. Duffy (eds), *Special Effects: New Histories/Theories/Contexts* (London: BFI Palgrave, 2015), pp. 45–61.

Coontz, Stephanie. *The Way We Never Were: American Families and the Nostalgia Trap* (New York: Basic Books, 1992).

'Coraline (2009)'. Animation Screencaps. https://animationscreencaps.com/coraline-2009/3/#box-1/152/coraline-disneyscreencaps.com-512.jpg?strip=all (accessed 31 January 2020).

'Coraline (2009)'. Animation Screencaps. https://animationscreencaps.com/coraline-2009/44/#box-1/16/coraline-disneyscreencaps.com-7756.jpg?strip=all (accessed 31 January 2020).

'Coraline in 3D: The *Dragon* Stop Motion Connection'. *Dragonframe*, 21 February 2009. https://www.dragonframe.com/blog/coraline-in-3d-the-dragon-connection/ (accessed 21 April 2020).

'Coraline – Tiny Knitting'. Focus Features/LAIKA, YouTube, 28 January 2009. https://www.youtube.com/watch?v=7wADZBNvA_s (accessed 10 October 2018).

Corrigan, Timothy, ed. *American Cinema of the 2000s: Themes and Variations* (New Jersey: Rutgers, 2012).

Crafton, Donald. *Before Mickey: The Animated Film, 1898–1928* (Chicago, IL: University of Chicago Press, 1993).

Crafton, Donald. *Shadow of a Mouse: Performance, Belief, and World-Making in Animation* (Berkeley: University of California Press, 2013).

Crary, Jonathan. *Techniques of the Observer: On Vision and Modernity in the Nineteenth Century* (Cambridge, MA: MIT Press, 1990).

Crockett, Zachary. 'How the Father of Claymation Lost His Company'. *Priceonomics*, 9 May 2014. priceonomics.com/how-the-father-of-claymation-lost-his-company/ (accessed 3 March 2020).

Culler, Jonathan. *The Pursuit of Signs: Semiotics, Literature, Deconstruction* (Ithaca, NY: Cornell University Press, 1981).

Decety, Jean, and Julie Grèzes, 'The Power of Simulation: Imagining One's Own and Other's Behavior'. *Brain Research*, vol. 1079, no. 1 (2006): 4–14.

Deleuze, Gilles. *Bergsonism* (New York: Zone Books, 1991).

Denson, Shane, and Julie Leyda, eds. *Post-Cinema: Theorizing 21st-Century Film* (Falmer: REFRAME Books, 2016). http://reframe.sussex.ac.uk/post-cinema/.

Desowitz, Bill. "'Corpse Bride: Stop Motion Goes Digital'. *Animation World Network*, 16 September 2005. https://www.awn.com/vfxworld/corpse-bride-stop-motion-goes-digital (accessed 1 May 2020).

Desowitz, Bill. 'Tadahiro Uesugi Talks "Coraline" Design'. *Animation World Network*, 23 January 2009. https://www.awn.com/animationworld/tadahiro-uesugi-talks-coraline-design (accessed 11 October 2019).

'Digital Cinema System Specification'. https://www.dcimovies.com/archives/spec_v1/DCI_Digital_Cinema_System_Spec_v1.pdf, p. 12 (accessed 20 April 2020).

Doane, Mary Ann. 'The Indexical and the Concept of Medium Specificity'. *differences: A Journal of Feminist Cultural Studies*, vol. 18, no. 1 (2007): 128–52.

Donovan, Moira. 'How Witchcraft is Empowering Queer and Trans Young People'. *Vice*, 14 August 2015. https://www.vice.com/en_us/article/zngyv9/queer-trans-people-take-aim-at-the-patriarchy-through-witchcraft (accessed 13 November 2019).

Earl of Ducie. 'Exhibition of Three "Mare-Stanes," or "Hag Stone"'. *Journal of the Anthropological Institute of Great Britain and Ireland*, vol. 17 (1888): 134–7.

Ebert, Roger. '*Coraline* (2009)'. RogerEbert.com, 4 February 2009. https://www.rogerebert.com/reviews/coraline-2009 (accessed 9 September 2018).

Elsaesser, Thomas. 'The "Return" of 3-D: On Some of the Logics and Genealogies of the Image in the Twenty-First Century'. *Critical Inquiry*, vol. 39, no. 2 (2013): 217–46.

Edwards, C. 'How Laika Pushed 3D Printing to New Heights with "The Boxtrolls"'. *Cartoon Brew*, 13 August 2014. https://www.cartoonbrew.com/feature-film/how-laika-pushed-3d-printing-to-new-heights-with-the-boxtrolls-101512.html (accessed 10 June 2019).

Eisenstein, Sergei. *Film Form: Essays in Film Theory*. Ed./trans. Jay Leyda (New York: Harcourt, Brace, Jovanovich, 1949).

Farquharson, Vanessa. 'Stop-Motion Putting End to CGI Domination; Technique Enjoys Resurgence in Animated Market'. *Calgary Herald*, 27 November 2009, p. E15.

Fass, Paula S., and May Ann Mason, eds. *Childhood in America* (New York: New York University Press, 2000).

Ferrari, P. F., C. Maiolini, E. Addessi, L. Fogassi and E. Visalberghi. 'The Observation and Hearing of Eating Actions Activates Motor Programs Related to Eating in Macaque Monkeys'. *Behavioural Brain Resaerch*, vol. 161, no. 1 (2005): 95–101.

Foá, Maryclare, Jane Grisewood, Birgitta Hosea and Carali McCall, eds. *Performance Drawing: New Practices since the 1960s* (London: I.B. Tauris, 2019).

Fordham, Joe. '*Coraline*: A Handmade World'. *Cinefex*, no. 117 (2009): 41–61.

Foster, Hal. 'Preface'. In Hal Foster (ed.), *Vision and Visuality* (Seattle, WA: Bay Press, 1988).

Foster, Joshua. 'Special Feature: Director's Commentary'. *Coraline 2-Disc Collector's Edition* (L.E.G. Productions, 2009).

Foutch, Haleigh. '*Kubo and the Two Strings*: Director and CEO Travis Knight on LAIKA's most ambitious film yet'. *Collider*, 30 June 2016. https://collider.com/kubo-and-the-two-strings-travis-knight-arianne-sutner-interview/ (accessed 12 August 2019).

Fraser, Hilary. 'Through the Looking Glass: Looking Like a Woman in the Nineteenth Century'. In Francesca Orestano and Francesca Frigerio (eds), *Strange Sisters: Literature and Aesthetics in the Nineteenth Century* (Bern: Peter Lang, 2009), pp. 189–213.

Freedberg, David, and Vittorio Gallese. 'Motion, Emotion and Empathy in Esthetic Experience'. *Trends in Cognitive Science*, vol. 11, no. 5 (2007): 197–203.

French, Lawrence. 'Phil Tippet: Stop-Motion May Be Going Extinct, but the Former Animator Is Alive and Well'. *Cinefantastique*, vol. 31, no. 1/2 (1999): 40–5.

Freud, Sigmund. *The Uncanny*. Trans. David McLintock (New York: Penguin, 2003).

Frey, Holly, and Tracy Wilson. 'Stop-Motion Animation History with LAIKA Studios'. *Stuff You Missed in History Class*, podcast recording, 10 April 2019. https://www. iheart.com/podcast/stuff-you-missed-in-history-cl-21124503/episode/stop-motion-animation-history-with-laika-studios-30806101/ (accessed 25 September 2020).

Frierson, Michael. 'Tim Burton's "Vincent" – a Matter of Pastiche'. *Animation World Network Magazine*, vol. 1, no. 9 (1996). https://www.awn.com/mag/issue1.9/articles/frierson1.9.html (accessed 9 August 2019).

Frost, James. 'Jan Svankmajer: Film as Puppet theater'. *Animation Studies*, 29 December 2016. https://journal.animationstudies.org/james-frost-jan-svankmajer-film-as-puppet-theatre/ (accessed 8 June 2020).

Gage, Carolyn. *The Triple Goddess: Three Plays* (lulu.com, 2009).

Gaiman, Neil. *Coraline* (London: Bloomsbury, 2012 [2002]).

Gaiman, Neil. 'Fairy Tales Are More than True: Not Because They Tell Us That Dragons Exist, but Because They Tell Us That Dragons Can Be Beaten'. *Tumblr*, 18 November 2014. https://neil-gaiman.tumblr.com/post/102947175291/fairy-tales-are-more-than-true-not-because-they (accessed 13 November 2019).

Gaiman, Neil. '@lesbiantrevorbelmont Asked: I Was Wondering, in The Kindly Ones, One of the Things Cluracan calls Nuala Is "La Belle Dame Sans Merci"'. *Tumblr*, 3 April 2018. https://neil-gaiman.tumblr.com/post/172565660631/i-was-wondering-in-the-kindly-ones-one-of-the (accessed 13 November 2019).

Gaiman, Neil. '@notdoingmywork Asked: What Was the Point of the Story Coraline?' *Tumblr*, 21 April 2017. https://neil-gaiman.tumblr.com/post/159843218331/what-was-the-point-of-the-story-coraline-because (accessed 13 November 2019).

Gaiman, Neil. '@reivaxm Asked: Hello. I Was Reading Coraline Again', '@aweirdvegan-blog Asked: Are Ms. Spink and Forcible Together?', and '@uwudroj asked: Hello I Was Just Wondering, Are Miss Spink and Miss Forcible a Couple?'. *Tumblr* posts, 31 August 2014, 24 October 2016, 6 July 2018. https://neil-gaiman.tumblr.com/post/96248654066/hello-i-was-reading-coraline-again-and-something, https://neil-gaiman.tumblr.com/post/152237746756/are-ms-spink-and-forcible-together and https://neil-gaiman.tumblr.com/post/175615960441/hello-i-was-just-wondering-are-miss-spink-and(accessed 13 November 2019).

Gaiman, Neil. *The Sandman* (New York: Vertigo Comics, 1989–96).

Gaiman, Neil. *The Sandman: A Game of You* (New York: Vertigo Comics, 1993).

Gallese, Vittorio, and Alvin Goldman. 'Mirror Neurons and the Simulation Theory of Mind-Reading'. *Trends in Cognitive Science*, vol. 2, no. 12 (1998): 493–501.

Galloway, Alexander S. 'Polygraphic Photography and the Origins of 3-D Animation'. In Karen Beckman (ed.), *Animating Film Theory* (Durham, NC: Duke University Press, 2014), pp. 54–67.

Giardina, Carolyn. '"Coraline" Makers Reveal How They Sculpted 6,333 Faces Fast', *Hollywood Reporter*, 12 February 2016. https://www.hollywoodreporter.

com/behind-screen/coraline-makers-reveal-how-they-863155 (accessed 3 November 2020).

Giardina, Carolyn. 'Oscars: "Kubo and the Two Strings" Is Rare Animated Feature to be Nominated in VFX', *Hollywood Reporter*, 24 January 2017. https://www. hollywoodreporter.com/behind-screen/oscars-2017-kubo-two-strings-is-rare-animated-feature-be-nominated-vfx-967979 (accessed 16 November 2020).

Giesen, Rolf. *Puppetry, Puppet Animation and the Digital Age* (New York: CRC Press, 2018).

Giles, Paul. *Virtual Americas: Transnational Fictions and the Transatlantic Imaginary* (Durham, NC: Duke University Press, 2002).

Gire, Dann. 'Creepy Stop-Motion Animation Highlights Fantasy Turned Nightmare'. *Daily Herald*, 5 February 2009, p. 19.

Giroux, Henry. *The Mouse That Roared: Disney and the End of Innocence* (Lanham, MD: Rowman & Littlefield, 1999).

Gooding, Richard. ' "Something Very Old and Very Slow": *Coraline*, Uncanniness, and Narrative Form'. *Children's Literature Association Quarterly*, vol. 33, no. 4 (2008): 390–407.

Goldner, Orville, and George. E. Turner. *The Making of King Kong* (New York: Ballantine Books, 1976).

Grant, Gavin J. 'Neil Gaiman Interview'. *Indie Bound*. https://www.indiebound.org/ author-interviews/gaimanneil (accessed 8 June 2020).

Gray, John. *The Soul of the Marionette: A Short Inquiry into Human Freedom* (New York: Farrar, Straus and Giroux, 2015).

Halberstam, J. *The Queer Art of Failure* (Durham, NC: Duke University Press, 2011).

Halberstam, Jack. 'Queer Gaming: Gaming, Hacking, and Going Turbo'. In Bonnie Ruberg and Adrienne Shaw (eds), *Queer Game Studies* (Minneapolis: University of Minnesota Press, 2017), pp. 187–201.

Hansen, Miriam. ' "With Skin and Hair:" Kracauer's Theory of Film, Marseille 1940'. *Critical Inquiry*, vol. 19, no. 3 (1993): 437–69.

Harris-Fain, Darren. 'Putting the Graphic in Graphic Novel: P. Craig Russell's Adaptation of Neil Gaiman's Coraline'. *Studies in the Novel*, vol. 47, no. 3 (2015): 335–45.

Harryhausen, Ray, and Tony Dalton. *A Century of Stop Motion Animation: From Méliès to Aardman* (New York: Watson-Guptill, 2008).

Hartmann, Margaret. '*Coraline*: A Freudian Fairy Tale That's Not Just for Kids'. *Jezebel*, 6 February 2009. https://jezebel.com/5148385/coraline-a-freudian-fairy-tale-thats-not-just-for-kids (accessed 12 December 2019).

Haynes, Emily. *The Art of Kubo and the Two Strings* (San Francisco: Chronicle Books, 2016).

Haynes, Georgina. Coraline's Closet [DVD], (USA: Universal Pictures, 2009).

Heinemann, Isabel. *Inventing the Modern American Family: Family Values and Social Change in 20th Century United States* (Frankfurt: Campus Verlag, 2012).

Hendershot, Heather. *Saturday Morning Censors: Television Regulation before the V-Chip* (Durham, NC: Duke University Press, 1998).

'Henry Selick in Conversation'. *Focus Features*, 9 February 2009. https://www.focusfeatures.com/article/henry_selick_in_conversation (accessed 12 December 2019).

'Henry Selick Interview: The Director of the Nightmare Before Christmas Reflects on His Biggest Hit and Discusses Next Film Coraline'. *DVDizzy*, 26 August 2008. https://www.dvdizzy.com/henryselick-interview.html (accessed 13 November 2018).

Higgins, Scott. '3D in Depth: *Coraline, Hugo*, and a Sustainable Aesthetic'. *Film History: An International Journal*, vol. 24, no. 2 (2012): 196–209.

Hoffmann, Heidrich. *Slovenly Betsy*, illustrated by Walter Hayn (Bedford, MA: Applewood Books, 2006; reprint from 1911). https://www.nypl.org/blog/2013/05/15/influence-str (accessed 9 December 2019).

Holliday, Christopher. *The Computer-Animated Film: Industry, Style and Genre* (Edinburgh: Edinburgh University Press, 2018).

Hosea, Birgitta. 'Made by Hand'. In Caroline Ruddell and Paul Ward (eds), *The Crafty Animator: Handmade, Craft-Based Animation and Cultural Value* (Cham, Switzerland: Palgrave Macmillan, 2019), pp. 17–43.

Hosseinpour, Saeede, and Nahid Shahbazi. 'Magical Realism in Neil Gaiman's Coraline'. *Prague Journal of English Studies*, vol. 5, no. 1 (2016): 87–101.

Howe, Tasha R. *Marriages and Families in the 21st Century: A Bioecological Approach* (Chichester: Wiley-Blackwell, 2012).

Huddleston, Tom. '*Coraline*'. *Time Out*, 5 May 2009. https://www.timeout.com/london/film/coraline (accessed 1 September 2018).

Huntingdon, Samuel P. *Who Are We? The Challenges to America's National Identity* (New York: Simon and Schuster, 2004).

Ikuma, John. 'Interview with Lead Animator/CEO Travis Knight', *Stop Motion Magazine*, no. 16 (2012): 21–31.

Johnson-Frey, Scott H., Farah R. Maloof, Roger Newman-Norlund, Chloe Farrer, Souheil Inati and Scott T. Grafton. 'Actions or Hand-Object Interactions? Human Inferior Frontal Cortex and Action Observation'. *Neuron*, vol. 39, no. 11 (2011): 1053–8.

Johnston, Keith. '"Three Times as Thrilling!": The Lost History of 3-D Trailer Production, 1953–54'. *Journal of Popular Film and Television*, vol. 36, no. 3 (2008): 150–60.

Johnston, Sheila. 'A Delicious Way to Scare Your Little Darlings to Death; The New Animation from the Director of *The Nightmare before Christmas* Is a Creepy Treat'. *Daily Telegraph*, 9 May 2009, p. 14.

Jones, Catherine. 'Starry Prequel'. *Liverpool Daily Echo*, 8 May 2009, p. 35.

Jones, Stephen. *Coraline: A Visual Companion* (New York: HarperCollins, 2009).

Kamen, Matt. 'How Boxtrolls Studio Revolutionised Stop Motion Animation'. *Wired*, 8 September 2014. https://www.wired.co.uk/article/boxtrolls-travis-knight-interview (accessed 10 June 2019).

Kaufman, Debra. 'Director Henry Selick on *Coraline*'. *Studio Daily*, 6 February 2009. https://www.studiodaily.com/2009/02/director-henry-selick-on-coraline/ (accessed 9 September 2019).

Kearney, Richard. *Strangers, Gods and Monsters: Interpreting Otherness* (London: Routledge, 2005).

Keeling Kara K., and Scott Pollard. 'The Key Is in the Mouth: Food and Orality in *Coraline*'. *Children's Literature*, vol. 40 (2012): 1–27.

Keveney, Roz. *From Alien to the Matrix: Reading Science Fiction Film* (London: Bloomsbury Academic, 2005).

Klein, Norman M. 'Animation and Animorphs: A Brief Disappearing Act'. In Vivian Sobchack (ed.), *Metamorphing: Visual Transformation and the Culture of Quick-change* (Minneapolis: University of Minnesota, 2000), pp. 21–41.

Klein, Norman M. *Bleeding Through: The Layers of Los Angeles, 1920–1985* (Los Angeles Labyrinth Projects at USC; Karlsruhe: Center for the Arts and Media, 2003).

Klein, Norman M. *Seven Minutes: The Life and Death of the American Animated Cartoon* (London: Verso, 1993).

Klein, Norman M. *The Vatican to Vegas: A History of Special Effects* (London: New Press, 2004).

Klein, Norman M., and Margo Bistis. *The Imaginary 20th Century* (Karlsruhe: Center for the Arts and Media, 2016).

Klinger, Barbara. 'Film History Terminable and Interminable: Recovering the Past in Reception Studies'. *Screen*, vol. 38, no. 2 (1997): 107–28.

Klinger, Barbara. *Melodrama and Meaning: History, Culture, and the Films of Douglas Sirk* (Bloomington: University of Indiana Press, 1994).

Knoblich, Günther, Eva Seigerschmidt, Rüdiger Flach and Wolfgang Prinz. 'Authorship Effects in the Prediction of Handwriting Strokes: Evidence for Action Simulation During Action Perception'. *Quarterly Journal of Experimental Psychology*, vol. 55, no. 3 (2002): 1027–46.

Kosslyn, Stephen M., William L. Thompson and Giorgio Ganis. *The Case for Mental Imagery* (Oxford: Oxford University Press, 2006).

Kozachik, Pete. '2 Worlds in 3 Dimensions'. *American Cinematographer*, vol. 90, no. 2 (2009): 26–39.

Kracauer, Siegfried. *Theory of Film: The Redemption of Physical Reality* (Oxford: Oxford University Press, 1974).

Krall, Dan. 'Coraline'. http://www.dankrall.com/coraline/ (accessed 5 July 2019).

Kristeva, Julia. *Powers of Horror: An Essay on Abjection*. Trans. Leon S. Roudiez (New York: Columbia University Press, 1982).

Kristeva, Julia. 'Word, Dialogue and Novel'. In Toril Moi (ed.), *The Kristeva Reader* (New York: Columbia University Press, 1986), pp. 34–62.

Lang, George. 'World of "Coraline" Worth a Visit'. *The Oklahoman*, 6 February 2009, p. 5D.

Lauchlans, Grant. 'A Hell of a Movie'. *Daily Record*, 29 May 2009, pp. 50–1.

Leader, Michael. 'Exclusive: Henry Selick on *Coraline*'. *Den of Geek*, 7 May 2009. https://www.denofgeek.com/movies/exclusive-henry-selick-on-coraline/ (accessed 12 August 2019).

'Lecture List: Term 2'. *Warwick English and Comparative Literary Studies*. 17 March 2016. https://warwick.ac.uk/fac/arts/english/currentstudents/undergraduate/modules/fulllist/first/en122/lecturelist-2015-16-2/shklovsky.pdf (accessed 8 June 2020).

Leitch, Thomas M. *Film Adaptation and Its Discontents: From Gone with the Wind to the Passion of the Christ* (Baltimore: Johns Hopkins University Press, 2007).

Lennard, Dominic. *Bad Seeds and Holy Terrors – The Child Villains of Horror Film* (New York: SUNY Press, 2014).

Lester, Catherine. 'The Children's Horror Film: Beneficial Fear and Subversive Pleasure in an (Im)Possible Hollywood Subgenre' (PhD thesis, University of Warwick, 2016).

Lester, Catherine. 'The Children's Horror Film: Characterizing an "Impossible" Subgenre'. *Velvet Light Trap*, no. 78 (2016): 22–37.

Levitt, Deborah. *The Animatic Apparatus: Animation, Vitality, and the Futures of the Image* (Washington: Zero Books, 2018).

Liberator, Paul. 'Movie Director Animates his "Weird Imagination"'. *Marin Independent Journal*, 4 February 2009.

Lloyd, Rebecca. 'Haunting the Grown-Ups: The Borderlands of *Paranorman* and *Coraline*'. In Ruth Hehold and Niamh Downing (eds), *Haunted Landscapes: Super-Nature and the Environment* (London: Rowman & Littlefield International), pp. 199–215.

Logie, Robert H. *Visuo-Spatial Working Memory* (Hove: Lawrence Erlbaum Associates, 1995).

Lord, Peter. 'Foreword'. In Ray Harryhausen and Tony Dalton, *A Century of Stop Motion Animation: From Méliès to Aardman* (New York: Random House, 2008).

Lord, Peter, and Brian Sibley. *Creating 3-D Animation: The Aardman Book of Filmmaking* (New York: Harry N. Abrams, 1998).

Loumenick, Lou. 'Darkness & Delight'. *New York Post*, 6 February 2009, p. 38.

'LunchBox DV: Summary'. *Animation Tool Works*, 10 August 2006. https://web.archive.org/web/20060810022321/http://www.animationtoolworks.com/products/lbdv_summ.html (accessed 30 April 2020).

MacCabe, Colin, Kathleen Murray, and Rick Warner. *True to the Spirit: Film Adaptation and the Question of Fidelity* (Oxford: Oxford University Press, 2011).

'Machine Vision Enables Stop-Motion Animation.' *Vision Systems Design*, vol. 14, no. 2 (2009), p. 9.

MacLeod, Anne Scott. 'American Girlhood in the Nineteenth Century'. In Paula S. Fass and May Ann Mason (eds), *Childhood in America* (New York: New York University Press: 2000), pp. 87–90.

MacKinnon, Carla. 'Autobiography and Authenticity in Stop-Motion Animation'. In Caroline Ruddell and Paul Ward (eds), *The Crafty Animator: Handmade, Craft-Based Animation and Cultural Value* (Cham, Switzerland: Palgrave Macmillan, 2019), pp. 99–126

Manovich, Lev. 'Understanding Hybrid Media' in Betti-Sue Hertz, *Animated Painting* (San Diego: San Diego Museum of Art, 2007).

Marks, Laura U. *Touch: Sensuous Theory and Multisensory Media* (Minneapolis: University of Minnesota Press, 2002).

Matlock, Maryna. '"What's in the Empty Flat?": Specular Identity and Authorship in Neil Gaiman's *Coraline*'. In Sara K. Day and Sonya Sawyer Fritz (eds), *The Victorian Era in Twenty-First Century Children's and Adolescent Literature and Culture* (London: Routledge, 2018), pp. 38–54.

McEachern, Martin. 'Myth in Miniature'. *Computer Graphics World*, vol. 39, no. 5 (2016). https://www.cgw.com/Publications/CGW/2016/Volume-39-Issue-5-Sept-Oct-2016-/Myth-in-miniature.aspx (accessed 24 August 2020).

McGorry, Ken. 'Cover Story: "Coraline" Animated Via Stop-Motion', *Post Magazine*, 1 February 2009. http://www.postmagazine.com/Publications/Post-Magazine/2009/February-1-2009/cover-story-coraline-animated-via-stop-motion.aspx (accessed 11 October 2019).

McLean, Thomas J. 'On the Set with "Coraline": Where the Motion Doesn't Stop'. *Animation World Network*, 16 September 2008. https://www.awn.com/animationworld/set-coraline-where-motion-doesnt-stop (accessed 5 July 2019).

Means, Sean P. 'Movie Review: Take a Trip to the Dark Side with "Coraline"'. *Salt Lake Tribune*, 5 February 2009.

Meeusen, Meghann. 'Framing Agency: Comics Adaptations of *Coraline* and *City of Ember*'. In Michelle Ann Abate and Gwen Athene (ed.), *Graphic Novels for Children and Young Adults: A Collection of Critical Essays* (Tarbox, Jackson: University Press of Mississippi, 2017), pp. 126–40.

Meister, I. G., T. Krings, H. Foltys, B. Boroojerdi, M. Muller, R. Topper and A. Thron. 'Playing Piano in the Mind-an fMRI Study on Music Imagery and Performance in Pianists'. *Cognitive Brain Research*, vol. 19, no. 3 (2004): 219–28.

Miller, Alice. *The Drama of the Gifted Child*. 3rd edn (New York: Basic Books, 1997).

Miller, Alice. *Thou Shalt Not Be Aware: Society's Betrayal of the Child*. 1st edn
(New York: Farrar, Straus and Giroux, 1998).

Miller, Madeline. 'From Circe to Clinton: Why Powerful Women Are Cast as Witches'.
The Guardian, 7 April 2018. https://www.theguardian.com/books/2018/apr/07/
cursed-from-circe-to-clinton-why-women-are-cast-as-witches (accessed 13
November 2019).

Mulvey, Laura. 'Visual Pleasure and Narrative Cinema'. *Screen*, vol. 16, no. 3
(1975): 6–18.

Murphy, Mekado. 'Moving Ahead in Stop Motion'. *New York Times*, 10 August 2012.
https://www.nytimes.com/2012/08/12/movies/with-paranorman-laika-aims-to-
push-animation-boundaries.html (accessed 30 July 2019).

Myers, Lindsay. 'Whose Fear Is It Anyway? Moral Panics and Stranger Danger in
Coraline'. *Lion and the Unicorn*, vol. 36, no. 3 (2012): 245–57.

Nadal, Marcos, and Anjan Chatterjee, 'Neuroaesthetics and Art's Diversity and
Universality'. *Wiley Interdisciplinary Reviews: Cognitive Science*, vol. 10, no. 6 (2019).

Nally, Claire. 'Grrly Hurly Burly: Neo-Burlesque and the Performance of Gender'.
Textual Practice, vol. 23, no. 4 (2009): 621–43.

Nelson, Victoria. *The Secret Life of Puppets* (Cambridge, MA: Harvard University
Press, 2003).

Neupert, Richard. *French Animation History* (Malden, MA: Wiley-Blackwell, 2011).

'New York Witches Place Hex on Brett Kavanaugh'. *BBC News*, 21 October 2018. https://
www.bbc.co.uk/news/world-us-canada-45928212 (accessed 13 November 2019).

Nodelman, Perry. *Words about Pictures: The Narrative Art of Children's Picture Books*
(Athens: University of Georgia Press, 1988).

North, Dan. *Performing Illusions: Cinema, Special Effects and the Virtual Actor*
(New York: Wallflower Press, 2008).

Owen, David. 'Neo-Burlesque and the Resurgence of Roller Derby: Empowerment,
Play, and Community'. *Canadian Theatre Review*, vol. 158 (2014): 33–8.

Pallant, Chris. *Demystifying Disney: A History of Disney Feature Animation*
(London: Bloomsbury, 2013).

Pallant, Chris, and Steven Price. *Storyboarding: A Critical History* (Basingstoke: Palgrave
Macmillan, 2015).

Parsons, Elizabeth, Naarah Sawers and Kate McInally. 'The Other Mother: Neil
Gaiman's Postfeminist Fairytales'. *Children's Literature Association Quarterly*, vol. 33,
no. 4 (2008): 371–89.

Pedersen, Erik. 'Watchdog Group Chides Laika for "White-Washing" "Kubo and the
Two Strings"'. *Deadline*, 23 August 2016. https://deadline.com/2016/08/kubo-and-
two-strings-protest-white-actors-japanese-characters-manaa-1201807914/ (accessed
12 August 2019).

Pelphrey, Kevin A., Teresa V. Mitchell, Martin J. KcKeown, Jeremy Goldstein, Truett
Allison and Gregory McCarthy. 'Brain Activity Evoked by the Perception of Human

Walking: Controlling for Meaningful Coherent Motion'. *Journal of Neuroscience*, vol. 23, no. 17 (2003): 6819–25.

Peters, Mette. 'George Pal's "Cavalcade of Colours, Music and Dolls": 1930s Advertising Films in Transnational Contexts'. In Malcolm Cook and Kirsten Moana Thompson (eds), *Animation and Advertising* (Cham, Switzerland: Palgrave Macmillan, 2019), pp. 55–71.

Pett, Emma. '"Blood, Guts and Bambi Eyes": *Urotsukidōji* and the Transcultural Reception and Regulation of Anime'. *Journal of British Cinema and Television*, vol. 13, no. 3 (2016): 390–408.

Pettigrew, Neil. *The Stop-Motion Filmography – A Critical Guide to 297 Features Using Puppet Animation*, Volume Two (London: McFarland, 1999).

Posner, Liz. 'You May Be a Witch and Not Even Know It: The Resurgence of W.I.T.C.H. Activism Under the Trump Administration'. *AlterNet*, 30 October 2017. https://www.alternet.org/2017/10/resurgence-witch-activism-and-witches-under-trump-administration/ (accessed 13 November 2019).

Pratchett, Terry. *Discworld* (New York: Penguin Random House, 1983–2015).

Priebe, Ken A. *The Advanced Art of Stop-Motion Animation* (Boston, MA: Cengage Learning, 2010).

Prince, Stephen. *Digital Visual Effects in Cinema: The Seduction of Reality* (New Brunswick, NJ: Rutgers University Press, 2012).

Prince, Stephen. 'True Lies: Perceptual Realism, Digital Images, and Film Theory'. *Film Quarterly*, vol. 49, no. 3 (1996): 27–37.

Purves, Barry J. C. *Stop Motion: Passion, Process and Performance* (Burlington, MA: Focal Press/Routledge, 2008).

Purves, Barry J. C. *Stop-Motion Animation: Frame by Frame Film-Making with Puppets and Models* (London: Bloomsbury, 2014).

Ramachandran, V. S. and William Hirstein. 'The Science of Art: A Neurological Theory of Aesthetic Experience'. *Journal of Consciousness Studies: Controversies in Science and the Humanities*, vol. 6, no. 6–7 (1999): 15–51.

Rapport, Nigel, and Andrew Dawson. *Migrants of Identity: Perceptions of Home in a World of Movement* (Oxford: Berg, 1998).

Rea, Steven. 'On Movies: "*Coraline*" Animator Started with the Story'. *Philadelphia Inquirer*, 1 February 2009, p. H02.

Richards, Linda. Interview with Neil Gaiman. *January Magazine*, August 2001. https://www.januarymagazine.com/profiles/gaiman.html (accessed 8 June 2020).

Rizzolatti, Giacomo, and Laila Craighero. 'The Mirror-Neuron System'. *Annual Review of Neuroscience*, vol. 27 (2004): 169–92.

Roberts, Jeanne Addison. *The Shakespearean Wild: Geography, Genus, and Gender* (Lincoln, NE: University of Nebraska Press, 1991).

Robey, Tim. '*Coraline*'. *Daily Telegraph*, 8 May 2009, p. 31.

Rocha, Ellen. 'Beyond Materiality in Animation: Sensuous Perception and Touch in the Tactile Existence of "Would a Heart Die?"'. *Animation Studies*, vol. 11 (2016). https://journal.animationstudies.org (accessed 17 March 2020).

Roper, Caitlin. 'The Man Who Brought Stop-Motion Animation to the 21st Century'. *Wired*, 18 September 2014. https://www.wired.com/2014/09/travis-knight-stop-motion-boxtrolls/ (accessed 23 September 2020).

Rose, Steve. 'Masters of Puppets: Charlie Kaufman and the Subversive Allure of Stop-Motion'. *The Guardian*, 7 January 2016. https://www.theguardian.com/film/2016/jan/07/subversive-allure-stop-motion-anomalisa-tim-burton (accessed 1 March 2020).

Rowe, Robin. '"Bride" Stripped Bare'. *Editors Guild Magazine*, vol. 26, no. 4 (2005): 1–8.

Rowntree, Grim. 'Hag Stone Lore'. *Cauldron Craft Oddities*, 30 October 2012. http://cauldroncraftoddities.blogspot.com/2012/10/hag-stone-lore.html (accessed 13 November 2019).

Rudd, David. 'An Eye for an I: Neil Gaiman's *Coraline* and Questions of Identity'. *Children's Literature in Education*, vol. 39, no. 3 (2008): 159–68.

Ruddell, Caroline, and Paul Ward. 'Introduction'. In Caroline Ruddell and Paul Ward (eds), *The Crafty Animator: Handmade, Craft-Based Animation and Cultural Value* (Cham, Switzerland: Palgrave Macmillan, 2019), pp. 1–15.

Saunders, Sarah. 'LAIKA's Brian McLean Talks about 3D Printed Faces for Studio's New Stop Motion Animation Film'. *3D Print*, 20 March 2019. https://3dprint.com/238607/brian-mclean-talks-3d-printed-faces-for-laika-stop-motion-animation/ (accessed 4 November 2020).

Savage, Mike, Gaynor Bagnall and Brian Longhurst, *Globalization and Belonging* (London: Sage, 2005).

Saygin, Ayse Pinar, Stephen M. Wilson, Donald J. Hagler Jr, Elizabeth Bates and Martin I. Sereno. 'Point-Light Biological Motion Perception Activates Human Premotor Cortex'. *Journal of Neuroscience*, vol. 24, no. 27 (2004): 6181–8.

Scott, Anthony. 'The Importance of Using Gages'. *Stop Motion Animation*. http://www.stopmotionanimation.com/page/the-importance-of-using-gages (accessed 1 May 2020).

Scott, A. O. 'Cornered in a Parallel World'. *New York Times*, 6 February 2009, p. C1.

Sedgwick, Eve Kosofsky. *Touching Feeling* (Durham, NC: Duke University Press, 2003).

Selick, Henry. *Coraline*, 'Feature Commentary' (Laika, Inc., 2009), DVD.

Selick, Henry. 'Henry Selick on Why Jan Svankmajer Matters', *Cartoon Brew*, 12 June 2016. https://www.cartoonbrew.com/ideas-commentary/henry-selick-jan-svankmajer-matters-140434.html (accessed 27 September 2020).

Selick, Henry. 'Henry Selick Winsor McCay Award Recipient 2020', YouTube, 2 February 2020. https://www.youtube.com/watch?v=i5-3I1ly0q8&ab_channel=ASIFAHollywood (accessed 27 September 2020).

Shadbolt, Jane. 'Parallel Synchronized Randomness: Stop-Motion Animation in Live Action Feature Films'. *Animation Studies*, no. 8, 9 June 2013. https://journal.animationstudies.org/category/volume-8/jane-shadbolt-parallel-synchronised-randomness/ (accessed 9 December 2019).

Shepherd, David. ' "Noah's Beasts Were the Stars": Arthur Melbourne Cooper's *Noah's Ark* (1909)'. *Journal of Religion & Film*, vol. 20, no. 1 (2016): 1–27. http://digitalcommons.unomaha.edu/jrf/vol20/iss1/20.

Shklovsky, Viktor. *Theory of Prose* (Elmwood Park, IL: Dalkey Archive Press, 1990).

Singer, Tania, Ben Seymour, John O'Doherty, Holgar Kaube, Raymond J. Dolan and Chris D. Frith. 'Empathy for Pain Involves the Affective but Not Sensory Components of Pain'. *Science*, vol. 303, no. 20 (2004): 1157–62.

Smith, Adam. *An Inquiry into the Nature and Causes of the Wealth of Nations*. 6th edn, vol. 1 (London: G. Bell and Sons, 1887; original 1776).

Smith, Damon. 'Star Trek'. *Oxford Times*, 6 May 2009.

Smith, Moira. 'The Flying Phallus and the Laughing Inquisitor: Penis Theft in the "Malleus Maleficarum" '. *Journal of Folklore Research*, vol. 39, no. 1 (2002): 85–117.

Smith, Vicky, and Nicky Hamlyn, eds. *Experimental & Expanded Animation: New Perspectives and Practices* (London: Palgrave Macmillan, 2018).

Staiger, Janet. *Interpreting Films: Studies in the Historical Reception of American Cinema* (Princeton, NJ: Princeton University Press, 1992).

Staiger, Janet. *Perverse Spectators: The Practices of Film Reception* (New York: New York University Press, 2000).

Stevens, Dana. 'Button Eyes'. *Slate*, 5 February 2009. http://www.slate.com/articles/arts/movies/2009/02/button_eyes.html?via=gdpr-consent (accessed 9 September 2018).

Švankmajer, Jan. *Touching and Imagining: An Introduction to Tactile Art* (London: I.B. Tauris, 2014).

Tatar, Maria. *The Hard Facts of the Grimms' Fairy Tales* (Princeton: Princeton University Press, 1987).

Tate, W. E. *The Enclosure Movement* (New York: Walker, 1967).

The Classification and Rating Administration (CARA). 'History of the Ratings'. *Film Ratings*. https://filmratings.com/History (accessed 9 September 2018).

'The Making of Coraline' (UK Blu Ray Release, 2013).

'The Making of the Nightmare before Christmas'. *The Nightmare before Christmas Special Edition DVD* (Buena Vista Home Entertainment, 2000).

Thompson, Gary. ' "Coraline" May Be Unnerving for the Kids'. *Philadelphia Daily News*, 6 February 2009, p. 38.

Tilley, Lisa, Ashok Kumar and Thomas Cowan. 'Introduction: Enclosures and Discontents'. *City*, vol. 21, no. 3–4 (2017): 420–7.

Torre, Dan. *Animation – Process, Cognition and Actuality* (New York: Bloomsbury, 2017).

Torre, Dan. *Carnivorous Plants* (London: Reaktion Books, 2019).

Tronick, Edward, et al. 'The Infant's Response to Entrapment between Contradictory Messages in Face-to-Face Interaction'. *Journal of the American Academy of Child Psychiatry*, vol. 17, no. 1 (1978): 1–13.

Troutman, Megan, 'It's Alive … AGAIN: Redefining Children's Film Through Animated Horror'. In Casie Hermansson and Janet Zepernick (eds), *The Palgrave Handbook of Children's Film and Television* (Cham, Switzerland: Palgrave Macmillan, 2019), pp. 149–65.

Tully, James. 'The Future Is Here!'. *The Argus*, 26 March 2009.

Turan, Kenneth. 'Review: "Coraline"'. *Los Angeles Times*, 6 February 2009. https://www.latimes.com/entertainment/la-et-coraline6-2009feb06-story.html (accessed 18 November 2020).

Turnock, Julie. *Plastic Reality: Special Effects, Technology, and the Emergence of 1970s Blockbuster Aesthetics* (New York: Columbia University Press, 2015).

Vancheri, Barbara. 'PG-Rated Movies with More Kick Are Catching Parents Off-Guard'. *Pittsburgh Post-Gazette*, 6 February 2009. https://www.post-gazette.com/ae/movies/2009/02/06/PG-rated-movies-with-more-kick-are-catching-parents-off-guard/stories/200902060205 (accessed 9 September 2018).

Vaughn, Stephen. *Freedom and Entertainment: Rating the Movies in an Age of New Media* (Cambridge: Cambridge University Press, 2006).

Vaz, Mark Cotta. '*The Nightmare before Christmas*: Animation in the Third Dimension'. *Cinefex*, no. 56 (1993).

Venker, Suzanne. 'Men Called. They Want Their Balls Back'. 30 April 2018. https://www.suzannevenker.com/relationships/men-called-they-want-their-balls-back/ (accessed 13 November 2019).

Venker, Suzanne. 'The Neutering of the American Male'. 9 March 2018. https://www.suzannevenker.com/feminism/the-neutering-of-the-american-male/ (accessed 13 November 2019).

von Kleist, Heinrich. 'On the Marionette Theatre'. Trans. Thomas G. Neumiller. *Drama Review*, vol. 16, no. 3 (1972): 22–6.

Warwick, Lynda. 'Feminist Wicca: Paths to Empowerment'. *Women & Therapy*, vol. 16, no. 2–3 (1995): 121–33.

Webber, Roy P. *The Dinosaur Films of Ray Harryhausen: Features, Early 16mm Experiments and Unrealized Projects* (Jefferson, NC: MacFarland, 2004).

Weisbuch, Robert. *Atlantic Double-Cross: American Literature and British Influence in the Age of Emerson* (Chicago, IL: University of Chicago Press, 1986).

Wells, Paul. '"Picture by Picture, Movement by Movement": Melbourne-Cooper, Shiryaev and the Symbolic Body'. *animation: an interdisciplinary journal*, vol. 6, no. 2 (2011): 149–62.

Wells, Paul. *Understanding Animation* (London: Routledge, 1998).

Wells, Paul. 'Wonderlands, Slumberlands and Plunderlands: Considering the Animated Fantasy'. In Christopher Holliday and Alexander Sergeant (eds), *Fantasy/*

Animation: Connections between Media, Mediums and Genres (London: Routledge, 2018), pp. 23–41.

Wilby, Emma. *Cunning Folk and Familiar Spirits: Shamanistic Visionary Traditions in Early Modern British Witchcraft* (Brighton: Sussex Academic Press, 2010).

Williams, Marietta. '[Familiars 2017: Part 4] How a Familiar Serves the Witch'. *Witchy Words*, 17 November 2017. http://www.witchywords.com/2017/11/familiars-2017-part-4-how-familiar.html (accessed 13 November 2019).

Wilson, Sean. 'Exclusive Interview: Early Man Director Nick Park Talks Aardman, Bristol and Eddie Redmayne'. *Cineworld*, 31 January 2018. http://www.cineworld.co.uk/blog/early-man-aardman-nick-park-interview (accessed 17 March 2020).

Wiseman, Dennis. *The American Family: Understanding its Changing Dynamics and Place in Society* (Springfield: Charles C. Thomas, 2008).

W.I.T.C.H. Boston (@witchboston). 'ANONYMOUS | INTERSECTIONAL | INCLUSIVE | UNIFIED'. Instagram Photo, 27 January 2017. https://www.instagram.com/p/BPx5jAFh5kj/ (accessed 13 November 2019).

W.I.T.C.H. PDX. 'W.I.T.C.H.: STARTING NEW CHAPTERS'. PDF File, No date. https://static1.squarespace.com/static/58bc4014db29d66bb3b20966/t/59c6e45fd7bdce9acafab603/1506206816220/NEW-W.I.T.C.H.-CHAPTERS.pdf (accessed 13 November 2019).

Wloszczyna, Susan. '3-D and Stop-Motion Find "Coraline"; Visuals Pop with Old, New Images'. *USA Today*, 18 November 2008, p. 1D

Wolff, Ellen. 'Digital Puppeteers: Pete Kozachick and Brian Van't Hul on *Coraline*'. *Millimeter* (January/February 2009), pp. 18–21.

Wolff, Ellen. 'Systems Go for Stop Motion'. *Daily Variety*, 13 November 2009.

Wyness, Michael. *Contesting Childhood* (New York: Falmer Press, 2000).

Young, Graham. 'Animation May Be the First X-Certificate'. *Birmingham Evening Mail*, 8 May 2009, p. 31.

Zahed, Ramin. *The Art of Missing Link* (San Rafael, CA: Insight Editions, 2019).

Zamir, Tzachi. 'Puppets'. *Critical Inquiry*, vol. 36, no. 3 (2010): 386–409.

Zeki, Semir. 'Art and the Brain'. *Journal of Consciousness Studies: Controversies in Science and the Humanities*, vol. 10, no. 3 (1999): 76–96.

Zipes, Jack, tr, ed. *The Great Fairy Tale Tradition: From Straparola and Basile to the Brothers Grimm* (New York: W. W. Norton, 2001).

Zone, Ray. *3-D Revolution: The History of Modern Stereoscopic Cinema* (Lexington: University Press of Kentucky, 2012).

.

Filmography

The 7th Voyage of Sinbad (1958), Dir. Nathan Juran, USA: Columbia Pictures.

The Amazing Adventures of Morph (1980–1), [TV] Dir. Peter Lord and David Sproxton, UK: Aardman Animations.

A Boy's Dream (1903), Dir. Arthur Melbourne-Cooper, UK: Alpha Trading Company.

A Town Called Panic/Panique au Village (2009), Dir. Stéphane Aubier and Vincent Patar, Belgium: La Parti Productions.

Alice/ Něco z Alenky (1988), Dir. Jan Švankmajer, Czechoslovakia: Film Four International.

Anomalisa (2016), Dir. Charlie Kaufman and Duke Johnson, USA: Paramount Animation.

Antz (1998), Dir. Eric Darnell and Tim Johnson, USA: DreamWorks Animation.

Ballet Mécanique (1924), Dir. Fernand Léger and Dudley Murphy, France: Synchro-Ciné.

Bambi (1942), Dir. Ron Clements and John Musker, USA: Walt Disney Studios.

Betty Boop in Snow White (1933), Dir. Dave Fleischer, USA: Fleischer Studios.

Bobby Yeah (2011), Dir. Robert Morgan, UK: Robert Morgan.

The Boxtrolls (2014), Dir. Graham Annable and Anthony Stacchi, USA: LAIKA.

The Breakfast Club (1985), Dir. John Hughes, USA: Universal Pictures.

The Cabinet of Jan Svankmajer (1984), Dir. Stephen and Timothy Quay, UK: Channel Four.

The Cameraman's Revenge/Mest' kinematograficheskogo operatora (1912), Dir. Władysław Starewicz, Russia: Khanzhonkov Production Company.

Chicken Run (2000), Dir. Peter Lord and Nick Park, UK: Aardman Animations.

Child's Play (1988), Dir. Tom Holland, USA: United Artists.

Clash of the Titans (1981), Dir. Desmond Davis, UK/USA: Metro-Goldwyn-Mayer.

Coco (2017), Dir. Lee Unkrich and Adrian Molina, USA: Pixar Animation Studios.

Coraline (2009), Dir. Henry Selick, USA: LAIKA.

Corpse Bride (2005), Dir. Tim Burton and Mike Johnson, USA: Tim Burton Productions.

Daughter/Dcera (2019), Dir. Daria Kashcheeva, Czech Republic: Film and TV School of the Academy of Performing Arts in in Prague (FAMU).

The Death of Stalinism in Bohemia/ Konec stalinismu v Čechách (1990), Dir. Jan Švankmajer, UK: BBC.

Dimensions of Dialogue/Možnosti dialogu (1983), Dir. Jan Švankmajer, Czechoslovakia: Krátký Film Praha.

The Dinosaur and the Missing Link: A Prehistoric Tragedy (1915), Dir. Willis O'Brien, USA: Conquest Pictures Company.

Dolls in Dreamland (1907), Dir. Unknown, USA: Biograph.

Dolly's Toys (1901), Dir. Arthur Melbourne-Cooper, UK: Paul's Animatograph Works.

Donnie Darko (2001), Dir. Richard Kelly, USA: Flower Films.

Drag Me to Hell (2009), Dir. Sam Raimi, USA: Ghost House Pictures.

Dreams of Toyland (1908), Dir. Arthur Melbourne-Cooper, UK: Alpha Trading Company.

Duck Amuck (1953), Dir. Chuck Jones, USA: Warner Bros. Cartoons.

Et Cetera (1966), Dir. Jan Švankmajer, Czechoslovakia: Krátký Film Praha.

The Fall of the House of Usher/Zánik domu Usherú (1980), Dir. Jan Švankmajer, Czechoslovakia: Krátký Film Praha.

Fantasia (1940), Dir. Samuel Armstrong et al., USA: Walt Disney Studios.

Fantastic Mr. Fox (2009), Dir. Wes Anderson, USA: American Empirical Pictures.

Father and Daughter (2000), Dir. Michaël Dudok de Wit, the Netherlands: CinéTé Filmproductie BV.

Finding Nemo (2003), Dir. Andrew Stanton, USA: Pixar Animation Studios.

Footlight Parade (1993), Dir. Lloyd Bacon, USA: Warner Brothers.

Frankenweenie (2012), Dir. Tim Burton, USA: Walt Disney Pictures.

Ghost in the Shell 2: Innocence/Inosensu (2004), Dir. Mamoru Oshii, Japan: Production I.G.

The Great Cognito (1982), Dir. Will Vinton, USA: Will Vinton Productions.

The Hand/Ruka (1965), Dir. Jirí Trnka, Czechoslovakia: Krátký Film Praha.

The Haunting in Connecticut (2009), Dir. Peter Cornwell, USA: Gold Circle Films.

How I Live Now (2013), Dir. Kevin Macdonald, UK/Canada: Film4.

The Humpty Dumpty Circus (1898), Dir. Albert E. Smith and James Stuart Blackton, UK: Vitagraph Studios.

The Incredibles (2004), Dir. Brad Bird, USA: Pixar Animation Studios.

Independence Day (1996), Dir. Roland Emmerich, USA: Centropolis Entertainment.

Insects/Hmyz (2018), Dir. Jan Švankmajer, Czech Republic: Athanor.

Invasion of the Body Snatchers (1956), Dir. Don Siegel, USA: Walter Wanger Productions.

Jabberwocky/Žvahlav aneb šatičky slaměného Huberta (1971), Dir. Jan Švankmajer, Czechoslovakia: Krátký Film Praha.

James and the Giant Peach (1996), Dir. Henry Selick, USA: Walt Disney Studios.

Jason and the Argonauts (1963), Dir. Don Chaffey, USA: Morningside Worldwide Pictures.

Jasper and the Haunted House (1942), Dir. George Pal, USA: Paramount Pictures.

Jurassic Park (1993), Dir. Steven Spielberg, USA: Amblin Entertainment.

King Kong (1933), Dir. Merian C. Cooper and Ernest B. Schoedsack, USA: RKO Pictures.

Kubo and the Two Strings (2016), Dir. Travis Knight, USA: LAIKA.

Kung Fu Panda (2008), Dir. John Stevenson and Mark Osborne, USA: DreamWorks Animation.

Lawrence of Arabia (1962), Dir. David Lean, UK: Horizon Pictures.

Lemony Snicket's A Series of Unfortunate Events (2004), Dir. Brad Silberling, USA: DreamWorks Pictures.

Mary and Max (2009), Dir. Adam Elliot, Australia: Melodrama Pictures.

The Mascot/Fétiche Mascotte (1933), Dir. Władysław Starewicz, France: Gelma-Film.

Memento (2000), Dir. Christopher Nolan, USA: Summit Entertainment.

Mighty Joe Young (1949), Dir. Ernest B. Schoedsack, USA: Argosy Pictures.

Miss Hokusai/Sarusuberi: Miss Hokusai (2015), Dir. Keiichi Hara, Japan: Bandai Visual Company.

Missing Link (2019), Dir. Chris Butler, USA: LAIKA.

Moana (2016), Dir. Ron Clements and John Musker, USA: Walt Disney Studios.

Modern Times (1936), Dir. Charles Chaplin, USA: Charles Chaplin Productions.

Monsters, Inc. (2001), Dir. Pete Docter, USA: Pixar Animation Studios.

My Neighbor Totoro/Tonari no Totoro (1988), Dir. Hayao Miyazaki, Japan: Studio Ghibli.

The Nightmare before Christmas (1993), Dir. Henry Selick, USA: Touchstone Pictures.

ParaNorman (2012), Dir. Sam Fell and Chris Butler, USA: LAIKA.

Philips Broadcast of 1938/De Groote Philips Revue (1938), Dir. George Pal, the Netherlands/UK: Philips Radio.

Philips Cavalcade (1939), Dir. George Pal, the Netherlands.

Pinocchio (1940), Dir. Norman Ferguson et al., USA: Walt Disney Studios.

The Pirates! In an Adventure with Scientists! (2012), Dir. Peter Lord, UK/USA: Aardman Animations and Sony Pictures Animation.

Poltergeist (1982), Dir. Tobe Hooper, USA: Metro-Goldwyn-Mayer.

Punch and Judy/Rakvičkárna (1966), Dir. Jan Švankmajer, Czechoslovakia: Krátký Film Praha.

Ran (1985), Dir. Akira Kurosawa, Japan: Herald Ace.

The Sandman (1995), Dir. J. R. Bookwalter, USA: Suburban Tempe Company.

The Seven Ravens/Die Sieben Raben (1937), Dir. Ferdinand and Hermann Diehl, Germany: Puppentrickfilm.

Seven Samurai/Shichinin no Samurai (1954), Dir. Akira Kurosawa, Japan: Toho.

Sinbad and the Eye of the Tiger (1977), Dir. Sam Wanamaker, UK/USA: Andor Films.

Snow White and the Seven Dwarfs (1937), Dir. David Hand et al., USA: Walt Disney Studios.

The Spiderwick Chronicles (2008), Dir. Mark Waters, USA: Paramount Pictures.

Spirited Away/ Sen to Chihiro no Kamikakushi (2001), Dir. Hayao Miyazaki, Japan: Studio Ghibli.

Street of Crocodiles (1986), Dir. Stephen and Timothy Quay, UK: Atelier Koninck.

The 'Teddy' Bears (1907), Dir. Edwin S. Porter, USA: Edison Manufacturing Company.

Terminator 2: Judgment Day (1991), Dir. James Cameron, USA: Carolco Pictures.

The Tree (2018), Dir. Basil Malek and Han Yang, France: Gobelins, L'École de L'Image.

The Triplets of Belleville/ Les Triplettes de Belleville (2003), Dir. Sylvain Chomet, France/Belgium/Canada/UK: Les Armateurs.

Toy Story (1995), Dir. John Lasseter, USA: Pixar Animation Studios.

Urotsukidōji: Legend of the Overfiend/Chōjin Densetsu Urotsukidōji (1989), Dir. Hideki Takayama, Japan: Shochiku-Fuji.

Vincent (1982), Dir. Tim Burton, USA: Walt Disney Studios.

Waking Life (2001), Dir. Richard Linklater, USA: Thousand Words.

WALL-E (2008), Dir. Andrew Stanton, USA: Pixar Animation Studios.

Wallace & Gromit: The Curse of the Were-Rabbit (2005), Dir. Nick Park and Steve Box, UK: Aardman Animations.

The War and the Dream of Momi/La Guerra e il sogno di Momi (1917), Dir. Segundo de Chomón and Giovanni Pastrone, Italy: Itala Film.

Wreck-It Ralph (2012), Dir. Rich Moore, USA: Walt Disney Studios.

Westworld (2016–), [TV], USA: HBO.

Index

CPSIA information can be obtained
at www.ICGtesting.com
Printed in the USA
LVHW071307110323
741409LV00009B/23